A THEATRE OF THEIR OWN:
INDIAN
WOMEN
PLAYWRIGHTS
IN
PERSPECTIVE

DR. PINAKI RANJAN DAS

PARTRIDGE

To order additional copies of this book, contact
Partridge India
000 800 919 0634 (Call Free)
+91 000 80091 90634 (Outside India)
orders.india@partridgepublishing.com

www.partridgepublishing.com/india

CONTENTS

PREFACE

Situated in the cause and consequence of society, theatre as a dynamic space heterogeneously synthesizes a multitude of voices, viz. of the playwrights, directors, choreographers, stage and costume designers, light/sound operators, and also that of the audience. It not only intervenes into the cultural, political, religious structures of society, but also, almost always, challenges its equilibrium. But, historically theatre has failed to provide adequate representation to women as conscious subjects and often engaged in producing stereotypes. Feminist theatres of the 1960s sought to foreground the representation of women in theatre but were criticized for being essentialist and failing to address the differences that separate women in one context from women in another. But Tutun Mukherjee's 'Prolegomenon to Women's Theatre' in her anthology of plays by women playwrights *Staging Resistance: Plays by Women in Translations* (OUP 2005), introduced me to the gradual growth of a theatre by women in India that thematically and dramaturgically deviates from the feminist as well as male-dominated traditional Indian theatre conventions. Forays into the Indian Women's Theatre led me to explore not only its uniqueness in engaging socio-cultural crevices with respect to women in India but also the variety of forms they espoused to articulate their voices. In this book, however, I primarily focus on exploring themes and issues Indian women playwrights have broached in their plays, making a select study of women-authored plays. Appearing at different points in time, the plays have been brought together here on the basis of their theme/s that foreground women as the subject resisting stereotypes and thus voicing their desire and articulating a life of their own.

In the course of writing this book, I have received extensive support from the National School of Drama repertoire. Various editions of *Theatre India*, National School of Drama's Theatre Journal, have helped me structure and restructure my perspectives on the contributions of Indian women playwrights and directors. The Central Library of the University of North Bengal has provided me all the logistic and academic assistances that were necessary for the book to reach its desired end. Portions of/ related to this book have been presented in seminars/ conferences and published in the following seminar/ conference proceedings and peer-reviewed journals:

➢ "Negotiating the Abused Woman Body: A Study of Select Woman Authored Plays from the 1980s". *The Indian Journal of English Studies*. Vol. LVI. 2019. ed. by Khatri, C.L. Association for English Studies in India. 2019.

➢ "Let There be Light … There is No Light: Rereading the Gender – Caste Welfare Politics through Listen Shefali". *Globalization: Emerging Trends in English Language and Literature. 62nd All India English Teacher's Conference18-20 January, 2018. Osmania University Centre for international Programmes. Hyderabad.* ed. by Raju, B.V., A. Karunekar and K. Nageshwar Rao. Siri Publishers and Distributors Pvt. Ltd. 2018.

➢ "Images: Women in Post-Independence Male Oriented Indian Theatre". *Postcolonial Indian Drama in English and English Translation: Reading Themes and Techniques.* ed. by De, Uttiya and Sarkar, Jaydip. Authors Press. 2015.

➢ "Theatre's Intervention and Women Empowerment: Dina Mehta's Getting Away with Murder". *Women Empowerment in India Opportunities and Challenges. Sitalkuchi College, 27-28 November, 2015.* Comp. by. Sharma, Gopal. Rupali. 2015.

➤ "A Theatre of their Own: Indian Women Playwrights and Directors in Perspective". *International Organisation of Scientific Research –Journal of Humanities and Social Science Vol. 19, Issue 11.*ed. by Islam, M.S. et al. 2014.

➤ "Lesbian as the Absolute Other: Usha Ganguli's Rudali in Perspective" in The International Journal of Humanities and Social Studies Vol. 2 Issue 10 (Online). 2014.

I owe a debt of gratitude to my PhD Supervisor, Professor Ashis Sengupta, whom I feel honoured to regard as my Academic Father. He has not only mentored the theisis from which this book has germinated, but also steerd my growth as a scholar.

My sincere gratitude is to my teacher, Sri. Bhaskar Uday Ghose, who, opened up the world of academics to me. I feel indebted to Mrs. Mitra Sengupta, for her constant encouragement throughout the course of my career as a researcher. I am grateful to my parents, Sri. Pijush Das and Smt. Kajal Das for their continuous support and upholding my work over everything, my sister, Puja Das for pampering me with high sense of worth and my parents-in-law, Prodip Kr. Roy and Shila Roy for taking pride in my work. I would also like to thank Tirna Sengupta, my academic sibling, whose growth has inspired me in more ways than one. Finally, I owe a lot to my wife, Priyanka Roy, who shared all my pains. And my little daughter, Portia, has certainly helped in her own special ways!

DR. PINAKI RANJAN DAS

INTRODUCTION

Theatre, being a medium which speaks directly to the audience, among many other things, falls into the public domain; and women, being traditionally considered fit to occupy only the domestic space, were long kept away from articulating themselves through theatre. The same is true of Indian theatre also, which for centuries remained exclusive to men, but with the new surge of 'feminism' in the 1970s, effectively opened up for Indian women wide avenues for expressing their own voice. This newly found voice in theatre not only resisted 'devising' by men but also strove to form a 'feminist' theatre. But feminist theatre, globally, was critiqued for indulging in essentialism and failing to represent women in their contexts. Indian women playwrights and directors struck a different note by starting to construct a theatrewhich promised to uphold differences that separate women in one context from women in another. A study of Indian women playwrights (and directors), therefore, must be truly rewarding from historical, political and aesthetic perspectives.

Before examining the distinctive dimensions of "Indian" and then Indian women's theatre, let us try to understand why defining theatre has never been easy, especially when it is considered in relation to drama. At best it can be taken as a space where meaning is formed in performance on stage (be it proscenium or not), constituted through a complex interaction of the body, gestures, words and theatrical devices such as costumes, designs, lights, techniques, and affecting the emotion and intellect of the audience. Conventional discussions on drama and theatre have resulted in pronouncing sharp distinctions between the two. It has been generally observed that drama being primarily textual is a more 'serious literary mode'(Knowles 526) which exclusively belongs to the playwright (notwithstanding the poststructuralist notions of the author and the text); while theatre being audiovisual belongs to the audience and is seen as 'either the interpretative enactment of a stable, universal dramatic text or the translation of that text into different (usually unstable) codes of semiosis of enunciation, gesture, embodiment, design and so on'(526). The play text has often been claimed by drama to be meant for reading, which opens up new vistas of meaning but which suffers constriction when reduced to a particular condition of performance in the theatre. However to theatre, the play text is just a script to which live dimensions are added when it is performed. Critical understanding of drama/theatre has changed over the years. The play text is not just limited to black marks on white paper but everything that entails knowledge, even performance itself. Conversely, performance brings in the body, which writes itself on the stage. There may be textual dialogues that the body delivers, but then the body itself also has its own language; for a body is never reduced to such a sign which refuses any connotation whatsoever. It not just bears the mark and meaning of its gender being conditioned by socio-cultural perceptions of it in particular locations of performance, but also itself produces meanings on the stage. The body has both an objective and subjective presence on the stage. 'A performance takes one to another level of 'knowing'. What may be lurking within one in an incoherent shape, when echoed externally, comes sieved through a collective experience and changes its dimensions altogether. From the personal it becomes common knowledge – something that exists outside one – and being out in the open can be assuring as well as disturbing, if it challenges even a speck that lies dormant within.'(Subramanyam 146) Hence performance as text has initiated the emergence of a 'post-dramatic theatre', where contemporary theatre practitioners like Maya Krishna Rao perform on stage without any written script. Yet the advantage of having a well written script cannot be discounted.

The debate may be settled temporarily by recognizing the 'hybrid existence' of the play text, which is written in order to be read and also performed with multiple dimensions to it and with its difference with other genres.

'Theatre' of 'their own'

In an age where academic curriculum has essentially pushed theatre studies into 'post-script', and the cultural 'space' of making and watching theatre has been largely usurped by the immense popularity of television and 'mainstream' cinemas, it is important to understand why theatre still remains a 'space' to be reckoned as one's 'own'. And to argue for a 'theatre' of 'their own' for the Indian women playwrights (and directors), it is important to explore the possibilities that modern Indian theatre can provide as an instrument of subjective as well as social/ political/ cultural articulations and at the same time analyse the course of Indian theatre which gradually underwent broadening of thematic and dramaturgic scope in order to accommodate the independent voices of the women playwrights and directors.

Theatre's relation to Indian society (as it is in the case with most societies) has been an intriguing one. It has been so, not merely because of theatre's role in representing the nuances of Indian social and cultural life but also in its scope of being *interventional* in engaging with society's political, economic, ethnical, racial, temporal and contextual aspects. Here 'theatre' must not be seen as a mere form of art that puts the social events into performance, but as a mediator between the social issues and the audience, influencing and sometimes articulating the latter's response. But in such circumstances, theatre is often claimed by some 'performance' critics, as more of the performance studies than of mainstream literature. Being a cultural 'space' in itself, theatre has affinity with its location in a particular culture. This includes the uniqueness of its ritualistic and aesthetic forms. But even when social performances may become the content of theatre, it must continue to convert dramatic texts into performances, which exemplifies most of the modern Indian theatre traditions.

Performance studies free audience from the authority of play texts, and can even inform them of the nuances of performance in ways that liberate them from the control of 'modern stage realism'. Hence the audience may be lead beyond the page/stage constrictions. But the real, material conditions of theatre as separate from play-texts cannot be rejectedoutright because of theatre's location in between the cause and consequence of the society. It is both about being affected by the society and also affecting it. Ashis Sengupta in his book, *Mapping South Asia through Contemporary Theatre*, succinctly observes that "theatre in its creative constructedness", engages, "with (social) 'reality' at different levels of affirmation and interrogation, intervention and transgression, imagination and re-inscription. Thus representation in drama and theatre does not always indicate a fixed referent or a determinate position of the object represented. Instead, it can be strategic, exploring, interpretive, creative and redefining. It creates a live, organized, alternative version of a chaotic but dormant reality, past or present, and attributes contemporary, relevant meaning/s to it rather than merely seeking to dis-cover it for the audience."(13). Hence it is worth mapping how it is "as much a representation of offstage 'realities' as a space where 'realities' are equally formed and re-formed through human performance, exploring in the process a complex relationship between world, text, performance, viewing, and reception."(4) The 'human performance' here may take into account the performatives, but that is only to the extent of advancing a suggestion to the audience, who share the knowledge of the same. Performance has its own dynamics, which on stage would not put forward a mimetic representation of the 'offstage' referent, but would mediate with the 'reality', surely constructing reality/ies of its own.

Theatre in its engagement with the social reality may be inspired by issues political or economic, which either disturbs or reinstates its status quo. With its affective power of impressing the audience and even the possibilities of initiating them to action, theatre may take varieties of forms with multifarious names such as the 'progressive theatre', 'oppositional theatre', 'engaged theatre', 'applied theatre', 'theatre of liberation', 'street theatre', 'popular theatre' etc., depending upon the purpose it intends to serve. These forms of theatre are popularly known in India as 'political theatre', for it engages not just with the law makers but also with any form of authority, that identifies itself with the domination of the other, be it on the grounds of labor, class, caste, ethnicity, colour, or sex. Such political roles of theatre have often disturbed the authorities in such ways that history abounds with examples where they have fallen heavily upon it, be it the 1887 dramatic censorship act passed by the British Government on Colonial India, or the murder of Safdar Hashmi in broad daylight during the performance of *Halla Bol*, a street play against the exploitations of labor, targeted against both the Government and the Capitalist forces. Theatre, therefore emerges as a site which is both influenced by and in turn influences social and political performance, though, performance may not necessarily be translated into practice each time.

When women playwrights and directors are brought into 'perspective', the social politics concerning women again loom large. Though we come across women playwrights like Swarna Kumari Devi, Anurupa Devi or Bimala Sundari Devi in the pre-independence colonial period, it is only from the 1970s onwards that we find a significant population of Indian women playwrights and directors regularly participating in the process of 'theatre making'. Sushma Deshpande, Shanta Gandhi, Dina Mehta, Irpinder Bhatia, Manjula Padmanabhan, Varsha Adalja, Poile Sengupta, B. Jayashree, Shaoli Mitra, Tripurari Sharma, Usha Ganguli, Anuradha Kapur, Neelam Mansingh Chaudhury, Kirti Jain, Amal Allana are among many other women playwrights and directors who are not only composing/ devising plays/ dramas, but are also striving to produce a vocabulary of their own in theatre. But the accommodation of women's 'voice' in the 1970s Indian theatre was not an abrupt phenomenon. The 'event' may be placed in the context of the global and local ramifications of 'feminism' and feminist movements in theatre. According to Anita Singh, feminist theatre (a term sometimes used for the women-centric productions of the Indian women theatre practitioners) in India, was 'anupshot of an interface between postcolonial debates about language, interpellation, subject formation and forms of resistance and the feminist movements in the 1960's' (Singh 1)

The feminist movement of the 1960s (in the West), which had its roots in the socio-political and intellectual movements of the 1940s, has been termed in the feminist discourse as the 'second wave movement'; the 'first wave' being roughly associated with the post-1880s tothe 1920s, during which, among other achievements, the feminist movement across the West won franchise rights for women, making it possible for women to actively participate in the political system. The 1960s 'social revolution' which aimed at producing a 'counter-culture' to the traditional conformist cultures and championed the causes of socio-cultural liberations including the 'sexual' (that began in the U.S and subsequently reached the wider Western world) catalysed the abolishing of censorship in theatre in England. Freedom from censorship allowed theatre to engage with any immediate political struggles of the time. It is in response to the new feminist agitations and its allied movements, that in 1968, Lord Chamberlain's censorship against any 'explicit' heterosexual or homosexual behavior and 'bad language' (Wandor 76) was abandoned in England.

The 1968 impact on theatre initiated arguments to bring theatre out of the closets of the bourgeois, i.e. the performance of plays be discontinued in theatre buildings and instead performed among the common run of people, about and amidst their lives and struggles. Except the agitprop, all other proscenium theatre traditions were discouraged. The self-styled feminist theatre received the paraphernalia of the socialist touring groups, which used a TV like 'naturalist telling-it-like-it-is'(77) method to come closer to the people, which found a more effective medium in simple easy-to-understand satirical songs, and such visual imageries which were suggestive of certain peculiarities of a class or community. Hence the feminist plays that followed in the 1970s, looked at the woman 'question' from the socialist 'perspective', which was fraught with class consciousness and explicit Marxist connotations, taking into account the on-going reorientations of classical Marxist class analysis too. The scripted agitprop theatre of the time featured live experiences of working class women, and sexism both in public forums like the labor unions and in family at the domestic level. While agitprop theatre set to democratize theatre in all its aspects be it the subject matter, the form of theatre used or the audience addressed to, it initiated an internal democracy within the groups as well who 'wrote and performed their own work, instead of acting as hired labour, as would happen in traditional theatre' (77). But such movements do not really speak for any concrete impact of feminism on theatre for no such theatre which overtly dealt with feminist themes was produced; neither was there any proliferation of women playwrights harping on the feminist themes. It is only in the autumn of 1973 when feminist influence on theatre could explicitly be marked with the birth of 'Women's Theatre Group' out of the 'Women's Theatre Season' held in 'Almost Free Theatre' in London. Women's Theatre Group was a professional, all women's company, first of its kind in England. Such a formation had its impact on other established theatre works as well. In the mid-1970s, 'The Association of Community Theatres' formed by the touring groups, the 'Independent Theatres Council' formed by the small venues, 'Theatre Writers' Union' formed by the playwrights and 'Equity' by the performers' union, provided enough possibilities to the then active women's sub-committees. Those fringe theatres which remained out of these organizations lost most of their women theatre workers to the 'Feminist Theatre Study Group' set up in the late 1970s, in order to provide space for any independent/self-identified feminists. The Feminist Theatre Study Group became a forum which aimed at networking professionals, promoted feminist ideas and conducted consciousness –raising drives among women. Michelene Wandor notes that 'at one point, the group also demonstrated outside those West End theatres considered to be most sexist in the way they represented women as stereotypical characters' (bracketing mine) (78). Such consciousness drives resulted in increasing number of women coming up and openly voicing their discontent against the limited opportunities they were exposed to. Though much effort on the part of women theatre practitioners did not directly result in increased involvement of women at the 'National Theatre' and the 'Royal Shakespeare Company', both of which were largely male dominated, it increased the demand for more women-centered theatre groups in addition to that of the 'Women's Theatre Group', which would offer more opportunities to the women and other marginalized sexes. This resulted in the formation of 'Monstrous Regiment', a company which provided space to each of the sexes but privileged the women, and the 'Gay Sweatshop', which promoted gay and lesbian theatres along with the mixed theatre productions.

These groups, taken together, addressed two important issues – firstly, the women participation in theatre, which was not encouraging till then, and secondly, the aesthetic development in modern theatre, given the political transformation they had to undergo due to the post 1970s feminist influences. While none of these groups put forward any ideal pattern for theatre works, they did suggest some 'material working conditions which are...conducive or obstructive' to theatre productions 'informed by feminism' (80). The 'Women's Theatre Group' promoted collaborative and collective methods of producing plays, which must feature pro-women issues, even by way of politicizing the male/female relationship. Holding on to the policy of making more spaces for women, it not just employed only women in the company but also 'hired' women directors, stage managers, designers, etc. and produced plays centering on woman both as part of the past and the contemporary, which consequently entailed a reworking of history itself. Such efforts on the part of the 'Women's Theatre Group' challenged the traditional/ unquestioned contours of theatre, which till then reserved its space only for male performers and man-centric plays. This had an importance of its own, not just from the point of view of theatre but feminist politics as well, for it represented women's control over their own work. In keeping with the radical feminist principles, these women's groups banked on women's experiences and relationships and aimed at building women's autonomous yet organizational existence. This addressed not just the 'class conflicts' in relation to women but also the 'socialist-feminist elements in the way women interact, function, love and struggle with one another'(81).Though 'Monstrous Regiment' was better received by the theatre world because of its mixed sex structure, it underwent its own share of hostility in response to its privileging women over men. Though the intention behind such a formation was to challenge the normative order and provide a stage which is populated more by women than men, 'Monstrous Regiment' never sought to present man/woman relationship in subversion. The case is somewhat similar for the 'Gay Sweatshop' which, 'while being a mixed group, has chiefly challenged the closeness of the male gay... encouraging confidence among the gays in the audience, and linking gay with female oppression'(82).

But a new kind of performance-based theatre work, explicitly informed by feminism, developed from the 1970s. 'In the very early days of feminist agitprop at the beginning of the 1970s, bold visual imagery was used to satirize and question received notions of femininity and masculinity. Sexuality, make-up, fashion, the intimacies of the private lives were dragged out from behind closed doors, taken into the street theatre and exaggerated into visual shock tactics' (82). The decade ended with the basic questions already realized and the agitprop theatre fast losing its relevance. A 'new generation' of women theatre practitioners found their way into prominence, for whom the 'the climate' (82) was 'more relaxed' (82). 'They' began to 'build a new lively kind of performance theatre, in which the conventional, feminine, passive presence of the woman performer playing a secondary supportive female character' (84), was 'implicitly challenged with an alternative' (84). But given the patriarchal fabric of the society, it was 'not surprising that the more simplistic and unthreatening the feminism contained in a play, the more likely it was to achieve commercial success' (84). Hence,

> as a profession, theatre became a microcosm of the
> discrimination and inequalities operating in society

at large. In 1981, feminist playwright and critic Michelene Wandor, published an analysis of theatre and sexual politics which made explicit women's second class, 'understudy' status in a male dominated theatre industry... The lived professional experience of being consigned to the role of 'understudy' is what, in turn, encouraged women practitioners to form 'their own feminist-theatre groups'. (Aston).

Along with 'Monstrous Regiment' and 'Women's Theatre Group', which were 'seminal to the innovation of a feminist theatre tradition', many other groups like Clapperclaws, Cunning Stunts, Beryl and Perils, Clean Break and Mrs. Worthington's Daughters created a 'counter-cultural body of women's plays and performances' (Aston). The feminist groups, opened up more opportunities for women playwrights and 'by the mid to late seventies Caryl Churchill, Pam Gems, Bryony Lavery, Claire Luckham and Louis Page were moving the dramatic representations of women's lives and experiences centre-stage as a counter-cultural challenge and alternative to the 'malestream', canonical tradition of theatre'. (Aston)

Thereafter, women dramatists including Sarah Daniels, April de Angelis, Winsome Pinnock and Timberlake Wertenbaker earned recognition in the eighties. Owing to the emergence of a host of women playwrights influenced by Second Wave Feminism, Methuen Drama launched the *Plays by Women* series in 1982. This included Caryl Churchill's *Vinegar Tom,* which, with its stylistic and political innovations, along with other 'women's plays' by Churchill such as *Cloud Nine* or *Top Girls,* proved seminal in defining a 'feminist landscape in British Theatre'(Aston). Hence, when Helene Keyssar seeks to define the feminist theatre in *Feminist Theatre and Theory,* she observes that it is about 'productions and scripts characterized by consciousness of women as women; performance (written and acted) that deconstructs sexual difference and thus undermines patriarchal power; scripting and production that present transformation as a structural and ideological replacement for recognition; and the creation of women characters in the 'subject position'.'(1) According to Keyssar, this created a new audience for theatre. Among many other things, what it has most importantly proposed is the idea of a 'women's language' and its possibilities of creating altogether a new kind of narrative in theatre.

In India, the feminist theatre has also brought about a rethinking of plot/character configuration, putting into question the 'meaning and performance of character both on stage and in script' (Kapur 6). 'Direct Action', and consistency in logical building of plot gave way to indirect actions, inconsistencies and disjoints in plot construction. Non-linear plots, refusing any kind of resolution, aided in challenging the socio–political normativity which sustained the artificial boundaries between gender, class, race, culture etc. In her essay 'Performing Resistance, Re-dressing the Canon: The Emergence of Indian Feminist Theatre', Anita Singh conceptualizes the essential characteristics of Indian feminist theatre thus –

- Feminist theatre is a creative theatre that challenges representation of our dominant culture. The goal of almost all feminist plays/ groups is to subvert expectations, to enable or initiate positive changes in women's lives through political and theatrical representations (Singh 6).
- Feminist theatre focuses on female characters and explores concepts/ themes of feminist drama, relationships, sisterhood, sexuality and female autonomy (7).
- A Feminist theatre … brings in communal power structures – devising and collaborating writing process used by many communal/ cooperative companies, visual texts, small-scale commissions of new works by women authors and collaborative writing (7).
- Feminist plays deconstruct the emasculating structures of ancient legends and criticize the feminine myths still operating in Indian society. The content of their plays have ranged from re-working of traditional myths to current social issues (8).

Thematically, Indian feminist theatre came to be associated with the plays which dealt with the concerns of women such as the 'dowry deaths', 'eve teasing', 'rape', 'violence against women', 'economic dependency', 'compulsory heterosexuality' etc. But beyond these characteristics, Indian feminist theatre has been critiqued for being 'essentialist', that is, for reducing women to bodies, and for assuming that 'all women are the same'(Kapur 5). Hence, representation of women by way of producing stereotypes has continued in its own way, though the objective was to foreground women as subjects.

In the post-1970s period, we find the emergence of women playwrights and directors, who were initiated not only by explicitly political but also general concerns for gender relations. They drew upon women's experiences and aimed at 'consciousness raising' among women in order to bring about socio-political changes in their material conditions of existence. It is the 'feminine awareness' that is most strikingly aimed at in their plays. Though the Indian 'women's theatre' was initially influenced by the western 'feminist theatre' of the 70s, it gradually matured into a more conscious and confident 'female stage' from the 'feminist stage' in theatre. The latter, in its pursuit of political aims often appeared to be in absolute opposition to the conventional 'gender structure'.

In foregrounding women's experiences and sexuality on stage, not in opposition to the male counterpart but in focusing on their own exclusivity and uniqueness in perceiving the world at large, women's theatre presents the woman as a "speaking subject". Hence it throws into doubt the private/public divide where the 'public' ceases to be *exclusive* masculine domain. In presenting women as 'subjects'; as conscious choice and decision makers; women's theatre moves away from 'essentialism' in feminist theatre, for it takes into account multiple contexts of the women all over and the differences in their socio-cultural conditioning that mark off one woman from the other. Hence, women's theatre emerges as an alternative to the conventional theatre even though it was not necessarily taking a political stance against it.

In the Indian context, the role of women's theatre is more crucially conceived than in the West because of the complex locations of women amidst the cultural diversity of the country. Plays by the women playwrights who gradually populated the landscape of Indian theatre from the 1980s, strive to present the varied women experience which is not devoid of their struggles against socio-patriarchal domination, their hopes and aspirations, fulfillments or frustrations, subject to the conditions they live in. These can be further correlated with lived experiences of the playwrights and directors themselves. In order to dramatize these issues effectively, they use history, mythology or ancient accounts of life and society by way of reinterpreting them from women's perspectives. They have consistently used folk themes and motifs to their own advantage, and used drama as an effective medium to analyze socio-cultural differences and issues concerning gender discrimination. Hence, the Indian women theatre practitioners seek to enhance the scope of theatre in Indian in order to produce a more inclusive dramaturgy that can accommodate the interests of the 'people' living in the fringes as those in the centre of socio-political discourse. Thematically, women's issues remained the primary focus but were heterogeneously dissolved with other socio-political concerns. In *Listen Shefali* (1975), Varsha Adalja situates Shefali's struggle against the backdrop of a caste oriented 'modern' society which has its own political strategies to perpetuate gender subordination. In *Harvest* (1996), Manjula Padmanabhan posits the questions of motherhood and procreation amidst the themes of amputation, body-parts transplantation, reification and economic exploitation. In representing women in their contexts, the Indian women playwrights go beyond the feminist representations of women as 'victims' of socio-cultural, political injustices. They project women as 'conscious' individuals who not only challenge the *status quo* but also actively participate in the social discursive processes in order to produce the desired changes. Azizun Nisa in Tripurari Sharma's *A Tale from the Year 1857: Azizun Nisa* (1996) considers the 1857 'sepoy mutiny' as an opportunity for her to be part of a nationalist struggle (mostly considered to be a masculine affair) and rejects being categorized as a docile courtesan who is 'expected' to remain far from the machineries of war and political struggles. Manasa in Mamta G. Sagar's *The Swing of Desire* (1990) is as much a mother as a woman desiring to establish her career as a successful dancer. With the enlargement of thematic scope in women's drama, the dramaturgy too gradually evolved as the women dramatists experimented with the forms and techniques of dramatic compositions and theatrical representations. Borrowing from Alice Walker, Tutun Mukherjee calls this 'inclusive' dramaturgy as 'womanist dramaturgy', which is neither the outright rejection of traditional forms of theatre (because they also can be renovated to present the nuanced locations of Indian women in diverse, and by that means, more complex frameworks), nor is it the merely experimental theatre forms and non-linear plays exemplifying feminist theatre. It rather projects the 'consciousness' of women as women and what it means to be in the position of the 'subject' while being constantly made aware of the socio-sexual otherness. Tutun Mukherjee argues that in representing women as subjects, the womanist dramaturgy is interstitially located 'between realism and Brechtian non-realism' (Mukherjee 18). She explains that 'by its very nature ...womanist dramaturgy would find itself incompatible with unproblematized depiction of realism because realism tends to naturalize the status quo of the patriarchal system and covertly positions the reader/ spectator within that ideology' (18). A womanist drama-text therefore seeks to disrupt the equilibrium, create tension in the minds of the audience and deny the 'sacred' tradition of providing emotional purgation at the end. Hence, a play by woman playwright often weaves together threads of contradictions and engages multiple viewpoints in place of producing 'compulsory' narrative unity and closure. Such dramaturgical innovations and thematic concerns of contemporary Indian women theatre practitioners have constructed a theatre of their own that speaks of women in wider perspectives. Hence the 'in perspective' in the title of this book is not about imposing and then exploring a single perspective on the works of Indian women playwrights but perspectives that emerge from the plays composed (and directed) by Indian women playwrights (and directors), who not only deny being branded as feminists but also consciously construct an identity of their own. For example, Mallika Sarabhai believes that 'being a feminist and being a feminine are one and the same. "Our strength lies in our being women. The moment we de-sex ourselves and try to be something we are not – men – our defeat is writ large."'(Ahuja 17). Her theatre aims at making women conscious of their own potentials and at the same time critique their limitations. Sarabhai denies projecting men as responsible for the subordination of women.

Usha Ganguli, too, rejects the label of the 'feminist' and opines that "it is by working with both the masculine and the feminine that we will, at a point, reach harmony" (qtd. by Lieder F. K. in "Not-Feminism" 608). However, it must be mentioned that even when the women playwrights and directors reject being defined as feminists, they continue to contribute towards the discourse on women's rights to liberation from socio-cultural orthodoxies, religious taboos and the patriarchal *controls* embodied in hetero-normative relations. In an interview given to Anjum Katyal, Usha Ganguli makes her position clear as a non-feminist.

> I feel that I differ from the way people tend to use the term feminism. This term has nowadays become a fashionable one, and I don't believe in a particular brand of feminism. Therefore I don't want the play [Rudali] to be labeled as feminist. On theother hand, I believe in the liberation of women and their freedom, and I'm trying my best as a person, as a teacher, and as a theatre worker to work towards that. (Katyal 2)

The rejection of 'feminism' as an ideology and denying being identified as feminists, can generally be traced in the nature of feminist discourse in India, which at its inception was spearheaded by male reformists, with women joining the movement only at the end of the 19th Century. Hence, feminism in India had its commencement as part of larger social reformist movements. And it continued to be so in the 1960s and '70s with the contribution of Gandhian socialists and the Ultra leftists.

The formation of women's trade union was the result of one of the political movements initiated by the Gandhian socialists in the post-independence period. However, these unions neither considered them feminists, nor did they encourage any feminist discussions. But women's groups which emerged in Left outfits around 1975 initiated feminist debates and associated feminism with other social movements of the time. With the repealing of 'Emergency' in 1977, several other women's groups were formed mainly in the metropolis, which did not have any apparent similarity with each other but members of these groups largely hailed from that section of the society which was educated, belonged to the middle or 'upper-middle-class' and was located in the urban. Hence they lacked the authentic sensibility of the underprivileged, rural, poor, lower caste/class women who comprised the majority. But as active participants in the Left political processes, the members of these groups who were oriented in the Marxist understanding of class and society, sought to represent and bring together women from different sections, irrespective of their caste and ethnic identities. By the late 1970s and early '80s, women's groups caught the media attention with their repeated struggles against oppression of women, such as the protests against dowry murders, rapes, not just by the civilians but also by the police/army especially in troubled areas of the country, honour-killings, women trafficking etc. Hence the public and private collided in providing agendas for women's movements. But it must also be noted that in spite of enough enthusiasm in such movements, they did not produce expected results because of the essentially patriarchal structure of the law and administrative institutions in the country. Hence struggles continued against the administration as well, soon to be usurped by the major political parties. This in course led to the drowning of independent feminist voices amidst the loud cacophony of the national parties. From being the sole demand, women's issues became one among the other associated political demands. Demonstrations, street theatres, consciousness raising public campaigns informed by feminist ideologies were almost discontinued and women's centers were formed, with the aim to provide legal, health and counseling assistance. Increasingly influenced by the western feminist movements, women's groups such as the *Saheli* or *Salehi*, took up trans-cultural issues recurring in the daily idiom across India throughout the 1970s: rape, dowry deaths, wife-beating, bride-burning, mothering, housekeeping etc. Hence the productions of such plays as Dina Mehta's *Brides are Not for Burning* or *Om Swaha* by Anuradha Kapur and Maya Rao, presented by Stree Sangharsh, a Delhi based women's group, in the early 1980s. Also must be mentioned the production of *Mulgi Zali Ho* (A Girl is Born) by the Bombay based women's group, *Stree Mukti Sanghatana*. No less pertinent here is to consider a women's group from Manipur, *Meira Paibi* which was composed of women only above forty-five years of age, who believed that beyond a certain age, women's lives must be spent in the service of the society. These women patrolled the roads of Manipur at night and hunted places where men took alcohol and drugs. Later, the same women protested against the army when they forcibly took away their men. In an interview with Lakshmi Subramanyam, Tripurari Sharma mentions a few other women's groups from the 1980s which deserve to be mentioned here; *Sewa Mahila* and *Vimochina*, based in Bangalore, *Action India* and *Ankur* in Delhi, *Chattisgarh Mahila Mukti Morcha* in Raipur and *Mahila Manch* in Kanpur (Subramanyam 143).

The women's centers took up such issues which were more intimate with the public and hence met with severe hostilities from the traditional patriarchal institutes of the societies. The feminists were popularly critiqued as the 'latest offshoots' of western capitalism, having no respect for the traditional Indian ethos. They were considered ignorant of the essential social structure in India and were accused of making forays into it by making out false meanings out of witch-hunting, human sacrifice, forcible widow immolation etc. All of these contributed to the discontinuation of women's centers and the resultant vacuum was then occupied by the political parties' women's wings, which were promoted to show solidarity towards women primarily with the intentions of electoral politics.

The feminist debates in India, primarily encouraged by the women's groups, therefore began with demands relating to women's suffering across private and the public spaces. But a definite change can be noticed in the post 1980s period where celebrating the strength of the 'new women' supplemented the traditional discussions on women depravity and domination. The camps now gave way to *melas* which initiated large scale discussions of women's issues but ushered in a light mood of festivity too. With the spread of such events, they soon lost their seriousness in mere mechanical imitations of things customary to *melas* and underwent a process of fragmentation which is common to most of the feminist proceedings in the Indian subcontinent. Such fragmentation, which was exemplified in the open display of differences among the feminist organizations (often heavily loaded with different political ideologies), ushered in an inevitable collapse of 'sisterhood'. This led to doubt the very basis of 'feminism' in the Indian context, where fragmentation and multiplicities are operative in such layered ways that they seek to defy any sort of unified organization dedicated to women's issues alone. In the light of above discussion, it seems pertinent to note that Chandra Talpade Mohanty, one of the pioneer Indian feminists, understands 'woman' as a 'cultural and ideological composite Other constructed through diverse representational discourses' (19), while considering women as 'real, material subjects of their collective histories'(19), and opines that seeking the relation between the 'woman' and 'women' is one of the main objectives of feminist scholarships, though the relationship is 'not of direct identity, or a relation of correspondence or simple implication. It is an arbitrary relation set up by particular cultures' (19). Mohanty argues that assumptions of privilege and ethnocentric universality on the one hand, and inadequate self-consciousness about the effect of Western scholarship on the 'third world' in the context of a world system dominated by the West on the other, characterize a sizable extent of Western feminist work on women in the third world.' She further says that 'an analysis of "sexual difference" in the form of a trans-cultural singular, monolithic notion of patriarchy or male dominance leads to the construction of a similarly reductive and homogeneous notion of what I (she) call(s) the "Third World Difference"—that stable, ahistorical something that apparently oppresses most if not all the women in these countries. And it is in the production of this "Third World Differences" that Western feminisms appropriate and 'colonize' the fundamental complexities and conflicts which characterize the lives of women of different classes, religions, cultures, races and castes in these countries (19) (bracketing mine).

But third world feminism in itself is again a monolithic meta-narrative that imposes itself upon the women of colour, irrespective of their social, political, cultural, religious, ethnic and racial differences. The 'third world', conceived in the light of colonial history, has been defined as the non-enlightened, non-white, racially inferior exotic; but with the new surge of feminist criticism from the 1980s, a new sensibility has been vouched for the third world women, whose material conditions have already been ignored by Western feminism in privileging the white women. Julie Stephens however in her essay *Feminist Fictions: A Critique of the category 'Non-Western Woman' in Feminist Writings on India,* voices a transnational unity among women arguing: 'what unites women…must be something beyond culture. So cultures can be different; women cannot. Sameness, or what links women to each other, is the 'experience of being a woman', according to the discourse, because it is the same despite differences in culture. Cultural (i.e. historical) differences are irrelevant to any understanding of this 'experience', which is thereby situated in something universal to all human cultures and beyond the pale of history. The concept of 'universal sisterhood' or women's liberation on a truly international scale' is based on an essentialist notion of womanness beyond history, nation and class.'(Stephens 109) But in foregrounding multiculturalism as a point of departure from the West, traditional feminism may deem ineffectual, for as Susan Moller Okin argues in *Is Multiculturalism Bad for Women?*, feminism and multiculturalism cannot be reconciled.

South Asia being a mosaic of different cultures is again a break away from the 'third world'. Though women have sometimes been considered index to the progress or retreat of a society, and the women question has been one of the central political issues in the nation 'building' processes in South Asian countries, it would be a mistake to assume the existence of an overarching feminism in the entire region. Comprehending South Asia has its own complexities, for, though it is a constellation of post-colonial nation states separated by shared political boundaries, they relate to each other on grounds of economic, geographic, linguistic and social realities. Despite similarities, no single perspective can define the 'enormous geographical space comprising the nation states of India, Pakistan, Bangladesh, Nepal and Sri Lanka.'(Sengupta 1) While for the feminists in India or Bangladesh, 'anti-colonial struggles and post-colonial nation-making seem to be the point of departure' (Menon 220), they find no resonance among the feminists in Nepal. The 1947 partition may have had a huge impact on India, Pakistan and Bangladesh, but countries like Sri Lanka and Nepal had other 'histories of national and ethnic divisions to deal with' (Menon 220). Even the practice of religion has constituted and still continues to contribute differently to the national identities in different nation-states in South Asia. Moreover, as Nivedita Menon argues in *Seeing like a Feminist* (2012):

> ...within the countries themselves, political struggles are inflected by local dimensions, whether of class, religious or caste identities, regional aspirations within nation-states and so on. In addition, relationships among these nation-states are unequal and contested; they are further complicated by geopolitical developments and the differential effects of globalization and imperialist expansion on each country. It is within this variegated terrain that feminist struggles and concepts have shaped

themselves and engaged with various formations of power.(Menon220).

The feminists have engaged with most of the social discourses simultaneously, but, 'history' has continued to be the central realm of inquiry owing to the peculiarity of postcolonial politics in South Asia. In their essay, *South Asian Feminisms: Contemporary Interventions*, Ania Loomba and A. Ritty Lukose, observes that the 'spectacular rise of communalism, sectarian violence, and militarism has necessitated a continued feminist engagement with histories of religious identity, community and social memory' (Loomba and Lukose 5).They argue that Urvashi Butalia's exploration into the 'gendered aspect of the communal violence of the 1947 Partition of British India into India and Pakistan' (5) can be considered to have 'catalyzed... the horrific escalation of such violence in the 1980s, and specifically the anti-Sikh riots that erupted in Delhi after the 1984 assassination of Indira Gandhi by her two Sikh bodyguards' (5). Feminist historians in India were compelled to 'engage anew with the long lineages of Hindu cultural nationalism following the destruction of the Babri mosque in 1992 by Hindu fundamentalists, an event that ushered in an era of heightened anti-Muslim rhetoric and practices' (5).

In Sri Lanka, the whole agency of gendered history comes from the ethno-nationalistic struggle that is unique in its own right in South Asia, while in contrast, Pakistani feminists for the most of time remain occupied with their struggles against Islamic orthodoxy, rather than engaging themselves in nationalist debates. Hence, South Asia in its existence as a politically charged postcolonial space is divided into such discontinuities among the constituent nation states that no homogeneous feminism that can uniformly address its trans-cultural women's issues is plausible.

Similar critical issues ensue when feminism is considered in relation to India, for India as a federal nation state essentially unites its regions, politically putting together multiplicities, disjunctions and fragmentations on the one hand and recognizing the differences among the parts on the other. India as a nation emerges as an overarching narrative that seeks to homogenize the differences in Indian society that is torn on grounds of plurality in caste, class, ethnicity, race, religion, culture, and region. Therefore in a country of such diversity, conceptualizing feminism in Western terms would be impossible but reading the 'local' to frame multiple feminist perspectives based on issues that are unique to a specific locale instead of forming a singular perspective on the entire geography that invariably ignores the differences in women's issues must be encouraged. The term 'local', especially when it is to be mediated through women's theatre, must therefore entail the analyses of the actual empirical realities that contribute to the material conditions of women. Feminist activists have traditionally used theatre as a medium to 'strategically use and create social spaces to generate collective dialogue and critical reflection on issues of patriarchy and violence' (Nagar, 341). 'Activists working at the grass-roots level theorize the inter-relationships among their own political actions, their vision(s) of empowerment, and the everyday gendered spaces they seek to transform.'(341). But such activism always has to mediate with the 'socio-economic and political realities that define women's struggles'(342) typical to that region. Though the issues addressed by women's theatre are seldom intimately connected, critical idioms concerning them have evolved centering on violence against women both in their intra and extra-household relations. However, 'the focus has gradually shifted from the relatively narrow concerns of "women's welfare" to the new ideology/program of 'women's empowerment' and the question of individual autonomy' (Sengupta 22). Therefore the women theatre activists put forward 'questions of political consciousness and self-identity', which, for Mohanty, are crucial in defining 'third world women's engagement with feminism'. Hence theatre can directly participate in 'raw activism', where active political struggles may not consider any aesthetic contribution, but women playwrights and directors responded to this changed social situation, by writing, directing, and producing plays, telling '*their* stories of suffering, resistance, and dreams' (Sengupta 22). Though the increasing enthusiasm for spectacle attracted the audience more towards television rather than theatre, Indian women theatre practitioners innovated their dramaturgy to bring theatre close to people by producing non-linear, anti-realist plays and staging them amidst the orchestra of life, where struggle for existence *co-exists* with desire for entertainment, instead of waiting for people to come to theatre. Although this initially germinated in the form of street theatres of Utpal Dutta, Badal Sircar, and Safdar Hashmi, such innovations on the part of women playwrights and directors brought activism and aesthetics in close proximity with each other. One such example is Sushma Deshpande's *Whay Mee Savitribai*, which was performed in railway platforms, 'under a tree, in the temple, anywhere' (Deshpande) before audience which would require the director's intervention as a story teller, and also in international conferences, before 'elite' spectators. The same is also with her *Teechi Aaichi Ghosta*, a Tamasha play on the living conditions of prostitutes, and *Baya Daar Ugadh*, a play on women saint poets. While each play speaks on women empowerment and has been performed by the women activists to present women as they are (without stereotyping them), they are also brilliant pieces of theatrical and literary values.

The women playwrights and directors must be credited with merging diverse forms of performance and theatre. One of the most important names in this regard would be Mrinalini Sarabhai whose *Darpan Academy*, primarily devoted to training in different classical dance forms, has produced around 150 plays. For Mrinalini, dance and drama are no two separate entities. In choreographing more than 300 dance dramas, Mriniali has raised choreography to the level of theatre direction. One of her most glorious ventures is the production of *Swapanvasudattam*, a Sanskrit Classic in English for an American audience. Considered one of the pioneers of experimental theatre in India, Mrinalini's bold innovations, especially in her portraying Gowri, Chitrangada, Shakuntala, Mira, Savitri etc, not only showcases the Indian womanhood but also forms of 'iconoclasm – woman's questioning, challenging, demolishing the values and institutions, created by man.' (Ahuja 17). Mrinalini's daughter Mallika Sarabhai, who has the same knack for experimenting with theatre and dance forms as her mother, 'uses her dances to challenge her audiences and make them sit up and think about women's place in society or about cultural atrophy'(17). Though an exponent of classical dance forms at its pristine purity, Mallika has also showcased 'how to coalesce the classical and the folk, the oriental and the occidental' (17). Chaman Ahuja puts it best:

> At best it is creative choreography that rejects the moods and themes of classical dance but draws from it certain elements which are fused with the rhythms of folk dances, the aggressiveness of martial arts, the dramatic material from life, the narrative skill, and the stylized version of gestures and movements from everyday existence, the ultimate aim being to create a community art which may facilitate social change through awareness. (18)

In her role as Draupadi in Peter Brook's *Draupadi*, Mallika discovered herself as an essential fearless Indian woman for whom 'heroism' lies in 'her defiance' (18), much like the Draupadi of the epic, *Mahabharata*. 'Living with Draupadi was a wonderful experience – being forced to find the essential and the fearless in me. With her, my political, ideological and artistic lives merged. And have remained so.'(18). Rooted in the Indian context, Mallika's experience in the context of Indian theatre may be seen as defining the shift in approach of the modern Indian women's theatre (and social) activists, which is characterized by translating experience into activism. 'Mallika believes that being a feminist and being feminine are one and the same. In *Sita's Daughters*, Mallika uses narrative strategies as diverse as the mask, dance, music, mime monologues etc, to question the portrayal of few exemplary women from the Indian mythology and history. She identifies Sita's example as typical to the traditional Indian womanhood, who can establish their 'voice' only when subjected to extreme male social tyranny. The play however moves beyond Sita and browses through a number of exemplary

Indian women including the Rani of Jhansi and Meera Bai, in order to question the patriarchal strategy in projecting women in roles that has facilitated and defined masculine interpretation of women's roles. In her attempts to work with socially relevant issues, Mallika's dramaturgic innovations lend uniqueness both to her dance and the traditional techniques of communicating social concerns with the audience. She takes up the theme of violence in *V for* …and evolves a drama 'using case histories, video-images, quotations from violators and peacemakers' (19). Chaman Ahuja defines her work as the 'theatre of social purpose' and considers them as representing 'the theatre of tomorrow' (19).

Moving beyond the traditional methods of theatre making, some of the Indian women playwrights and directors discovered playwriting as a collaborative art. The changing socio-cultural position of women in the early 1980s promoted collaboration of women through women's groups and workshops. Reference to Tripurari Sharma's experiences in her formative days as a playwright-director, may exemplify the gradual process of shift towards collaborative theatre. In an interview with Lakshmi Subramanyam, published in *Muffled Voices Women in Modern Indian Theatre*, Sharma speaks of a theatre workshop at Nagda (Madhya Pradesh) in 1979. She was asked by a trade union to produce a play which would reflect the struggles of their lives without indulging in the political rhetoric. There was no script. Therefore they had to 'evolve' (138) one. She started by picking and choosing with trial and error method from the folk tales, stories, enactments and narrations, suggested by her team. The questions she raised during the process are important in understanding the shift in technique of evolving a play-from the singular to collaborative composition and direction, substituting the subjective for the objective, yet preserving the preferences and priorities; from text to experience; from the author to the actor; from an organic production of a play to piecing together fragments/ snaps/ shots/ dialogues/ performances/ songs/ dance, etc.

'The question is – can a person or an incident not be the subject of a text, unless a playwright picks it up and places it in a written structure? After all, life exists and any moment in it can develop into a play. But what if a writer does not pick it up? What if one fails to see it or chooses to ignore it? Priorities are different for each person. What may be meaningful to one group may seem mundane to another group. Is it possible to sift and recreate and enact something of your experience? After all, the first play, the archetypal play, was a recount of the hunter's experience to the community. It contained the essentials of the relationship between an actor and audience. Can some such performance not be designed in contemporary times? Theoretically 'Yes' and in practical terms somewhat difficult. The actor would then define and create the content and not be a medium for something that exists beforehand. It also implies that the text would not exist on paper but be shaped as the actor/ actors build upon their ideas, feelings or reactions. The actor no longer learns lines – he simply utters them. Nor does he interpret a text for it is created by him or her. It is a reversal of an actor's conventional training wherein he imbibes a character from the text – here he builds the character and the text simultaneously. The actor's stature is enhanced, but the moulding and remoulding is not without frustration. But we struggled and managed to piece together a performance loosely held together by songs and the theme.'

This was a small simple workshop, but in many ways significant for me. It affirmed my faith in the collective process, in the belief that there are layers of creativity within each person and that talent has no single form. I saw drama being born in the form that it is actually performed – a three dimensional reality. It seemed closer to the oral rather than the written tradition of expression. It transcended the restriction of reading, (hence writing), skills and thus was not bound by literacy. This further widened the scope and nature of possibilities. (Subramanyam 138 – 139)

Tripurari Sharma speaks of a number of such workshops, where she collaborated with students, trade unions, women's groups from slums and rural areas, to evolve drama texts out of their daily experiences. Sharma's endeavour therefore was to bring into practice a form of theatre which engages with incoherent and living experiences and dramaturgically reproduce them amidst the commotion of daily sprint of life. Theatre evolved as a 'design' suitable to be performed in college compounds, bastis, street squares, market places, terraces etc. Hence, 'the tone of the plays was not didactic but experiential. Often first person accounts were incorporated and hence the narration had an undertone of intimacy. Each play was different and representative of the group. Structurally the plays denoted sharing of experience, composed by exchanging notes – women talking to each other and the audience. Theatre then was also dialogue' (Subramanyam 144).

Evolving scripts out of conversation in groups, is provided a further dimension by Anamika Haksar whose directorial technique sought access to the inner recesses of the participants in a way that the latter is lured directly into confronting himself/herself and rediscovering his/her position amidst his/her socio-cultural condition. (Subramanyam 160). One can refer to her production of *Raj Darpan*, a script that she evolved in congress with a group of young students who were made to face a number of questions that in turn made them question the colonial attitude still prevalent in the matters of language, culture, ethnicity, class structure, administration, censorship, judiciary etc. Haksar had her training in direction from Russia, and it is her knowledge of the Stanislavskian school of acting that influenced her work with the actors in India, for whom, Haskar teased out their inner self in a manner that no other director ever did. In her production of *Antaryatra*, Haskar displayed how dramaturgic adjustments may emerge as metaphor to the thematic aspect of the play. Reworking the Tamil epic, *Silappadhikaram*, for the modern stage has its own challenges, but Haskar made it an opportunity to – 'explore the journey of women – the wife, the courtesan, and the ascetic' (Subramanyam 160).

> … as a metaphor for the journey she chooses an open air dramatic space enclosed on two sides by a dome like structure, opened at the back providing a depth that seems infinite. While some primary narrative is being enacted in front, a variety of actions are magically lit up at different distances at the back, for almost 300 feet, almost taking you on a journey into the inner world of these characters. The world thus evoked is full of images, of associations, of dreams, and the inner psyche. In her presentations there is a multiplicity of meanings – in the action, in the blocking, in the use of space, in the characterization and in its open-endedness. Here the narrative is not definitive but exploratory and forms a rich layering of meaning and emotions' (Subramanyam 160).

Though evolving texts out of dialogues and conversations with ordinary men and women became regular for various women directors in the 1980's and 90's, playwright – directors like Kirti Jain, Neelam Mansingh Choudhry, Maya Krishna Rao and Veenapani Chawla displayed even more varied ways of theatre production, ranging from the adaptation of contemporary classics to building scripts while acting on the stage. Kirti Jain's *Aur Kitne Tukde* may be mentioned here, for the director shares in *Muffled Voices: Women in Modern Indian Theatre*, the experience of putting on stage Urvashi Butalaia's book *The Other Side of Silence,* which is essentially a documentary that brings together interviews of few women who underwent traumatic violence during partition. For Kirti, it was both an opportunity to stage authentic flakes of history before a generation of audience which was fast losing the painful memory of partition, courtesy the politics of nationalism that survived on promoting hatred against the neighboring countries, and a challenge to fit the unconventional script into theatre. She had to evolve a form that would suit the staging of 'real life interviews, retaining the sense of the whole trauma that was Partition. The process therefore was naturally full of apprehension, restlessness and excitement of trying to discover a form. This also necessitated full participation and collaboration of the entire team,...' (Subramanyam 161).Neelam Mansingh Chowdhry's productions on the other hand reveal the fusion between modern traditions of acting and the age-long Punjabi folk traditions of the Naqqal actors. Though trained in conventional modes of theatre production, Neelam's endeavour was to discover an idiom that would 'synthesise' the rustic and the urban, both in its dramaturgic and thematic aspects. The Naqqals who worship Jawala Mai as their deity, are a community of performers who 'perform in a range of contexts and spaces: they follow Sufi traditions and perform at a dargah every week. They also participate in Ramlila performances and further enact stories of the Sikh Gurus and Sants. This eclectic performance tradition relies on female impersonation for the most part. Importantly, 'becoming female' is a matter of training for traditional actors as well as an instance of 'switching into a gender' (Mangai, 121).Neelam's theatre group, *The Company*, has produced plays where both the urban actors and the Naqqals have simultaneously performed for a range of characters, but for Neelam, the use of female impersonators does not account for the representation of gender on stage. For the Naqqals, however, 'doing' woman on stage is both informed by and continuously fraught with tensions of being men in real life. Neelam's works, however, are not exclusive of this tradition. In a number of plays produced in the 1990s and the first decade of the new century, Neelam has explored facets of women's desire, sexuality, the motherhood anxieties, the reluctance to follow the 'rules' of womanhood, the strategic use and abuse of femininity, passionate emotions in conflict with socio-patriarchal norms etc. In most of these plays, texts have evolved from Western classics, and adapted for the stage. In her *Fida*, which is an adaptation of Jean Racine's *Phaedra*, Neelam recounts the irresistible passion of a step-mother for her son. The play is a collaborative work where the script has been developed by Surjit Patar for dramatic adaptations and music composed by B. V. Karnath. While producing the play for the Bharat Rang Mahotsav in National School of Drama, New Delhi, Neelam did not restrain herself from displaying passionate love as bearing selfish, and 'negative' results when pitted against the socio-culturally determined forms and dimensions of love. Based on Dorris Lessing's collection of short stories, Neelam's *An Unposted Love Letter* is a bilingual monologue. Set in the green room of a theatre, an artist unleashes layers of her experiences as an actress in the play. Neelam collaborates again with B. V. Karnath as the musician, Sujit Patar as the scripter, and Sumant Jaykrishnan as the set designer. However, from exploring a woman's psyche in *Fida* to an artist's in *An unposted Love Letter,* Neelam's works features her unique style of experimenting with the traditional forms of narratives in theatre. While *Fida* unfolds from the middle of the plot and follows a linear path towards its climax, *An Unposted Love Letter* has no linearity of narrative or situation. Woven as if a continuous process of 'dressing and undressing, creating and wiping off, assuming and shedding', the *letter* gives the audience access to an actress's on-going theatre of the mind. The stage suggests a theatre changing room – a mirror with bulbs fixed to its four sides, is placed at the centre, costume stands are disorderly arranged and 'spaces' discretely marked for last minute rehearsals. The actress gradually strips her elaborate dress on stage evocating a cerebral process of 'becoming' someone, caricaturing the person and finally dissociating from him/her. The official website of *The Company* informs that 'Its productions are characterized by the use of spare props – sticks, fire, rice, washing poles– which evoke the ambience of an Indian village, and incorporates music, ritualistic elements and the presentation of poetic images that communicate as strongly as words' (Chowdhry). The *Kitchen Katha* too is an ensemble of such props. Essentially a culinary romance, the play is staged with cooked foods viz. *pakodas, roti, chutney, jalebis, popcorn* etc. being served before the actors. Scripted by Sujit Patar, the play is based on Laura Esquivel's *Like Water for Cholcolate and* Isabel Allende's *Aphrodite*, but Neelam has brought a unique sensation to the play with her use of vegetables and food, which is suggestive of various moods, 'thoughts and feelings of sensuality, pain, happiness and rejection' (Chowdhry). Neelam's productions therefore feature unconventional settings, elaborate and intelligent use of stage space, props that induce audience's tangible attachment with the action on stage and unique configurations of plot and character which unsettles the conventional portrayals. What is explicit in the works of these Indian women playwrights and directors is that there is a certain shift in the vocabulary of theatre productions. After a recent production of *Nachiketa* in London, in which she experimented with a form of opera, Neelam Mansingh Chowdhry spoke about her directorial style: 'I don't do homework or follow any school. For me, the play emerges when actors' bodies move in spaces. I improvise and give meaning to the air in those spaces. Everything has to be instant' (Deepak).

Though the 'instant' is never entirely 'renunciated' from its immediate/ gradual past (the context may be suspended but not destroyed); there is a constant attempt to shelve the traditional methods and techniques of theatre direction and production, and embark on improvising not only the dramaturgic but also the thematic. Hence trained in Kathakali, Maya Krishna Rao negotiates the 'instant' in her performances which mixes the classical Indian dance form with modern performance forms like the stand-up comedy, jazz, rap, tap dancing, rock and roll etc. in order to have a nuanced approach to the 'contemporary'. In an event titled SAHMAT in 2002, just after the Gujarat riots, when the communal tensions were running wild throughout the state and country at large, Maya Krishna Rao produced a comic piece structured on a popular cookery show in television. During her performance, she planted a mixer-grinder on the stage and exactly demonstrated the process of making chutney as a t.v. demonstrator does. 'As she puts chillies and adds turmeric and lets the mixer-grinder run, the chutney changes colour and emerges saffron in colour!' (Mangai, 205). This is only one amongst many instances where Maya explores the moment in a way which teases out her propaganda from an extremely different setting and technique that the audience is almost walloped over. In another instance, where Maya works on the mythical story of Ravana, *Ravanama*, she takes the kathakali dance form to a different level of performance where dance and theatre collaborate to form a new vocabulary. With a minimum amount of props, viz. a table, a lamp and newspaper, she creates a narrative that questions the mythic past, the politics of history/ the history of politics and the immediate contemporary that defines the popular *Indian* approach to Ravana, the 'ten headed monster' from *Ramayana*. Performing solo in most of her performances that range from comedy on 'serious' issues such as the Hindu – Muslim riot in Gujarat to extempore that not only questions but comments on more-than-tragic events like the gang rape of Jyoti Singh on a Delhi bus in 2012, Maya in a way completes the trajectory of Indian women theatre practitioners from being 'women alone' to 'woman alone'. However, being alone on stage does not necessarily isolate the performer from any sort of collaborations on and off the stage. In almost all her recent performances, she has mixed music and film in order to produce plays that synthesize spectacle and social activism. In *A Deep Fried Jam*, she weaves a comedy in collaboration with film maker Surajit Sarkar and sound designer Ashim Ghosh to produce a comedy that combines humour with nostalgia and makes subtle commentary on contemporary Afghanistan and Gujarat. Notable here is Maya's profound understanding of theatre as an art form in making comedy out of serious political events. In her solo productions such as *Khol Do*, *A Deep Fried Jam*, *Heads are Meant for Walking Into*, *The Non-Stop Feel Good Show*, *Hand It Over*, *Perspectives on Masculinities*, *Are You Home*, *Lady Macbeth*, *Ravanama* and *Walk*, Maya, as an actor, has explored the 'tension' that is inherent both in the performance and in the content of drama. In a conversation with Anuradha Kapur and Navtej Singh Johar, Maya says that going beyond the conventions of kathakali as a classical dance form that requires the performer to be absolutely ready to *receive* the traditions as they are, is not merely about improvisation – it is about 'creating a space between performance and non-performance; of being just there... It's about stepping into the unknown... It's not even there – it's going to be' (Rao). It's about not knowing the immediate future but at the same time preparing for it right on the stage. Exploring this 'unknown' has its own freedom, because of the absence of the director to lead the actor through it. The immediate historico-political condition lends the actor the present, which may produce an extempore-theatre creating a performance space which accommodates the present along with the immediate future. The actor (without the director), according to Johar, has to be open to the mind of the body. The body resists the traditional techniques. Hence there is always an element of discovery in and during an extempore theatre. Maya refutes the whole idea of *making* theatre; for according to her, 'making' is nothing but entering a 'precentered box'. One has to conform his thoughts and ideas according to a 'given' which is somewhat different from the true nature of being and is essentially uncouth, obscure, outlaw and all about sensations and seeking. The body therefore creates an intense personal moment in an extremely public space.

Exploring the body has been the forte of Veenapani Chawla too. In almost all the productions of her theatre group, Adishakti, Chawla strives to create an aesthetics that primarily focuses on relooking into the ancient Indian texts through performing arts involving extensive yet subtle use of breath. For Chawla, it all started with the explorations of the Indian classical form of Koodiyattam, a physical craft that has kept the aesthetics of Indian Sanskrit theatre alive. Trained at the Royal Shakespeare Company in London, and having learnt in India art forms like the Mayurbhanj Chhau, Kalaripayattu, Koodiyattam and Dhrupad singing, Chawla was asking herself, 'Why are we doing Western texts and what is the language of theatre? What is this realism in representation? ... What about us? What about historical India? Where are we culturally? Are we going to be constantly thinking derivatively or referring to Europe?' ("Theatre: Classical Meets Contemporary"). Koodiyattam provided her the answers she was seeking for. Watching the performances of Usha Nangiar, an exponent of the Koodiyattam she discovered that Usha uses her breath not only to animate her face during the performance but also to 'essentially create the satvika, which is the psychological state or emotional state from which this expression would come. It would come spontaneously' ("Theatre: Classical Meets Contemporary"). Veenapani's productions henceforth came to be characterized by the extensive use of breath which created a different language of the body. However, along with the modulation of breath in order to make the body behave in particular ways, her performances also derived *movements* from the Marshall Arts. To Chawla, the Marshall Arts provide the fundamentals of bodily movements but when performances are created out of it, 'you have to start putting in breath which is very different from the functional breath that they use … The moments of silence, the transition, the quick changes, evocation of emotion which it does essentially' ("Theatre: Classical Meets Contemporary"). Produced out of elaborate body movements, postures and modulation of breath, Chawla-directed performances synthesized the classical and the contemporary. In *The Hare and the Tortoise* Chawla uses the popular story of the hare and the tortoise competing with each other to win a race, in order to explore the 'contemporaneity' of time on the one hand and comment on the competing pairs from mythology to classics – Ganapati and Kartik, two popular siblings from the Hindu mythology, Ekalavya and Arjuna and Hamlet, the former a Pandava prince from the Mahabharata and the latter, the prince of Denmark from Shakespeare's classic dramatic work, Hamlet. The director herself comments:

> Adishakti's *The Hare and the Tortoise* is a dramatic meditation on the ethical possibilities inherent in the notion of contemporaneity. All too often our lives are over-determined either by the past or by the future, by the strictures of tradition, on the one hand, and of progress on the other. In this battle between the condition of nostalgia and the desire for achievement,

the present is forgotten or, worse, left unthought and unconsidered. Yet it may be the case that it is only in the recurring stillness of the present, of the moment, of what is now, that we can encounter ourselves as we truly are, untrammeled by the burdens of the past or the distorting pressure of the future. So too, it may well only be in the stark integrity of the present time – when we are not concerned about falling behind or getting ahead – that our relationships with others achieve a new equity and companionability. Thus, being contemporary, of the time, is linked to the notion of being coeval, of the same time, or, thence, of being together in the same time, or, of keeping time together, and so on. So too, being of the present carries within itself a kin set of etymological resonances, in this case, of being present to both oneself and to others. (Chawla)

Staged in consonance with mizhavu drums (as is traditionally done with Koodiyattam), her production of *Brhannala* is characterized by building a rhetoric that puts the human anatomy as the site of exploring time while preserving the main storyline at the same time.

'The answer is in being the hybrid, to nurture old knowledges but also to always be pluralistic – not to be conditioned by positions and ideologies'("Theatre: Classical Meets Contemporary").

Explicitly then, there has been a shift in theatre making for Indian women theatre practitioners from the late 1990s onwards. The authority of the play texts has gradually receded in order to focus exclusively on performance oriented theatres. The history of Indian women's theatre from the 1970s onwards reveals that initially women playwrights like Dina Mehta, Manjula Padmanabhan, Varsha Adalja, began to compose plays on women's issues but from the mid-1980s onwards the stress on collaborative 'theatre making' saw the emergence of playwright-directors like Tripurari Sharma, Usha Ganguli, composing/ devising plays to be performed on stage.

The final turn however, was provided by the women directors like Neelam Mansingh Chowdhry, Maya Krishna Rao, Veenapani Chawla whose primary focus has been *performance* on stage. But categorizing women theatre practitioners as playwrights, playwright-directors and directors is not about rejecting the evolution that most of the practitioners have undergone and are still undergoing. It is also not about denying the fact that composing plays, devising them out of conversations, directing the male/female authored texts for stage have coexisted and still coexists with resistance towards the primacy of texts for theatre performances. For example, Anuradha Kapur has initially co-scripted, devised and directed street plays like *Om Swaha, The Rape Bill, Amba* in the 1980s for Theatre Union, Delhi; later as a member of 'Dishantar', she acted in plays like *Adhe Adhure, Kanjoos,* etc. and with *Vivadi,* directed numerous plays, which include Rabindranath Tagore's *Ghar aur Bahar* (1989) and *Gora* (1991), Mirza Hadi Ruswa's *Umrao Jaan Ada* (1905) Dinesh khanna's *Sundari: An Actor prepares* (1998) and Bertolt Brecht's *The Job* (1997).

In this book, my primary focus is concentrated on the contribution of women playwrights in producing a canon separate from their male counterparts. The main proposition behind choosing play-texts over critically engaging live performances is that in order to produce and sustain an exclusive 'space' for women theatre practitioners, playwrights must continue composing plays and directors translate the play-texts into performance. Theatre may have the best possibilities of asserting its significance in live interaction with the society but plays composed to be performed on stage and read in print has its own importance. Tutun Mukherjee argues in her *Prolegomenon to Women's Theatre* in *Staging Resistance,* 'Playwrights in any culture or society form the backbone, the muscle, and the fibre of its theatre movement and without their creation a theatre can be neither born nor sustained' (Mukherjee 22). Though Mukherjee piles metaphors to define the playwright as a 'creator', I consider playwrights as authors for whom the socio-cultural, political, ethnical, national and gender consciousness provide the 'backbone', 'the muscle' and 'the fibre' for the plays they compose. However, in considering the Indian women playwrights as authors, I do regard them to have authority over how the 'story' is presented before their readers. But this does not deny the directors their 'authority' over how the play is presented before their audience. Therefore, when a play is composed by a playwright or devised in collaboration with other playwrights/ authors (of source texts) and directed by a different director/ group of directors, the authority is shared. But, most of the time, plays are associated with single authors, which generally goes against the grain of theatre making. For example, in her anthology of plays by Indian women playwrights, *Staging Resistance*, Tutun Mukherjee credits Neelam Mansingh Chowdhry, a Punjabi director for the play, *Fida* (adapted from Racine's *Phaedra*). But in an interview with K. Francis Lieder, Chowdhry's lead actress, Ramanjit Kaur insisted 'Chowdhry had simply commissioned an outside translation of Racine's *Phaedre* into Punjabiand that the text in *Staging Resistance* was simply a translation of a translation, from English to Punjabi and then again into English (Lieder 599). Therefore, the question arises, who must have been credited for *Fida*: the translators, the author of the source text or the director who presented it on stage? According to Leider,

> The texts of plays like *Fida* are not direct representations of their "playwright" speaking; rather, one must view the performance as a whole – the collaboration between text, director, actors, designers, and so on – in order to understand how Chowdhry uses *Fida* to invoke not just her own aesthetic and political stances, but also those of her collaborators. Chowdhry obscures her own voice within the translation and the collaborative devising process. (Leider 599)

Therefore, when a play-text is printed, 'playwright' may not always be an adequate term for referring to its 'author'. Leider suggests Aparna Dharwadker's use of the term 'auteur' as 'one who did not write the text on which the play is based but who has substantial control over how the story is told in the performed play (Leider

597). Though I have considered in detail the collaborative role of women playwrights and directors, I use 'playwright' for the authors of the texts I chose mainly because most of the texts are translated versions of the plays composed by playwrights alone. Also pertinent is to mention that the plays mostly appear in anthologies like Tutun Mukherjee's *Staging Resistance: Plays by Women in Translations* (OUP, 2005), *Body Blows: Women, Violence and Survival* (Seagull Books, 2000) and *Drama: Contemporary India* (PAJ Books, 2001), where each play-text is attributed to a particular playwright.

The texts that I have chosen, range from the 1970s to the early 2000s, for, in these three decades may be traced the major shifts toward 'theatre of their own' for Indian women playwrights (and directors). However, these shifts have not been documented well. Even contemporary play anthologies, such as Chandrashekhar Kambar's *Modern Indian Plays* (NSD, 2000) ignore women playwrights altogether, while G.P.Deshpande's *Modern Indian Drama: An Anthology* (Sahitya Akademi, 2000) gives space only to a male translated version of Mahasweta Devi's *The Mother of 1084*. Only Erin B. Mee in her *Drama: Contemporary India* (PAJ Books, 2001) presents two women playwrights among the six she selected for her anthology. However, some recent publications such as *Women, Centre, Stage* (Routledge, 2010), *Body Blows: Women, Violence and Survival* (Seagull Books, 2000) and *Staging Resistance: Plays by Women in Translation* (OUP, 2005) exclusively deal with plays written by women, although they are far from being adequate. The increasing popularity of women directors too has not redressed the problem, since much of their success has depended on adaptations of plays written by male playwrights. Critical explorations in this field, such as Nandi Bhatia's *performing women/performing womanhood* (OUP, 2010) or Tutun Mukherjee's 'Prolegmenon to Women's Theatre' in her book *Staging Resistance* are far from being adequate for they do not as such address the issue of constructing 'a theatre of their own' for the women theatre practitioners in India. Nandi Bhatia's *performing women/performing womanhood* 'looks at women's relationship to modern Indian theatre and how that relationship has been articulated in twentieth-century

India' ("Performing women/ Performing womanhood'). She examines 'representations of female actors, housewives, dalits, and courtesans in literary, cinematic, and autobiographical texts and in plays and performances. By tracing the effectiveness of theatre in foregrounding women who publicly challenged familial, nationalist, and reformist ideologies and confronted caste biases, the book demonstrates the radical potential of this genre in modern India. The book engages textual analyses alongside examinations of archival documents, political statements, reviews, interviews, and journalistic debates, to demonstrate the deeply intertwined links between gender, colonialism, nationalism, political dissent, and theatre' ("Performing women/ Performing womanhood").

In her 'Prolegomenon to Women's Theatre' in *Staging Resistance*, Tutun Mukherjee probes into the problematic relationship of women and theatre both in the eastern and western contexts. 'Drama and theatre are two...cultural products', she argues, 'in which the bias of gender generics and sexual difference are in evidence as social and psychic reality. Placing the forms within the discourse of 'gender as genre' reveals the way [the] sex-gender system operates in the art and practice of drama and theatre and controls their cultural reproduction'(4). "Unlike the autonomy and comforting privacy of print, the public, performative, collaborative, and materially demanding medium of theatre places women at a distinctive disadvantage, especially in India, where the vast majority of them are still circumscribed within the domestic sphere. However, while acknowledging the virtual absence of women from 'the documented history of modern Indian theatre as a cultural process and drama as a literary genre' (7), Mukherjee also recognizes new strides in women's theatre since the 1970s"(Dharwadker 155,156). Hence the aim of her 'collection', is 'to explore the imbrications of gender in the history of Indian theatre... [and] to explore the relationship between theatre, society and gender'(156).

Denial of women's role in Indian theatre has also been taken up by Lakshmi Subramanyam's *Muffled Voices: Women in Modern Indian Theatre* (Har-Anand 2002). The book provides an insight into the image of women in the written and performance texts in post-Independence theatre of India. The first section interrogates this image in the written or dramatic text of mainstream male playwrights while the second section articulates the diverse voices of women playwrights/directors and foregrounds the performative elements. In *Acting Up: Gender and Theatre in India, 1979 Onwards* (LeftWord, 2015), A. Mangai has explored how issues such as class, caste, ethnicity, myths, nationalities, etc. contribute to the intersections of gender and theatre in the works of Indian women theatre practitioners. However none of these texts go on to elaborate the aesthetics of Indian women's theatre, thereby leaving unaddressed the issues of constructing the women's dramaturgy which in theatre, voices women's resistance to stereotypes, provides space to articulate their desires and explores the varied experiences that contribute to their lives.

My 'argument' in this book is to address *these* lacunae through an examination of plays, thematically clubbed together in couples. It explicates women's theatre's engagement with issues like nation, war, class, caste, body, abuse, desire and freedom through critical discussions of select plays, some originally written in English and others in regional languages. Since Indian theatre cannot be said to be a coherent body which has a singular, monolithic national theatre, the presence of multiple theatre traditions, pluralities of language and differences in appeal and reception must be addressed by any research undertaken on Indian theatre. Though English has with time become an 'Indian' language, in public life as well as in writing, theatre in English finds its acceptance only to a limited 'urban/cosmopolitan, socially advantaged, educated individuals' (Mukherjee T. 21). Regional language theatre, on the other hand, not only finds a wider acceptance but is also richer at times in presenting the complex location of women amidst the multilayered and densely textured Indian society. However, it is to be mentioned that the present study takes into account English translations of regional language plays due to convenience of understanding and lack of general 'access' to the widely different languages of the country. Although translations into an 'alien' language may lack 'vernacular experiences' and 'linguistic nuances of the 'bhasa' (21), it is important to use them so that the regional works find a medium to transcend the 'regionalism' they are usually subject to. However, it is important to see that the translation of women's drama from regional languages into English, involves knowledge of the language of the source-text as well as sensitivity towards gender issues concerning the region.

This book studies the images of women as constructed in the male dominated Indian theatre in Chapter I, and in the following four chapters focuses on exploring themes and issues Indian women playwrights have broached in their plays, making a select study of women-authored plays. Appearing at different points in time, the plays have been brought together here on the basis of their theme/s that foreground women as the subject resisting stereotypes, questioning the legitimacy of gender neutral pronouns and voicing their desire to articulate life of their own.

Images of women: male and female playwrights (and directors)

Right from the inception of IPTA (Indian People's Theatre Association) in the 1940s to the consumerist 'neo-liberal' society in India in the 1990s and 2000s, women have been one of the subjects of playwriting for male practitioners of the modern Indian theatre. But the three dominant images – maya (seducer), mata (comforter) and victim — have remained central to their presentation of women in their theatre. Initially women's problems were seen as the problems of the family, identifying woman only in relation to man, either as his mother or sister or wife or 'kept'. Hence the frame of reference was essentially the domestic space. With the left politics in its heyday in both immediate pre and post-independence times, and the formation of a new political nation-state with redefined territories, women's issues came to be looked upon more as part of larger social issues than gender trouble in particular. In the post-60s, gender perception became political, with women being located at the interlock of social, political and cultural forces. However, sporadic representation of women as active participants in the socio-economic political structure appeared in the works of playwrights like Girish Karnad and Vijay Tendulkar. But wherever women were presented as strong, individual subjects, it was made sure that it spoke of patriarchal legitimization too. Though popular theatre still continued endorsing and encouraging stereotypical representations of gender relations rather than countering and annihilating them, attempts at least were made to recognize women as 'conscious' individuals. Though the image of woman as loyal, sentimental and self-abnegating was done away with, exclusivity of women's experiences in the Indian context still remained to be explored. Though male theatre activists like Utpal Dutta, Badal Sarkar, Safdar Hashmi, and other mainstream male playwrights and directors like G. P. Deshpande, Mohan Rakesh, Girish Karnad and Vijay Tendulkar addressed the women question in their plays, the works of Indian women playwrights and directors claimed better recognition. For, women in their plays are not merely constituents of a category to be taken up for question but emerge as makers and movers of family and society on the one hand and on the other, sites of struggle between conventional socio-cultural constructions and the desire not to be undone by such institutions.

The Indian women playwrights avoided drawing 'images' of women (either stereotypical or iconoclastic), presenting them as 'living' characters, responding to life as it comes to them. But this is neither about a stoic acceptance of what comes sieved through patriarchal and socio-conventional mores, nor is it about politically subverting the institutions so as to project a discourse opposite to the male. Instead, these playwrights located women amidst the varied socio-cultural contexts, studying the uniqueness of their lived experiences, struggles, resistances, frustrations, fulfillments, forced recognitions, liberations, and empowerments, to arrive at a critical distance both from the Indian male theatre practitioners and the West informed feminist traditions. This chapter serves as a prelude to my foray into the making of women's theatre in India.

Nation and War

Virginia Woolf's lexis in *Three Guineas* '...as a woman, I have no country. As a woman I want no country. As a woman my country is the whole world.'(99) may have heralded a new feminist approach in the early 1920s, but women's struggle in relation to the idea of 'nation' has never been restricted to vouching against acquiring political rights to citizenship. Such a 'conclusion' would require ignoring not just the history of the suffragette but also the Second Wave Movement's proposition of identifying the 'personal' as the 'political'. Women have continued their struggle for greater and more relevant spaces in politics and the public. In the South Asian context, women's role in politics is of greater significance; for in India, Pakistan, Sri Lanka and Bangladesh, electoral politics has for most of the time revolved around issues concerning women and continues to be periodically spearheaded by women leaders. Hence, when I study the role of Indian women's theatre in meditating on 'nation' in chapter II, I critically look into the constructions of woman and nation in relation to each other, especially at the behest of pre-colonial history of the Indian subcontinent, British colonial rule in India, partition and the post-partition nation building processes. In doing so, I locate 'war' at the intersection of nationalism and fear of cross border sexual atrocities. *Aur Kitne Tukde,* scripted by B. Gauri and directed by Kirti Jain, is a seminal play on this issue, for it looks at partition from the perspectives of four women. 'Patriarchal nationalism' has usually performed itself on women, by ways of sexual violence, religious conversion, and 'martyrdom and state violence', transforming their bodies into 'political artifacts' (Mohita). Unlike traditional feminist focus on women's victimization during war, the chapter takes up two women who actively participate in the politics of war and rise above the common run. Varsha Adalja's *Mandodari,* a play based on one of the most ignored characters of Indian mythology, reinterprets the Ramayana myth and explores complex dimensions of the character of Mandodari, who apparently attempts to end war even at the cost of sacrificing her conjugality.

The play in itself is a narrative against the conventional image of meek and possessive Indian wife who would compromise with the moral standards in order to hang on to her husband even when he ignores her. She emerges a woman whose sensibilities are not limited to personal 'benefits'. In the self-devised game of pawn she apparently loses to Kaaldevata. Her attempts of stopping the war go in vain, but at the end of the game, she reveals that her real intentions were to get Ravana killed: 'No, I was waiting for my lord's death... Well to read a woman's heart one has to be a woman perhaps! How could you understand the agony of being the wife of such a lustful yet blind man? ... Through Seeta's abduction and the ensuing war, I sought redemption of my clan. The arrow that killed Ravana actually released his soul and gave the egoistic man his salvation. Though I am widowed now, I am a happy woman. I succeeded in what I set out to do...' (Adalja114). Hence she comes out both as an avenger (to a 'lustful man') and a protector (of her 'clan', 'country'). Presenting one of the most 'insignificant' mythic characters as a politically aware strategist, Varsha Adalja renegotiates the question of woman and nation, portraying an oppressed and objectified woman triumphing in a trade which is essentially masculine. Though the play ends with an indictment against war, as Mandodari questions its credibility and argues that it is the hunger for 'power' which is central to the reasons behind such a 'needless violence' and 'destruction', she herself comes out as a political woman, who defies the traditional images of the victims of war.

The chapter also takes up for critical discussion, Tripurari Sharma's *A Tale from the Year 1857*, which is developed around the Sepoy Mutiny of 1857. It is a reading of how a courtesan moves beyond the limits of her art and sexuality, and emerges a soldier for the sake of her country. The play brings together multiple parallel developments, projecting the growth of an apolitical woman Azizun into a politically aware rebel alongside Zubaida who is happy to remain sheltered within the 'feminine' indoctrinations. The play also invokes debate on arts as a mere means of entertainment or as an effective instrument for specific political purpose. Amidst these, remains the presentation of war, which affects each and every character in the play. While war transforms Azizun into a political rebel, it prepares Sarwar for a noble death and proves Md. Ali resolute only in his loyalty to Nana Sahib. Harping on the essential temporality of the event, the play subverts master-slave dichotomy between the Indians and the British to such an effect that after being staged for the first time in National School of Drama in New Delhi in 1999, further productions had to be suspended on the charge of misrepresenting history (Sharma Interview).

Class and Caste

Having accounted for the intersection of woman, nation and war, the next chapter gives critical attention to woman in relation to class and caste, which is fundamental to the complexity of social framework for a large section of South Asian Society. In the Indian context, it is difficult to understand class and caste in isolation from each other, for there are numerous points of convergence, which overlap in the two apparently different social systems. Having its inception in the *varna-system*, caste is fundamental to 'status groups' (Weber186), which is defined essentially in terms of 'styles of life' (Betille 188). But I look at caste here as a *performative* – codes that have come into being through regular practice of subordination on one section of the society by the other based chiefly on entitlements, duties, access to even the minimum of necessities/opportunities/ benefits, producing a clearly defined hierarchy that has predominantly brought forth the pure/ polluted matrix in the Indian society. Though class has never been decisive in caste identity of an individual, it has surely influenced his/her caste experiences. Within the traditional caste structure, class proliferated itself in such ways that class-caste association proved to be the most vicious hindrance for the empowerment of the Dalits (a popular terminology for the 'lower' caste sub-humans in India), but with economy increasingly shaping the social structure in India (especially in the post-neoliberal society of the 1990s), elevation in class has emerged as one of the escape routes for people under caste oppressions. Hence, when perspectives on caste in class where 'class structure has cut across the caste hierarchy forming new alliances and antagonisms' (Mukherjee R. 338) are taken up in order to study the experiences of women, they appear as cultural sites where socio-economic changes are played upon in mediation with politics.

The two plays that the chapter discusses: Usha Ganguli's adaptation of Mahasweta Devi's novella *Rudali* and Kusum Kumar's *Listen Shefali*, question the class-caste nexus in subordinating women and developing narratives of resistance at the same time. *Rudali* deals with the pathetic condition of poverty-stricken women who have no choice but adopt 'untoward' ways of survival. Some adopt the profession of crying at the demise of rich people in villages, while the others are ready to embrace prostitution for which they are 'well paid'. The play is also a reading of a woman, namely Sanichari whose struggle against economic oppression is coupled with caste discrimination. It is primarily about resisting against economic and sexual dependency. With her long lost childhood friend Bikhni, Sanichari takes up a rudali's job. Though initially dependent on her grandson for economic support and companionship, she learns to earn by her own. Having found a true partner in Bikhni, with whom she shares a richly textured emotional relationship, she ignores male dependency in all forms and emerges a free agent in her own right. The play abounds in stereotypical images of women, but they are only used as backgrounds to emphasize Sanichari's gradual surfacing as an empowered entrepreneur.

Rudali is dealt with in relation to Kusum Kumar's *Listen Shefali*, which speaks of resistance on the part of a lower caste girl, Shefali, against being married to Bakul, the son of an influential politician, Satyamev Dikshit, who wants to marry his son to her, only to accrue political gains by earning himself the title of protector and emancipator of the Dalits. The play is about the frustrated desires of a woman, who valued self-respect over sanctioned material benefits. The play highlights questions of caste and the complex social position of Dalit women and exposes the politics surrounding them. The play informs that Shefali has continued resisting against being identified a Dalit, right from her childhood, but, ironically, her own mother marries off her sister to her erstwhile 'lover' Bakul, on the ground of a 'better future' at least in terms of their class positions. Though aware of the objectification that would follow, such a compromise only refers to the wretched Dalit experience that prepares for subordination in one form or the other.

Body and Abuse

Simone *de* Beauvoir in *The Second Sex* argues that 'woman is her body as man is his, but her body is something other than her'(42). What is central to such an understanding is that women's experience of their bodies is different to men, for, women lack control over their bodies and is instead managed by men. Traditions, customs, rituals, marriage, religion, history, literature, science and other socio-cultural artifacts and discourses have conventionally put the female body under male subordination. It has therefore emerged as a site which is at once the location of male desires and fantasies, and vulnerable to violence. Hence the feminists have looked upon violence as gendered. Sexual harassment, rape, pornography, prostitution, sati, dowry deaths are some of the forms of violence that women have traditionally suffered. Theorists have defined violence as force (physical/sexual/emotional/ psychological/spiritual/cultural/verbal/financial), which a person/ community/race/nation uses to control the other's actions and cause fear, which may amount to the latter's death/destruction.

Though 'violence' is associated with use of force to control, 'abuse' (the term that I use in place of violence in chapter III) minutely focuses on the victim as a subject. I argue here that when women's living experiences are taken into consideration, psycho-sexual abuse may lead to more varied and unexplored areas of critical understanding. These may account for the anguish of being 'misused' on the one hand and on the other, argue that based on the socio-cultural location the abused psycho-sexual condition may or may not have the 'potential' to change the situation s(he) is pitted into. The narratives of abuse would project women as victims, but at the same time account for the complexity of their experiences, struggles and even survival.

This chapter discusses two plays – Manjula Padmanabhan's *Lights Out* and Dina Mehta's *Getting Away with Murder*, which delineate women's abuse in two different contexts. Both the plays examine questions on sexuality and explore the vulnerability of women in situations where even sexual abuse is made to seem 'normal' and 'commonplace'.

Manjula Padmanabhan's *Lights Out* builds on a real incident of routine abuse of women in a colony in Bombay. The plot follows the disturbance in a domestic household while being exposed to the brutality. Leela, the lady of the house is constantly agitated with the hapless cries of women from the under-construction house opposite her; Bhasker, her husband, however, prefers remaining passive. Leela's agitation develops into anguish as her repeated appeals to Bhasker and Mohan, the guest (male) for dinner, to help the victims are frustrated by the pseudo-rationalization of their inactivity in the face of 'sexual torture': 'unless they actually call for help, is it our business to go?' (20) 'After all, it may be something private, a domestic fight, how can we intervene? Personally, I'm against becoming entangled in other people's private lives' (20); 'unless it is murder. I don't think anyone should come between the members of a family' (20).But Leela is empathetic towards the victims, for she is transformed into a helpless victim as herself. With Naina's arrival on the scene, Leela finds a partner, but they are persuaded by the men in believing that the women molested outside may be prostitutes and that, "a whore is not decent, so a whore cannot be raped" (40). The question of rape being applicable for only 'decent' women and not for those in the flesh trade disturbs the audience. Padmanabhan here throws light on the patriarchal ideas of the 'decent' and distinguishes them from the 'whores' in order to project patriarchal understanding of rape as the act of violating the 'dignity' of an individual, and ignoring the claims of those who are considered 'undignified'. Rape is also seen from two different perspectives in the text: for the men it is only about violence which can have domestic, ritualistic, or moralistic dimensions or can be unquestionable religious taboos etc, while for women it is about the gross violation of a woman's body, psyche and freedom as they are forced to inaction and sought to be controlled by the men folk. Hence, for women, rape emerges as a gendered violence that is organized socially to fracture, control and subordinate women to men. However, the play ends with Nina's husband Surinder making his appearance on stage and the three men finally deciding to act, suggesting again that women's liberation is possible only through the agency of men.

This chapter further takes up for discussion Dina Mehta's *Getting Away with Murder* which presents the life of three friends as they journey through their own 'private hells'. The play throws up issues like 'child sexual abuse', 'discrimination', 'infidelity', 'insecure relationships', 'incest', 'female infanticide' and 'harassment at the work place'. It begins with Sonali's fear psychosis tormenting her: 'someone indoors is watching me' (Mehta 59). The play traces it back to her childhood experiences of being repeatedly watched naked by the uncle and being inflicted countless sexual abuses. Instead of sharing her pain, her mother made her 'run her errands, mouth her opines, feel her feelings' (59). But Gopal escaped all 'because he was born with an extra set of accessories' (59). Sonali further confides that she is pregnant and wants amniocentesis done, and that she had already aborted once when she found she was going to give birth to a girl. This is because her past experiences left memory of discrimination and deprivation and she had been indoctrinated with the idea that 'a woman's failure to bear a son is just retribution for the misdeeds in her past life" (63).

While such is the condition of Sonali, Mallika has to deal with her own 'private hell' on being compelled to keep office with a male chauvinist, Mr. Pingley, and cope with the 'insecurity' in her relationship with Gopal, who is younger to her for the society ordains that only a "man has the right to the body of a woman younger than he" (78), not a woman. The third friend, Razia, who is apparently an empowered woman in being a doctor, is in an even worse condition. Her husband Habib is all set to marry a nineteen-year-old girl in the hope of having a child. The situation seems absolutely 'normal' to Razia, for she finds "an ancient tyranny at work within me (her) that man's desire for children must be satisfied"(78). Though she acknowledges that it is only patriarchy which is to be blamed for this, she tells Mallika "don't fool yourself that you and I are so different Malu! Or that by identifying man as villain we have won our fight for equality! The enemy is within, don't you see? It's in our minds, Mallika that we are underlings!"(78) However, the play ends with Sonali succeeding in getting over the trauma of childhood sexual abuse, as a "bad human experience", and Mallika defying patriarchal reduction in her own way.

Desire and freedom

Chapter V revolves around the questions of desire and freedom as probed by the contemporary Indian women playwrights (and directors).Traditionally women have been identified according to stereotypes constructed by patriarchal projections of myths, socio-cultural institutions and literature. Accentuated by such media, women's desires have always been conditioned by repressions. Hence, the freedom of being 'desiring' has generally been glossed over by the patriarchal productions of women as 'desirable'. Indian women's theatre engages with the idea of new age women who desperately hold on to their desires even if socio-patriarchal thought in family and society at large continue frustrating them. The chapter locates freedom as a state of being, where authentic human existence, is mediated by both individual and collective experiences of desire. Dealing with Neelam Mansingh Chowdhry's *Fida* and Mamta G. Sagar's *The Swing of Desire*, the chapter critically looks into the norms of complex Indian society which has traditionally preserved 'desiring' only for men. The two plays coupled together are actually contrary to each other: while *Fida* speaks of the frustration of the desires of a woman ending in the tragedy of almost all the characters, thereby reinforcing the idea that woman's desire may lead to an obvious tragic end, *The Swing of Desire* is about a woman's success in attempting to break free from the shackles of womanhood and fulfill her own desire, even at the cost of her own family. The play speaks of the conscious efforts of a woman to attain subjecthood by rejecting the reification imposed by stereotypical gender roles.

Basing on Surjit Patar's adaptation of Racine's *Phaedra*, Neelam Mansingh Chowdhry presents Fida's unconventional love and desire for her stepson, Harsan. She finds it difficult to shelter her passions within her tormented mind. With the news of the king's probable death, Fida finds a temporal liberty to foster her desire and confide to Harsan only to be left confused by his silence. She continues to lure him with promises of throne and kingdom, for she is drawn into believing that desire for power is inherent in man. However, the news of the king still alive makes Fida conscious of the social expectations and she is anguished with the guilt of betraying her husband for the sexual desire of possessing Harsan. The play ends with the death of Harsan, after being falsely accused of trying to sexually possess Fida. Hence, the play deals with 'matters of convention and tradition, transforming the lustful desire of a woman into a negative experience, for society and its deep rooted attitudes seek to determine whom she should desire and to what extent' (Chowdhry). Fida's love, combined with her moral conscience and her superhuman efforts, are powerless against the fatality of passion.'(Chowdhry)

Mamta G. Sagar, on the other hand, presents a different reading of female psyche and sexuality in *The Swing of Desire*. It explores parallel complexities in the relationship of two couples. Manasa, once a dancer, wants to regain her status as a dancer, but is bound by the patriarchal desires of an extremely nagging husband, Pratap. An autocratic husband who wants her to be an 'object of your (his) wanton desires'(Sagar 233), Pratap has been trying to stifle the desires of his wife by branding her dance as a prostitute's art used only in order to seduce men, but the equally strong-willed Manasa refuses to remain a "child-bearing machine"(233). The other couple-Bhava and Pratap's sister, who remains anonymous throughout the play, is caught in a different crisis. Bhava regards his wife a misfit for him and expects her not just to 'satisfy' him 'in bed', but his 'intellectual needs as well' (239). In a brawl between the two, Bhava complains that "You have suppressed yourself so much that I can't see you as my companion at all" (239). While the 'feminine' wife frustrates Bhava, the 'lack' of femininity in Manasa irritates Pratap. However, Manasa transcends social constraints and re-establishes herself as a professional dancer, leaving Pratap in a terrible anguish of knowing that one of his two children is not his own without being told which one. Defeated by his own false masculine institutions that continue to torment him, Pratap approaches Manasa with the promise that he is ready to 'forgive and forget' (247), if she decides her return to the family. Manasa is quick to recognize Pratap's intentions which hide his male ego. However, that the play ends in Manasa rejecting Pratap's proposal and asserting own choice in deciding her life thereafter. Putting two entirely different characters (viz. Fida and Manasa) in the same frame, the chapter therefore explores the critical nuances of women's relation to desire and freedom.

The book concludes suggesting that women's theatre in India has opened up new vistas at the thematic as well as aesthetic level, where woman ultimately emerges as a speaking subject. It is not only about achieving personal freedom through theatre but also about the responsibility of voicing the socio-cultural and political 'reality' of the condition of women in India. This is not only about creating a sisterhood against oppression but about recognizing and celebrating the differences that contextually distinguish one woman from another and show their complex positioning in the family, institutions and society. "The social relevance of a play, as well as its aesthetic appeal, depends largely on the intersection of several factors such as issues of address, the dynamics of representation, the historical time and locus of performance, and the orientation of the audience potentially affecting its reception" (Sengupta13-14). The plays discussed stand testimony to women practitioners' endeavour to redefine the Indian theatre traditions from the perspective of women playwrights and directors, as they take an insider's look into issues which subjugate women socially, culturally, physically, psychologically and even historically. The study therefore questions the traditional place of woman in Indian theatre and tries to find out a niche for women theatre practitioners, contributing towards the formation of a canon of their own.

CHAPTER

Images of Women in Male-oriented Indian Theatre Traditions

Indian Theatre: History, Tradition, Women

Any attempt towards writing the history of India usually confronts the alleged lack of authentic historical documents. India's existence as a non-coherent and fissured political ensemble before the birth of 'modern' India with the advent of Islamic rulers generally ignored the 'historical' documentation of its constitution in any social, cultural, political or academic sphere. In place of a well-defined unitary nation, India in its more than 4000 years' history – right from the days of Indus Valley Civilization to that of the post-Independence territorial settlements with Pakistan, Nepal, Bhutan, China and Bangladesh— has emerged as a political body, constantly under the process of re-formation with its boundaries shifted and re-shifted under different kings, races, colonizers, and uni/multi party/parties electoral politics, creating spaces for several languages, thousands of dialects, and a mosaic of diverse cultures. But as to the tradition of theatre in this country, it has a long and living history, which is at once diverse in its response to the dramaturgical variety with assortment in linguistic, racial, religious and cultural plurality and 'uniform' in its sharing of the ethno–social specificity and preserving the uniqueness of identity as Indian. Any discussion on woman and her representation in Indian theatre, therefore, must situate her amidst the evolution of Indian sensibilities with respect to women in different contexts.

That Indian theatre has a long tradition which dates back to its obscure and mythic origin. It can be explained through Bharata Muni's *Natyashastra*, an exhaustive theoretical treatise on dramatic poetics. This *Shastra* is addressed to playwrights, poets, directors, actors, musicians and dancers, for, in India, drama (Sanskrit, *nataka*) traditionally is a form which brings together poetry, music, dance, and acting (*abhinay*).All these elements in harmony are further enhanced by elaborate make ups, designs, costumes, painting, sculpture etc., in order to express the *rasa-s* (emotions) and *bhava-s* (moods). Hence theatre in India, unlike the Greek or the Western Theatres of the antiquities, has been a combination of genres that evolved with the progress of its allies.

Though the Indus Valley Civilization left evidences of dance and music as their mainstay both in entertainment and in performing 'religious' rites, there exists no such confirmation of formal theatre. Hence the earliest form of theatre that can be accounted for is the Sanskrit theatre (1500 to 1000 BCE). However, some of the advocates of ancient folk theatre forms argue that a living theatrical tradition has always been in India. But with the Aryans invading the vast stretches of Indian mainland, conceptualizing, 'narrating' and 'imagining' an essential and unified geographical space, Sanskrit theatre became the definition. It essentially obliterated other forms of theatre, which may have existed in the vernaculars. This was further accentuated by the pride in Sanskrit for contemporary Brahmin scholars. Hence, European historians like Sylvan Levi and H. H.Wilson, who wrote theatre histories of India in the context of Indology (where Europeans were eager to understand India and its past from the native scholars), invariably privileged Sanskrit and essentially advocated Sanskrit theatre in place of theatres in India, ignoring the extraordinary diversity of *bhasha* traditions. However it must be mentioned that though Sanskrit theatre strictly adhered to the poetics of Bharata and enjoyed privilege on grounds of linguistic superiority, it also provided space for other dialects/ languages for the actors of 'lower' castes. Kalidas's *Abhijnana Sakuntala* may be a masterpiece in Sanskrit theatre but also consists of dialogues in *Maharastri, Magadhi* and *Sauraseni.* Playwrights like Bhasa, Shudraka, Vishakhadatta, and Bhavabhuti also followed the same tradition of composing multilingual plays though oriental scholars traditionally projected it as uniform, essential and unilingual. In doing so, they either totally ignored the existence of a strong folk tradition in India or sought a sharp division between the Sanskrit and folk theatres as elite and non-elite. Having their roots more close to the rural milieu, folk theatre was more simple, immediate and flexible in not being restricted by any conventions. Later, with the decline of Sanskrit theatre around 1000AD, folk theatres gained more prominence, and continued to be so for the next 700 years. Founded mainly on songs, recitations, dialogues and dances of particular regions, folk theatre broadly practiced two forms: religious and secular, which respectively gave birth to ritual theatre and the theatre of entertainment. These regional theatres took different shapes and forms in different parts of the country in relation to the variety of flora and fauna, culture, language, literature, ritual, myth, religion, history, etc. However, they lost their prominence to a great extent with the change in political scenario *a propos* the establishment of British colonialism in India.

The modern Indian theatre refers to the theatre that emerged in the late-eighteenth century and incorporated Sanskrit, traditional and the European theatre practices. 'By and large they borrowed most heavily from European playwriting and staging practices; they also sporadically and very selectively adapted a few features from their region's traditional theatre; and they copied, although sometimes only nominally, some elements from the Sanskrit theatre.' (Solomon 16). The British introduced 'proscenium' to Indian theatre which gradually changed the theatrical discourse and its structure. Though the establishment of the Playhouse (Calcutta, 1753) and Bombay Theatre (Bombay, 1776) was intended to exclusively cater to the British population, they ushered in a new trend of English plays in India, which was 'designed not only to shape artistic activity but to impose on Indians a way of understanding and operating in the world and to assert colonial cultural superiority.'(Mee 1) Hence the modern Indian theatre marked a shift from the traditional, non-textual, performance-based theatre to the West influenced, text-based dramatic theatre, necessitating a shift from Indian theatre's conception as a 'community event' referring to 'annual harvests' and 'religious occasions' to 'dramatic literature' (2).However, to say that dependence on text did not exist before such developments would be a misnomer, for, theatre forms like Jatra, Bhavai, Tamasha, Kathakali etc. often used literary texts, mythic and religious stories commentaries to be staged before the public, though 'literature that walks'(2) was never encouraged for theatrical performances. But modern Indian theatre is different from the traditional in ways more than one; for as Erin B. Mee observes,

> 'modern theatre came to be defined in terms of plot-driven plays that stemmed from a single author. It was expected to have human characters, conversational dialogue, behavior that was psychologically motivated, events that were causally linked, and realistic settings that allowed spectators to believe in the present tense reality of the action on stage and to identify with the characters, eliminating anything that would shatter the illusion of the fictional world of the play' (2).

Ananda Lal in his essay *A Historiography of Modern Indian Theatre* identifies social criticism as one of the standards for modern Indian drama that precedes the social dramas of Ibsen and Shaw (33).

Traditional Indian theatre, was, as Macgowan and Melnitz observe in *The Living Stage,* the 'theatre of symbolism' (293). The western theatre 'heightened physical reality into an illusion of life', or even when an expressionistic play is taken into account, 'though the settings and lights were usually arbitrary, mannered, bizarre, we (one) could see or sense that this distortion of reality was intended to make the reality more dramatic, more powerful'(293)(bracketing mine). But in India, 'the whole look and meaning of their (Indian) drama is symbolic to the last degree. The acting is either extravagant in its studied violence, or repressed into a masklike repose. Gestures have an esoteric meaning. Voices are usually shrill or pitched in singsong cadences. Scenery is either nonexistent or full of mannered elaborations. If the actor doesn't wear a mask, his face may be painted with extravagant and symbolic patterns.'(293). However, theatre in India, under the colonial influence, rejected such intricate symbolism in order to stage social dramas which upheld fidelity to fact not just in their themes, but also in their presentations.

Professionalism was another development that accounted for Indian theatre's 'maturity' into the modern, for it essentially transformed the non–commercial Indian theatre into a 'commodity'. This 'created a cultural divide between what came to be seen as high/ English/ urban/ modern/ theatre and what was categorized as low/Indian/rural/traditional/performance' (Mee4), though the 'divide' was not as sharp as it appears now. However, in the post-independence period, the 'theatre of roots' movement in its assertion of Indian identity defined the modern Indian theatre in its own terms and hence challenged 'acultural definition of modernity and modern theatre in and on Western terms' (5).In the conscious attempt to decolonize the modern Indian stage, theatre itself turned out to be not just a 'theatre of roots' but also a 'theatre of identity'.

However, right from the pre-Sanskrit ritual 'theatre' to the post-independence 'theatre of roots', Indian theatre has never held enough space for women to articulate their voices through it. Be it the dramaturgy, or thematic negotiations with women's issues, Indian theatre has held a 'sanctioned' ignorance in relation to women. This has its roots in theatre's socio-cultural mediations as well, for Indian society predominantly has been patriarchal and constantly upholding sharp distinctions between the public and the private in relation to the position of man and woman. Hence in theatre traditions of India, be it the non-scripted folk theatres or the Sanskrit theatre and colonial and postcolonial modern theatres, women's absence in the theatrical trade is clearly visible, even though we find male authored women characters in almost all the forms. In *Natyashastra*, Bharata Muni informs that ancient theatre reserved *samskara* (Muni 327) for learned men, while men from the 'lower' class/caste and women were made to speak in *prakrta* (327) on stage. In accounting for the professionalism of theatre practitioners, Bharata also informs that 'common women', elaborately 'made up', were used to cater to the taste of that audience which wanted 'light' entertainment in place of serious dramatic ventures. Hence classical Indian theatre preserved women only for the 'populist' theatre performances. The same practice continued in the folk theatre tradition as well. For, women were used here as stereotypes, sometimes for the sake of enhancing the melodramatic effect of the stage play. Though often young boys without beards were made to perform women's roles, whenever there were women actors performing, they attracted huge audience. This tradition was exploited by the Parsee theatre and the early 20th century modern Indian theatre as well. The Parsee theatre used women to enhance its commercial value; consequently, early 20th century theatres featured such women actors as BinodiniDasi, Sukumari, Tinkari and Tarasundari, who were looked upon as celebrities and therefore helped project theatres as posh haunts for the *novieau riches*. Also, behind and off stage, women contributed as script writers, singers, composers and authors, in the likes of Indira Devi Choudhurani, Bimala Sundari Devi, Ashapurna Devi etc. Also there are such examples as Arundhati Devi, Angurbala, Banabiharini who at once donned multiple roles of script writing, acting, singing, dancing, and even sometimes performing male roles.

But amidst all these graces, it must also be mentioned that though Indian theatres can boast of having one of the highest shares of women performers in different roles in the early 20th century, they lacked the seriousness of dealing with authentic women's issues and women performers never earned respect in society as they were looked upon as 'public women', meant for entertainment. In being open to the public (male) gaze in theatres, the women performers therefore were reduced to their bodies. The question of honour associated with family and woman therefore emerged as one of the important mores in the redefinition of patriarchal hegemony concerning women. However, this doesn't blind the attempts of IPTA and the Theatre of Roots movement that (re)presented women and their concerns at once in proscenium and street theatre, both in the pre and post-independence period. Though the IPTA was formed primarily with the aim to politically revitalize the Indian theatre and the Roots movement aspired to revive the elements of ancient Indian tradition in theatre, the woman question gradually got associated with them, for they looked upon women as political constituents of the oppressed parts of a greater 'whole'; woman as part of a class, a society, a tradition, and a state. The IPTA demanded performing in streets, railway platforms, and other public places. This gave a severe jolt to the conservative ideals of 'respectability', for women who were politically aware and motivated by left ideologies, joined the activists who looked upon theatre performance as a vital extension of their political activism in order to make their agendas more visible to the public. To add to this is the very nature of the performance space itself, which demanded transgression of 'social boundaries of caste, class and gender' (Singh, 63). Most of the women who were associated with IPTA came from 'progressive' families. But the liberty granted was based on several parameters which in their own ways were obstacles to be transcended. The accounts of Sheela Bhatia, Dina Gandhi, Reba Roy Choudhury, Shanta Gandhi, Rekha Jain are extraordinary struggles against family and patriarchy that worked together to confine them under narrow domesticity. The narratives of their struggles were uniquely drawn because unlike the earlier women of theatres who primarily hailed from the family of professional entertainers, they arrived in IPTA through 'political journeys' (63). IPTA therefore was a home to the rebels who struggled against class stratifications and diverse forms of patriarchal hegemonies. Organizational works compelled the IPTA to work and live in different socio political conditions which necessitated overcoming orthodox gender separations. In their regular tours of various parts of the country, be it the 'literate villages of Kerala, or politically conscious Bengalees or the illiterate rural folk of Bihar' (Srampickal 154), the actors had to stay in *ghettos, bastis, slums* and share room with both their co-actors and the (often) poor organizers.

Sadly, the IPTA disintegrated in the post-independence period. 'But it spawned smaller units all over the country. Notable among these were: The Indian National Theatre (INT, Kamaladevi Chattopadhaya), the Little Theatre Group (LTG, Utpal Dutt), Kerala People's Arts Club (KPAC, Thoppil Bhasi) and several other state units of IPTA existing independently, but carrying on the crusade begun by IPTA. A number of playwrights like Habib Tanvir, Lakshmi Narain Lal, Badal Sircar, P. L. Deshpande, Sarveswar Dayal Saksena, Tripurari Sharma and others have faithfully continued the unique tradition of IPTA.' (47) Though less organized, the people's theatres in India continued political dramatizations and throwing up socio-cultural issues. Some of the most notable performances may include Patna based Gathividhi's *Yeh Natak Nahin*, which was a satire aimed at the aspiring politicians, Janam's (Delhi) *Aurat*, dealing with oppression of women, Theatre Union's *Marzka Munafa* on Multi National Companies' trade with banned drugs in third world countries, the UP based IPTA's *Cricket match*, a political satire on Congress and Janata Dal (now, *Bharatya Janata Party*), and Alarippu's *Reshmi Rumaal* which dealt with the living conditions of women in cloistered houses. Along with these, several SAGs (Social Action Groups) who work with fringe communities like the tribals, the fishermen, the landless labourers, the slum dwellers and rural women, harp on themes such as 'unity, cooperation, small savings, alcoholism, communal harmony and superstition' (179).

Hence women's participation in Indian theatre follows a trajectory from social invisibility to political visibility. From the non-women theatre traditions of antiquity to the theatres of independence, Indian theatre covers a huge ground to make women visible on stage. The post-independence modern Indian theatre, an organic ensemble that brings together the works of a host of regional language and Hindi/ English male playwrights and directors, primarily focused on social issues concerning class, caste and gender. For, India came into existence as an independent nation state as a 'collusion of the capitalistic forces of development and the traditional feudal forces', doing 'nothing to destroy the unequal power relations in the caste system and patriarchal order' (Pandit, 39). In their engagement with these issues, the playwrights have offered dimensions which has accounted for the enhancement of these discourses in relation to theatre. But in course to this, several 'images' have been constructed, worshipped and sometimes even deconstructed.

Images: Women and Post-independence Male Theatre Tradition

In his essay, *Rhetoric of the Image*, Roland Barthes notes that the term 'image' is etymologically related to '*imitari*' (152). This immediately refers to the idea of 'copying' in the process of image formation, thus initiating the question of credibility for 'analogical representation (the "copy")' in producing 'true system of signs' (152). When looked upon as representation, image, especially in the context of literature, ceases to be a mere reference to the signified, but undergoes a complex process of transformation in mediation with the author's sensibility and technique. Hence an image acquires two referents in the process of its representation; one refers to the surface element which Sonja K. Foss would call 'presented' and the other is the implied element which she would call 'suggested' (147).This may have some proximity with what Barthes refers to as 'denotation' and 'connotation'. The surface element therefore denotes the meaning of an image at its literal level, while the implied element connotes what is available to the viewer only in suggestions. Though the surface element works as a 'signifier' to the implied, the construction of an image is in teleological relation to the author's association with the 'signified'. But in this symbolic relation of the image, the sign may refer to an empty 'signified', for the 'signified' is a construction in itself. But in the present context of analyzing plays, meaning is more critically conceived; for, in such a production, image is always in a process of construction which mediates between the author's recreation of the process of signification and its acceptance to the readers. But this process of recreation is never disjoined from the association of an author's individual 'pattern of memory, desire, and dream' and 'the ideas of society as a whole, of family, peers, country, the age' (Ferguson, 3). Therefore the 'empty' signified is an assortment of the subjective and objective sensibilities where authentic material existence may give way to essential constructions. Hence, images emerge as figments that find no authentic connotations. They are signifiers that refer to another set of signifiers instead of an unproblematic given.

In literature, images are rhetorical constructions that condense what society identifies as stereotypes and which is recognized as 'archetypes' in popular discourses. Considered inferior to men, women have been traditionally stereotyped as docile silent girls, wives, mothers, sex objects, seductresses, beautiful muses, old maids, vamps, witches and victims. But with stereotypes being social constructions built in order to confine women to certain definitions that supplement patriarchal dominations on them, the images find no real 'signified'. With literature's role in social processes sometimes looked upon as an agency that goes on to 'naturalize' conventions as real, the images of women are crucially conceived as unchallenged representations of mere patriarchal assumptions in place of concrete individuals. Similarly, the male–oriented Indian theatre from the era after independence to the end of the twentieth centuryhas projected an evolution of women characters from representing 'invisible' social existence groping in enforced ignorance to representing confident, self–assertive 'new age women'. The male authored plays in this era, looked at from the perspectives of women, present narratives of subordination either as a subject of engagement or for the purpose of critiquing the hetero-patriarchal social structures that locate women as secondary to men. Such evolution in (re)presenting women probably is a resultant of the gradual transformation in the measured alterations in the roles performed by women in society. But even in this transformation, images of women, regularly supplemented by socio-cultural political archetypes, continued to be produced in the male dominated Indian theatre canon. Hence, a critical survey of select plays by male playwrights from the post-independence theatre may lend a greater scope for conceptual clarity and serve as a prolusion to my foray into the making of women's theatre in India. Selection of plays and playwrights may always be criticized as arbitrary, but given the 'huge' population in the male theatre canon in India I have considered representative women characters of a few male playwrights only to thematically build my argument towards the uniqueness of Indian women playwrights (and directors) in producing new 'images' of women.

Vijay Tendulkar: Silence as narrative 'reality' for women

Having composed plays in the last four decades of the 20th century, Vijay Tendulkar is known for dealing with the socio-political flux of the period with an unsympathetic criticality. In the process, Tendulkar's plays have also engaged with the emerging women's issues as well. But, while projecting the inherent 'gloom' in a discriminatory society, he is often blamed for portraying women as mere victims. His women characters find themselves caught in a vicious circle of narrative reality accentuated by a network of patriarchal, cultural, psycho-social, economic and political 'sutures'. While Benare in *Silence! The Court is in Session* (1967) is 'silenced' by the society's patriarchal shams, Kamala in the eponymous play (1981) being projected a woman slave had no voice of her own. Again, Gauri in *Ghashiram Kotwal* (1972) is the epitome of silence, who suffers masculine oppression without even making any significant sound.

Silence! The Court is in Session is a play centering on Miss Leela Benare who is an apparent 'deviant' with a zest for life. The spontaneity in her character makes her incur the wrath of a society that reserves its rights against women. She is the one who would not play the 'game' of social hypocrisy, but ironically she is dragged into it in the form of a convict put in a mock trial aimed at laying bare her private life. Tendulkar may seek to evoke sympathy for his women characters, but they find themselves helpless before chauvinistic oppression. Miss Benare is an appropriate embodiment of Tendulkar's conception of 'progressive' woman. She is single, an activist and a member of a theatre group, 'The Sonar Moti Tenement (Bombay) Progressive Association', and hence she is more easily 'claimed' as a public personality. Tendulkar initially projects her as a self-assertive woman who rejects living in the shadow of life:

> I, Leela Benare, a living woman, I say it from my own experience. Life is not meant for anyone else. It's your own life. It must be. It's a very very important thing. Every moment, every bit of it is precious. (Tendulkar "Silence!" 61)

As the mock trial begins, Miss Benare is made to face a volley of questions from the accusers. She is charged with infanticide, an illicit relationship with professor Dalme and above all her lifestyle and the decision to remain unmarried till thirty. As Benare remains silent, Mrs. Kashikar, another notable woman in the play questions 'Free! Free! She's free all right – in everything! Should there be no limits to how freely a woman can behave with a man? An unmarried woman? No matter how well she knows him? Look how loudly she laughs! How she sings, dances, cracks jokes! And wandering alone with how many men, day in and day out.' (100). Tendulkar intelligently puts comments in the form of questions. An epitome of social indoctrinations, Mrs. Kashikar is the typical 'vamp' who is opposed to 'granting' social liberty to women. The play therefore is poised between the desire of a woman to be liberated from the 'fixed' socio-normative hindrances and the desperate attempts of another woman to re-instate the expected social 'habitus'. But in his presentation of Benare, Tendulkar has failed to portray a woman who can defend herself at the face of social criticism. Even though her defense is presented through a soliloquy, it suggests the failure of social articulation for individually lulled thoughts. But, even in her apparent silence, Benare is among Tendulkar's most powerful women characters, for in other plays like *Kamala* and *Ghashiram Kotwal*, the image of victim is more profoundly drawn.

Kamala probably is the symbol of exploitation in Tendulkar's oeuvre. She is presented as a slave who is devoid of any institutional education except that she must be unquestioningly loyal to her master. Kamala grew with the apprehension of being sold someday. When she is brought to the city by Jairaj her sensibilities do not undergo any change. Tendulkar presents socio-patriarchal hegemony in two dimensions in the play. Represented through Kamala and Sarita, the educated wife of Jai Singh both the dimensions invariably project women as sufferers. While for Kamla, the socio-sexual domination is both invoked and destined, in Sarita, socio-patriarchal indoctrination is exemplified in her incapability of asserting her independence. Hence the play hints at the woman's space as of compromise and endurance. Kamla's 'visibility' in her house, especially amidst the entire politics of initially hiding and then broadcasting her to the world, stirs Sarita, as she herself becomes increasingly conscious of her 'invisibility'. This leads to the central question in the play which puts Sarita into an 'existential' crisis: 'How much did he buy you for?' (Tendulkar, "Kamala" II 34). Reduced to an 'object' of male possession and closeted along with Kamala in a patriarchal space, Sarita confronts the 'reality' of hetero-sexual marriage. The two women therefore emerge as 'sisters', who must keep their 'master happy' (35). Waking to the verity of cohabiting in a similar space, Sarita decides to 'speak' up for Kamala but fails to articulate in its entirety the context of Kamala's life and 'desires'. Tendulkar's unproblematised representation of such a sisterhood only reinforces the stereotyping of women with the contextual differences being surrendered for representing victims of patriarchal subordination.

The image of victimhood is reinforced in Tendulkar's *Ghashiram Kotwal*, where Gauri, Ghahiram's daughter, emerges as the epitome of silence and gendered subordination. The play revolves around a politics of power that centers on Ghashiram's selling his only daughter to Nana Phadnavis for political gains. Ghashiram, once the victim of the corrupt power structures of Pune, becomes the fountainhead of all corrupt practices. Amidst the entire power sharing between Nana and Ghashiram, Gauri is used as a pawn. She is presented as a mere 'sex object' whom Nana desires but Ghashiram possesses. Tendulkar's critique of woman's objectification can be appreciated at this point but the play engages with building stereotypes in more subtle ways. In the entire play, Gauri speaks only once when Nana makes sexual advances towards her during one of her daily prayers to Ganapati. She amorously complains Nana, 'he will see'. Replete with sexual innuendos, the scene shows Gauri's naive faith in the patriarchal structure and authority.

Gauri's silence is infective – almost all other women in *Ghashiram Kotwal* are silent. The Brahmin wives speak but in no individual voices of their own. Ironically, the only independent woman voice is Gulabi, the courtesan, who claims a separate identity by asserting her body. She claims her separate identity. Hence, Vijay Tendulkar's oeuvre is representative of the narratives of silence for women, who are projected as mere victims in a male dominated social structure.

Girish Karnad: Breaking the 'Silence'

Girish Karnad is one of the few playwrights in Modern Indian drama who are also exponents of the theatre of roots movement. Hence in delineating the contemporary sensibilities relating to the social and cultural life, Karnad took recourse to myths, folklores and historical legends. Recreating episodes from the Indian epics and classic anthologies, Karnad situated man–woman relationship as the nucleus of Indian society. In the process, women are conceived in two principal dimensions – as a symbol of patriarchal domination and as representing resistance against the phallic authority, be it in terms of the social or the psychosexual.

Yayati explores the predicament of women in a patriarchal world of ideal father-son relationship. Yayati, the father of Puru, incurs upon himself the curse of old age as a result of his erotic liaison with Sharmistha even though he was married to Devayayni. Though both Devayayni and Sharmistha undergo sexual subordination to Yayati, it is Chitralekha who is reduced to a non-entity in the exchange of youth between Puru (Chitralekha's husband) and Yayati. In sync with the ideal family tradition, the play is a narrative of the loyal son; but at the same time it is also of a failed husband. Puru fails to acknowledge the matrimonial aspirations of a wife while Yayati, in his fit of sexual pleasures, not only destroys Devayani and Sharmistha, but also the conjugal life of Chitralekha, who eventually commits suicide. Hence, amidst the masculine operations in an essentially patriarchal society, women are generally identified as 'patients' who are acted upon by the male 'agents', performing/acting out their wanton roles. Although Karnad begins with reference to Devayani's attraction towards Yayati in his first play *Yayati,* the play soon shifts focus towards portraying Sharmistha as the traditional seducer and Chitralekha, as the ultimate victim of patriarchal subordination, who fails to produce any authentic meaning in a male-dominated world. While Sharmistha ushers in domestic turmoil, Chitralekha is rejected both emotionally by her husband and sexually by her father-in-law, whom she has offered herself after Puru's willful metamorphosis into old age. The plays that followed situate women in more complex orientations. For instance, in *Hayavadana,* a relationship saga of three – Devdatta, Padmini and Kapila – flourishes, matures and later destroyed centering on Padmini's desire to have a perfect combination of brain and brawns. In an interview with James Bernett, Karnad says 'In Sanskrit, any person whose name you do not know is addressed as 'Devadatta'. Kapila means dark and therefore earthy and Padmini is the name of one class of women in Vatsayana's Kamasutra' (Bernett, 339).

Hence, Devadatta even after his marriage with Padmini, remains 'anonymous' to her, for failing to satisfy her carnal desires, and Padmini is irresistibly pulled towards the 'dark' passions symbolized by Kapila. The motif of darkness is also drawn in the presentation of goddess *Kali*, in front of whom, Devadatta commits suicide; Kapila beheads himself and Padmini performs the rites of reinstating head on a body in order to bring back to life. *Kali* being conceived as the custodian of all dark passions, grants magical powers to Padmini, who in a fit of the moment, interchanges heads of the two men, producing her desired combination of mind/intellect (Devadatta) and body/passion (Kapila). Hence the main conflict in the play centers on the complexity of women's desires. Though Karnad can be criticized for drawing stereotypical image of Padmini's (dark) desires, he can also be credited with the portrayal of woman as desiring in place of the traditional 'desirable'. While Padmini's desire is critically negotiated in *Hayavadana* as a subjective wish for producing the hybrid between her husband and his friend, Rani's desire in *Nagamandala* surfaces from the traditional expectations of a conjugal life and a longing for union.

Rani is the neglected newly-wed wife, who is constantly ignored by her husband, Appanna. The social bond of marriage which apparently promises love, protection and togetherness turns out to be a virtual 'prison' which not only cages her body but also aspirations. Neglected, she has to *suffer* the bond alone, but her 'parched' heart is soothed by a 'Naga' whose show of love towards her in the disguise of her husband gives her the opportunity to enjoy sexual 'liberty'. The Naga here refers to the mythic tradition of *icchadhari* (as one desires) snakes, who could take human forms as they wished. Hence he emerges as a foil to Rani, but this desire of the snake to unite with her is not propelled from within, instead it is brought about by an accidental operation of magical herbs. The play therefore seems to suggest that it is only on magical intervention that a woman's desire is understood, reciprocated and fulfilled. But the Naga becomes a mere contrivance in Rani's achievement of sexual liberation. The *mandala* of *Nagamandala* therefore is not the coil of the snake as it literally suggests, but of woman's desires, which passionately winds around the 'masculine'. However, important is it to mention that when Rani becomes pregnant and is brought before the village panchayat to prove her fidelity, she vows placing her hand on the naga inside the snake burrow (a popular belief that any person lying would die of snake bite) and says that she has never touched any other male than Appanna, her husband and the naga coiled within the burrow. Therefore, the play also suggests that Rani is sympathetically cheated by the naga even when he tries to satiate her sexual passions. In this regard, the play points towards forming an essential image of the domesticated Indian woman for whom her husband remains the be-all and end-all of all desires even when she is ignored by him.

While Rani attains her 'subjecthood' at the end of the play, Vishakha in *The Fire and the Rain* (originally composed in Kannada in 1989), becomes the 'object' of possession and she is used as an instrument of vengeance under a ubiquitous patriarchal control. Karnad draws Vishakha in the image of a 'failed' wife by the Indian standards but an ideal beloved who allows herself to be exploited by her lover. Vishakha is married to Paravasu without her consent. Considering her a misfit in the public and competitive realm of intellect, she is left alone by her husband, Paravasu to be neglected in his absence for seven years, when he is to head the team of priests performing *yajna* to appease *Indra*, the god of rains. Bereft of Paravasu's companionship, Vishakha is subject to her father-in-law Raibhya's lust which confronts the 'sacrosanct' conventions behind the father – daughter-in-law relationship. Desperate in her desire for a companion, Vishakha is seduced by Yavakri, her former lover, and makes her bait to wrought vengeance on Paravasu and Raibhya. Karnad juxtaposes caste issues with women oppressions, for in the Indian context gender coercion go beyond caste divisions. Vishakha, though an upper-caste Brahmin girl, suffers from patriarchal subordination similar to a tribal woman, Nittilai. Though representing extremely opposite socio-cultural contexts, Vishakha and Nittilai share a common identity of being 'woman' and are equal subjects to male authority. However, Karnad goes a step ahead in presenting Nittilai as a stronger character to Vishakha, for she evinces larger growth than the latter. Her caste experiences make her less critical of the gender bias and the repressions of desires appear commonplace to her. Throughout the play she evinces enormous growth in her character. Her questions, 'Why didn't Yavakri ask for a couple of good showers?'(Karnad 10); 'What is the point of any knowledge, if you can't save dying children' (11) echo her response to the contemporary Brahmin scholarship. The play therefore is a narrative of two contradictory worldviews in Vishakha and Nittilai. Vishakha remains confined within the essential framework of a gendered society, but Nittilai goes beyond being ghettoized into an extremely backward community in order to establish herself as a 'subject' in her own right.

Karnad's women characters therefore acquire various dimensions as they take on different roles in different contexts, but stay rooted and responsible to the socio-cultural, ethnic, racial and sexual realities. His presentation of women follows a marriage between the traditions of staging archetypal women and an individual honest attempt of projecting images of women, who undo their anatomical definitions to produce a meaning of their own.

Mohan Rakesh: Closeting Resistance

If Vijay Tendulkar recreated the image of 'ideal' woman on modern Indian stage in portraying women as mute sufferers, Mohan Rakesh, a contemporary of Tendulkar, is important in presenting strong, determined women who are capable of fighting against patriarchal conventions and asserting themselves. In Mallika, Savitri and Sundari, Rakesh has sought to draw such extraordinary steadfastness that their male counterparts seem irresolute, weak and hesitant. But even in his portrayal of women characters in such positive lights, Rakesh has been criticized for being driven by stereotypical assumptions of women, for in spite of their vitality, his women loved to remain confound within the traditional social expectations. They can be epitome of sacrifices, emotional and affective to the extent that they fail to move beyond the definitions of their biology.

In love with Kalidasa and his art, Mallika in *Ashadh Ka Ek Din* (1958), is conceived as a 'free spirit', who is reluctant to bind Kalidasa to the social and domestic realm of marriage. For Mallika, marriage is just a convention that socially identifies a private commitment. Mallika's progressive ideals are brought into relief by her mother, Ambika, who was a widow herself. Ambika knows society's response to a woman who has no husband. Hence she is unsure of Mallika's predicament in her refusal to marry. In the process, Rakesh is critical of a society, which seeks to subject single self-assertive women to the masculine sexual desire, imagination and abnegation. However, in spite of the social stigmatizations, Mallika emerges as a 'liberated' woman who defies the 'social' in favour of the 'personal'. Her decision to remain unmarried is also brought to test by Kalidasa's surrender to the lure of marriage when he marries the Gupta princess. With Mallika unmoved by such news may claim audience's admiration but the play also provides for a sense of sacrifice and deception in Mallika's fruitless and patient wait for Kalidasa to return. 'Mallika is neither passive nor self-effacing, but paradoxically yet typically, her self-assertion takes the form of self-sacrifice' (Juneja 182).

The play also reads *ashad* (rain) in a different light, where rains are symbolic of Kalidasa's return to creativity. As Kalidasa awakes to the influence of rain, he also recognizes that Mallika is his ultimate desire and inspiration. The association of fertility with Mallika is obvious here. The separation of art and love in Kalidasa is figurative of the divide between culture and nature, where intellection of culture invariably is associated with Kalidasa himself and the emotion of nature with Mallika. But culture's recognition of nature cannot stay for long. Kalidasa leaves Mallika the moment he comes across her 'child', the symbol of her fecund creativity. For Kalidasa, Mallika's image as the 'mother' therefore is a stronger denotative image to Mallika, the defiant lover. Hence the play is a brilliant reading of archetypes, which ironically goes on to show Rakesh's unmediated imposition of stereotypes in presenting Mallika as a woman who traverses from self-sacrifice to motherhood.

With *Lehron ke Rajhans* (1963) Rakesh returns to the same conflict between man and woman but in a different context. The conventional associations with feminine and masculine that even relate to the separation between woman and man is again found in Rakesh's response to characters like Nand and Sundari. The man, Nand, is in a spiritual quest, while the woman, Sundari is bound to the domestic, assigning more importance to the body and its coordinates than on the mental faculties. 'Rakesh's archetypes are rooted in familiar stereotypes about men and women' (184), hence, the play begins with Sundari preparing for a *Kamotsav* (festival of love), to hold back her husband Nand to the domestic chores of life. Nand is conceived as a man who is in a 'higher' intellectual pursuit, while Sundari is busy in her emotional and corporeal works. Sundari represents the typical seductress when she tries to lure Nand at his return in the 1st Act, disturbed in his philosophical conflict. Rakesh portrays in her a seasoned actor who is trained in the art of *shringara*. She conforms to the 'societal definitions of the feminine' and is 'subjective and immediate in her apprehension'(185).

Rakesh projects women as an obstacle against renunciation for men. Essentially conceived, attraction towards a woman makes him more masculine, 'while her repulsion makes him enlightened'(185). Rakesh presents this in relation to the similar suggestion made in the Buddha legend. But what makes him more vulnerable, is his unproblematic representations. Even in Yashodhara, Rakesh invokes the audience's sympathy but never really endows 'life' in her. Yashodhara is seen to follow her man, waiting years for his return, but never asserting her existence. Rakesh also brings in the motif of jealousy through the portrayal of Sundari, who is propelled to resent Yashodhara, for allowing Buddha to carry on his renunciation. But it must be appreciated that Sundari conceives the 'higher' masculine quests as subject to women's discretions in allowing them to be gained.

Sundari was initially instrumental in Nand's consistent failure to resolve the conflict he was in, but it is she who sends him in the pursuit of Gautama, for she rejects living with Nand's irresolution. But the appreciation gained now is lost in the last act again when she turns away Nand, who remains indecisive even under the direction of Buddha. The audience is propelled to question Sundari's consideration of a trouble-torn Nand and her failure is seen as typical to her. In her final reproach to Nand she reduces herself to the archetypes of impulse and emotion that goes on to define her. Hence the play draws end with the sexual instead of psychological limitation of Sundari being exploited to covertly refer to the conflict between Nand and Sundari.

In Savitri of *Adhe Adhure* (1968), Rakesh portrays a 'half feminine' woman, who loses all her personal relations because of her defiance against the traditionally prescribed gender roles. But even in his depiction of a woman who has the potential to transform the gender matrix of the society, Rakesh has allowed himself to be limited by the 'contemporary' stereotypes. In the traditional Indian context, it was held ideal for a woman not to go outside to work, but even if she has to go for the economic necessity of the house, it must not be for her own career but for the sake of assistance to the male. In Savitri, we find a woman who seeks to balance the work and family, though she is the lone bread earner of the family, she must fulfill her feminine 'duties'. Rakesh therefore portrays Savitri in a double bind, where both the domestic and the professional commitments must be balanced.

Incapable of earning livelihood, Mahendranath is a foil to Savitri. He complains of an assumed disrespect in his household and, in his self-pity and conceit makes a show of male authority – an inevitable outcome of the fear of loss of control. Dominated and abused by her husband, Savitri, on the other hand, is an image of domestic violence and frustration. She is even bullied by Mahendra's friends, who consider her to be the reason behind Mahendra's failure and separation from his family.

Though mistreated by friends and family, Savitri lacks the courage to move out of her marital relation with Mahendra. In itself, this may suggest the vulnerability of women in a strict social structure which compels them to continue their marriage even when the entire love's labour is already lost. Savitri is never a self-effacing woman and the play also reports of an illicit relation with her boss, Shinghania. She uses her lures on him to produce enough economic opportunities for the family. She even wins a job offer for her son from Singhania. But with his self-pride being 'compromised' in his mother's attempts to get a job for him, Savitri's son criticizes her of having an insatiable thirst for wealth and status. Savitri therefore has a multi-layered presence in the play. She evinces the potential to go beyond the general limitations of the fixed gender roles but resists herself from doing so.

Hence, women characters in Mohan Rakesh are essentially self-assertive but suffer the lack of choice in a gendered world and finally end up conforming to their stereotypical image. As Renu Juneja puts it, his 'gallery of strong women has added a new dimension to modern Indian drama'. (191) 'In some measure, his portraits are responsive to the changes now taking place in Indian society. He handles his women with a sensitivity and awareness far beyond that of the average man. Yet his perceptiveness is limited by his reliance on somewhat archaic and stereotypical assumptions of the feminine. The unresolved quality of these images is, indeed, typical of the divided reality of women in contemporary India'. (191)

G. P. Deshpande: The 'social' woman

G. P. Deshpande, one of the noted playwrights of modern Indian theatre perceived gender as a product of social, political and cultural forces. Hence, gender in his plays emerges as a construction that is interlocked within the boundaries of class, caste and state. Deshpande looks at gender as a site where other forms of social structures unfold their power. Therefore, his reading of gender relations is always grounded on the social situations of his characters. Even when depicting personal relationships, he located them in the socio-cultural and political space. Hence in his portrayal of women characters, he chose the public over domestic spaces, thereby making their case more complex and politically stimulating. Unlike the preceding images of women portrayed by the pre and post sixties male playwrights, Deshpande's women are 'intelligent with an incisive sense of humour and sharp wit' (44). They are women of ideals, who value independence and in their affiliation to the left wing politics, attempt to dissolve both class stratifications and the public/private debate.

Saraswati in *Udhdhwasta Dharmashala* is a political activist who has high ambitions. She marries Shridhar Vishwanath Kulkarni because she finds in him a person who shares her political views and commitments. But she leaves him realizing that her political dreams may get frustrated in continuing the relation with him. She is intelligent enough to attract the attention of a senior party leader, Prayag, in order to rise higher in the party ranks from where she can influence and manage its activities. While Saraswati denies the traditional notions of soft, docile domestic woman, Madhavi, in the same play appears as a muse inspiring revolutionary words in Sridhar, the poet. She is impressed by his words but rejects the idea of putting them into practice; for, she refuses to be dominated by their political content. Finding Sridhar uncompromising in carrying on with his revolutionary creations, she manipulates Vitthal to render him companionless. Hence both the women, surface as virtual 'destroyers' of Sridhar, and are politically operative in their own ways to move beyond traditional images of women in the Indian context. But Durga in *Raste* appear as a foil to these women. In Durga, Deshpande portrays a true revolutionary leader for whom there is no separation between word and action. Unlike Saraswati and Madhavi, Durga is a non-scheming woman who goes by the ultra-left ideologies and dies in an encounter. With respect to the enormity of her death, the other members of her party seem dwarfish with their ideological standpoints lacking action and depending upon words to bring forth a sociopolitical change.

While Durga meets a tragic death as a result of her steadfast commitment towards the left ideology and her resilience against socio-political injustices, Vasundhara in *Andhar Yatra* arrives at the same fate even in her silent acceptance. She remains inactive and isolated and never in the entire play does she appear to bind herself with those who are attracted towards her. Daulat Rao, a politician; Shripad, an intellectual and Aswaththa, a revolutionary-all fall in love with her but she refuses to partner anybody. Her fundamental belief has been to live life and not share it. Hence, she rejects any relation that comes her way but in the process isolates herself. Even in her marriage, when she is sexually exploited by her husband; she refuses to protest and learns to overcome her anguish. The only political question that she asks is as to why are all political movements failing, when each try to change the world. The answer to which is probably she herself, 'all movements of social and political transformation are working in isolation from each other' (Deshpande, 17).

G. P. Deshpande is also in league with such playwrights and directors as Girish Karnad, Mohan Rakesh, Badal Sircar, and the like in renegotiating Indian history. In *Chanakya Vishnugupta*, he not only reads the historical story of the Mauryan Empire but also identifies Chanakya as a patriarch who uses Suwasini, a woman in love with Chandragupta, as a pawn in his scheme of things. Even though Chandragupta loved her, Suwasini is compelled to marry Nanda, after whose death she accepts the life of a Buddhist Bhikshuni. However, she is not drawn as a conventional tragic character because she overcomes it with her spirituality thereby projecting herself as an antagonist to Chanakya who represents materiality in the play. Hence Deshpande's women are fierce individuals who defy being measured by traditional paradigms. In moving away from the established images of women in male oriented Indian theatres, Deshpande heralds the emerging women in his plays, who are not only politically educated but also ready to challenge male authority in political and social institutions.

Though any survey of post-independence Indian theatre is not complete without discussing Mahesh Dattani, I deliberately keep him out of this list because gender and not woman remains the main focus of his works. For Dattani, patriarchy as a set of conventions that impose on women and men alike is an object of criticism but he refuses to hold any essential feminist conclusions in projecting the vague hypocrisies of socio-cultural institutions. *Tara* may be a story of deprivation for a girl child whose one leg is amputated for her twin brother; but, as Dattani himself says in an interview with Erin B. Mee, 'I think it's a play about the self, about the man and woman in self, but a lot of people think of it as a play about the girl child' (21). Though his other plays deal with diverse issues, situating the woman question as one among the many, *Final Solutions* projects in Hardika, woman's 'non-independent' experience of India's independence. Reflecting on the gendered experiences in post-colonial India and questioning the hetero-normative social and cultural institutions, Dattani avoided framing woman as the only sex to suffer discrimination in terms of social, political, cultural, racial, ethnical and religious participation.

Deviations: Indian Women Theatre Practitioners

The treatment of women in the male canon (of course with few exceptions), as it follows from the above discussion, has revolved around the images of women, be it the stereotype of the traditional voiceless or of the roaring, self-assertive or the relatively 'free.' However, the post-1980s period saw the crowding of Indian stage by women theatre practitioners across the country. This led to a gradual establishment of what can be called a theatre of their (women playwrights' and directors') own. But the formation of canonfor women theatre practitioners could only be after a gradual progress from imitating the male theatre counterpartsin the 1950s to the confident self-assertion in the 1970s.

In conscious attempts to build an exclusive niche for themselves in Indian theatres, women playwrights and directors deviated from the traditions of their male predecessors and contemporaries both in terms of dramaturgy and content. Even with respect to image formation, they arrive at a critical distance from the male practitioners as they altogether do away with the images, be it stereotypes in the traditional sense of the term or not. Their women are living characters who face life as it comes to them. But this philosophy of life does not refer to any stoic acceptance of what comes sieved through patriarchal and socio-conventional mores; neither do the women make conscious efforts to politically subvert the institutions that traditionally privilege the men. Instead, the playwrights sought unique socio-political, cultural, economic and racial loci for their women which would go on to shape their lived experiences, struggles, resistances, frustrations, fulfillments, earned recognitions, liberations, or empowerments. Hence the 'images' that emerge from their works do not essentially remain confined to a certain class of women. At its formative stage, any canon permits reworking of the traditional. Hence images of women as victims remained an important category for the early Indian women playwrights writing mainly in English. Dina Mehta's *Brides are Not for Burning* or Manjula Padmanabhan's *Lights Out* deals with gender oppression across the social, cultural, class and caste arrangements. However, with the regional and linguistic turns in Indian Women's theatre or theatres in India at large, the post-90s theatre productions focused mainly on women with respect to their contingent locations and renegotiated with issues unique to them. Varsha Adalja, Kusum Kumar, Usha Ganguli, Neelam Mansingh Chowdhry, Mamta G. Sagar and a host of other playwrights, some of whom are even directors and have private theatre troupes as well, speak of women, situating them amidst the experiences of nation, class, caste, race, culture and sexuality. Hence, they present contemporary authentic women by avoiding their ghettoization through essentialising and stereotyping and by making them indeterminate and evocative.

CHAPTER

Women, Nation, War: Mandodari and A Tale from the Year 1857

'... as a woman, I have no country.
As a woman I want no country.
As a woman my country is the whole world.'

(*Three Guineas*, 99)

For women, Virginia Woolf's lexis from the *Three Guineas* may initially seem to be an impressive *mantra* for negotiating their national identity but toeing such oversimplified feminist conclusions would result in ignoring the complex and 'paradoxical' relations between woman and nation. History accounts for a shift in perception, for women's struggle with 'nation' has never been restricted to vouching for disenfranchisement in constructing a separate identity of their own, and at the same time demeaning the political notion of citizenship.

Since its first formal turn in the post-French revolution period, when Mary Wollstonecraft appealed for the social recognition of women's rights to the Quebecois feminists'struggle for suffrage, women's criticism has been volleyed more against the patriarchal 'national' than nation in itself. But with prominence in complex nationalistic struggles in postcolonial nation states, women's relations with nation became increasingly problematic. Theatre, being inherently interventionist, responded to the woman–nation (dis)connects in its own way. In India, where the nationalist struggles essentially centered on the debates between the binaries of spirituality and materiality, moderates and extremists, home and the world; woman and nation became correlates referring to domestic spaces to be preserved. Hence, worth exploring is women's theatre's engagement with the nuanced location of women within the frame of Indian nationalism, which has continued to evolve from the pre-independence freedom struggle to 'hate mongering' (sometimes state-sponsored) both in the inter-national and intra-national contexts.

The use of theatre as an effective propagandist tool may be traced back to the *bhakti* movement (c.15th century) in 'Hindu' history, when poet-saints used theatre as a means of spreading and sustaining the movement throughout the country. However, the political role of theatre in India is most prominently realized only in the nineteenth century when theatre became a 'living' site for political struggle. Nationalism's primary condition was to make people conscious of their own life and times, national brotherhood, and more so of the political hindrances that thwart their national, social and communal progress. And theatre was often used unto 'ends' that propelled the British administration in India in taking suppressive measures on it. Dinabandhu Mitra's *Nildarpana* stands as one of such early attempts where the colonial procedures were severely criticized. Drawing on the 1858 revolutions in Bengal when the poor indigo cultivators refused to sow crops at the orders of the British planters, and were consequently put to death, the play marks the beginning of theatre's political tryst with the colonial government. It inspired a host of patriotic plays which were written to heighten the national sentiments of the mass. The British Government in India responded by the Dramatic Performances Act in 1876, which wielded strong censorial powers over the production of indigenous plays. Speaking on the political role of theatre in India, Farely Richmond argued that 'This period, marked by an unrestrained desire among Indian writers and producers to propagate independence, is also characterized by suppressive restrictions imposed by the colonial government on the publication and performance of plays' (Richmond 319).

Though throttled by the Act, Indian theatre continued producing nationalist plays employing newer strategies. While political allegories like *Kichak Vadh* (1907) used episodes from the epics to dramatize contemporary events and allegorize political personalities, a number of productions drew on 'historical figures who fought against political oppression' (322). Though most of the plays were banned by the Government, whenever staged (sometimes even by daring the ban) attracted unprecedented success. Therefore, political theatre's objective of igniting the popular imagination was somehow realized. The regional and folk theatres arose to the occasion as well.

> Elsewhere in India, other playwrights glorified their own local patriots. In Assam, the struggle of the Ahom kings with the Burmese invaders was dramatized. In Maharashtra, Shivaji's exploits came to symbolize Tilak's political struggles. In Mysore, Ecchama Nayaka, Tipu Sultan, Nargund Baba Sahib and Kittur Chennamma provided the subject for many nationalistic dramas. And all over India, the battles between Rama and Ravana in the *Ramayana,* as well as those between Krishna and Kamsa in the *Puranas,* provided Indian patriots with ample scope for symbolizing the struggle for freedom from foreign oppression. (322)

These nationalistic attempts in theatre not only showcased the colonial impoverishment of the natives, but also induced the general ideal of freedom. However, apart from congregating public sentiments and resisting against colonial oppressions, theatre as an instrument of propagating nationalism endeavored nation building by exposing and critiquing social prejudices prevalent in the Indian society. Hence, social and economic abuses, religious bigotry, socio-cultural oppressions in the forms of casteism and untouchability, and women's suppression in terms of the practices of *sati*, dowry and child marriage recurred thematically.

Owing to the changes in equations of global power and increasing international support over India's claim to independence alongside the heavy material and financial loss suffered by the British Government in the Second World War, the possibility of political freedom for India was already realized during the 1940s. These global changes, complemented by the enthusiastic 'Quit India Movement', growing apprehension of a second sepoy mutiny after the crushing of Indian National Army and an unprecedented political rise against the British Government whose decisions during the First World War led to artificial famines across the province of Bengal, resulted in the independence of India. As an emerging republic in the late 1940s and early 1950s, India as a newnation-state threw up issues which Indian theatre practitioners espoused broaching themes that directly pertained to its challenges and aspirations. The Indian People's Theatre Association (formed in 1942) sought to express the popular sentiments concerning both national and local issues. Converging folk into street theatre, the IPTA staged such plays as *Aaj Ka Sawaal* (The Problems of Today), *Swathantra Sangram* (Independence Struggle) and *Bhook ki Jwaala* (The Flames of Hunger). But IPTA's major success came with Sombhu Mitra's production of Bijan Bhattacharya's *Nabanna* (1944) as a protest against the 1943 Bengal famine. Though protest motif continued recurring in IPTA's productions, its Central Ballet Troupe produced *India Immortal* in 1945 which encompassed the last two thousand years of rich cultural heritage of the country. This was performed all throughout India, inspiring and appealing masses to rise to the occasion of freedom struggle.

The partition of India as a result of the two nation theory flaunted by the political leaders and the implementation of The Mountbatten Plan marked the 'labor' that caused an unforeseen amount of bloodshed amidst the biggest human exodus ever in the history of the world. The partition redefined the approach to 'nation'because it compelled the re-imagination of the 'self' as the 'other'. While Hindus and Sikhs in Lahore, Karachi, Islamabad, or Dhaka were forced to leave their homeland and enter the newly defined frontiers of India, most Muslims in India were pushed beyondthe borders to Pakistan and East Pakistan (though India still remained home to millions of Muslims owing to its secular identity).

The IPTA produced a host of plays in this period, notable among which are Khwaja Abbas' *Main Kaun Hun?* (*Who Am I?,* 1947) dealing with a wounded soldier's predicament in failing to remember his camp (Hindu or Muslim) and the eventual return to memory leaving all his persecutors with a sense of perennial guilt in their minds and R. Ghatak's *Dolil* (*The Written Deed,* 1947), which depicted the killings of innocent refugees who were preparing for a march to make their grievances known. Largely avoiding prejudices and religious fanaticism the IPTA took a secular approach positing social criticism as their mainstay. The post-independence period however is marked with IPTA's shift from nationalist propagandas to the left political ideologies, for its theatrical ventures became thematically synonymous with the demands of the left wing political parties. Ignoring the larger national issues, it increasingly became the instrument of left organizational fronts.

The first notable theatre event in the post-independence period, however, is the 1956 drama seminar organized by the Sangeet Natak Academy with the objective of framing 'guidelines' for the future of Indian drama. With S. Radhakrishnan citing Sanskrit performance tradition as the repository to pan Indian theatre, J. C. Mathur asserted Hindi theatre as its rightful heir and proposed that regional professional theatres must produce plays in Hindi along with their own vernacular productions (Mathur 10).

The notion being acknowledged by Sachin Sengupta (director of the seminar) and supported by Mulk Raj Anand, who advised the translation of vernacular plays into Hindi, a rush of translation works followed. Plays by prominent regional playwrights like Vijay Tendulkar, Girish Karnad, and Badal Sarkar among others, were translated into Hindi. But regional theatres preserved their individual identities, though folk traditions increasingly merged with the mainstream. Hence the Nehruvian dream of 'one India/ one art' was not realised, for such homogenisation would be a mere reiteration of the colonial system of affairs in Indian terms. In another seminar organised by the Sangeet Natak Academy (SNA) in 1971, when the cultural relevance of traditional theatre was debated, Suresh Awasthi, the secretary of SNA from 1965 to 1975 defined the predominant theatre practice in the then India as 'Theatre of Roots' for the productions of Urban theatre directors where traditional and folk elements converged with urban themes. 'Practitioners of such a hybrid aesthetic such as Girish Karnad, K. N. Panikkar, Habib Tanvir, Utpal Dutt, and Ratan Thiyam had somewhat unselfconsciously and organically been experimenting with integrating elements of Yakshagana, Sanskrit drama, Naccha, Jatra, and Thang-ta, Raslila, and Pung-cholom respectively.' (Mitra, 68) Retaining the heterogeneity of Indian theatre, these theatre productions therefore re-questioned the definition of national theatre in India. Making an exhaustive study of these performances, Erin B. Mee opined that the theatre of roots was 'a post-Independence effort to decolonize the aesthetics of modern Indian theatre by challenging …colonial culture … reclaiming the aesthetics of performance and by addressing the politics of aesthetics'. (Mee, 5) The same tradition continued and further developed throughout the 1960s and 70s which was further complimented by the unfolding of contemporary political events both in and around the country which forced it into war with the neighbors followed by the civic and political crisis of the 'emergency'. With the nation building process and attempts to preserve its civic and political integrity underway at the same time, theatre's engagement with nation became more nuanced.

This chapter probes into the same 'association' through the prism of Indian women's theatre. But making a comprehensive study of the relations between two such entities (India as a nation-state and Indian women's theatre), which are still in the process of 'becoming' both on theoretical and hermeneutical levels, renders the pursuit difficult if not impossible. Hence, I choose two important women productions—Tripurari Sharma's *Azizun Nisa: A Tale from the year 1857*(1999) and Varsha Adalza's *Mandodari* (1996) as evocative of approaches of women in engaging with nation especially in the time of war, when nationalism and patriotism emerge as essential correlates.

Nation, Imagination, Nationalism

Set in Kanpur, *A Tale from the Year 1857: Azizun Nisa* dramatizes the story of a courtesan, Azizun who responding to the call of the nation, readily renounces her career and becomes one among the sepahis during the sepoy mutiny and contributes against the British. Though Tripurari Sharma makes a deeper study into history through Azizun, Varsha Adalja in *Mandodari* reworks characters from the popular Hindu myth *Ramayana*, to build a plot that revolves around a relatively lesser known/important character Mandodari whose tryst with an imaginary Kaaldevtaa ultimately decides the outcome of the war between Rama and Raavana. Therefore, both Sharma and Adalja seek to redefine women's positions with respect to nation and war and in the process re-imagine the 'national'.

Benedict Anderson defines nation as 'an imagined political community' (Anderson 49). It is 'imagined as both inherently limited and sovereign' (49). Hence imagination, to Anderson, is constitutive of a nation, which is limited because 'even the largest of them (nations) encompassing perhaps a billion living human beings, has finite, if elastic, boundaries, beyond which lie other nations' (50) and sovereign because 'the concept was born in an age in which

Enlightenment and Revolution were destroying the legitimacy of the divinely-ordained, hierarchical dynastic realm' (50). However, such a definition entails a series of questions. Firstly, in looking at the nation as imagination, Anderson writes, it is 'imagined because the members of even the smallest nation will never know most of their fellow-members, meet them, or even hear of them, yet in the minds of each lives the image of their communion'(49). Hence, Anderson suggests that in general, a nation, however small, is large enough to shelter groups which can never have full-fledged inter-personal relationships with each other. To reinforce this argument, he further says that 'all communities larger than primordial villages of face-to-face contact (and perhaps even these) are imagined. Communities are to be distinguished, not by their falsity and genuineness, but by the style in which they are imagined.' (49). But to hold that 'communities larger than primordial villages of face-to-face contact' will use a particular 'style' of imagination to produce forth a nation is confusing, because 'it is after all a hermeneutic truism that all social relations – even those between 'primordial villagers – work through the shared understanding (and misunderstanding) of those involved' (Poole 11). Secondly, since the act of defining is 'political' in itself, Anderson's definition of the nation as sovereign is essentially fraught with Eurocentric sensibility of world history. He relates the sovereignty of nation with a period in Europe when 'the legitimacy of the divinely-ordained, hierarchical dynastic realm' (50) was substituted with the republic. In India, however, the concept of nation was realized way earlier when Chandragupta Maurya in 321BCE brought the entire region between Afghanistan and Myanmar together under one empire. Of course, empire is not coterminous with nation but with *political* imagination invoked upon, the political map of the then India (except the Deccan), was roughly synonymous with the Mauryan empire. Imagination for Anderson, is exclusively *creative* of the nation as a political community. But, since imagination is mitochondrial for any social existence, free play of unqualified imagination may produce ambiguous and multiple identities, delimited by no pre-existing essence of the national. Again, community and one's communal identity is never apolitically imaginable. Therefore, for the imagination to conceive of and then identify with a nation, it must undergo a nationalist education that results in a condition conducive to the production of a 'political community'as nation. Hence, instrumental imagination, initiated by the political discourse of nationalism fabricates the meta-narrative − nation. But this narrative is never fully realized unless the imagination is recognized collectively, which is arrived at only when most of the members of the 'community' is made conscious of it. Therefore nation becomes a product of collective instrumental imagination mediated by the aegis of social and objective consciousness. But mere production of 'nation' does not presuppose its re-production. Hence it is made possible through repeated performances of such national cultural and political elements as language, literature, history, tradition, myths, customs, institutions, heroes and icons, politics, symbols (national flag, emblems), constitution, legal, political and electoral structures, and sometimes religion or even secularism.

However, in *A Tale from the Year 1857*, Tripurari Sharma presents the waking up to the realization of nation in multiple provisos. Azizun here is not the traditional woman who is constructed in conformity to the national idiom. She is not the 'type' courtesan whose art ends in mere commercial entertainment. Sharma portrays her as an already inspired woman whose imagination of the nation needs no nationalist instrumental education. But while portraying Shamsuddin, the second most important character of the play, she makes nation appear to him as a part of the cultural, social, religious and political experience. For Mohd. Ali, nation becomes synonymous with Nana Saheb, while for Adila, Lucknow, under the custody of Nana is her nation. Hence if nation is conceived in terms of the collective performative instrumental imagination, it can also refer to the regional and the communal, which are politically conceived in their own rights. Anthony D. Smith addresses the problematic by defining the nation and *ethnie* (the term he uses for ethnic communities) separately.

> 'I propose to define the concept of nation as a 'named human community occupying a homeland, and having common myths and a shared history, a common public culture, a single economy and common rights and duties for all members'. The concept of *ethnie* can in turn be defined as 'a named human community connected to a homeland, possessing common myths of ancestry, shared memories, one or more elements of shared culture, and a measure of solidarity, at least among the elites'.' (Smith 13)

However, in explaining the proposition, he clarifies that 'these are really summaries of pure or ideal-types of 'nation' and '*ethnie*', derived from a stylization of the respective beliefs and sentiments of elite members of *ethnies* and of nations. They do not list common denominators.'(13) But he asserts that the definitions do 'highlight their distinctive elements and the key differences between them' (13).In a conversation with Shamsuddin where he complains about being 'robbed' of his religious sentiments while serving as a soldier for the British administration in India, Azizun is therefore seen confiding her concern and articulating conscience about her nation as 'homeland'. That she identifies with and owes her exclusivity to the nation is betrayed in her anguish in the thought of being increasingly captured by the outsiders (here the British):

> Now Avadh has also fallen to them... I tremble to think...the way our entire homeland is being taken over by strangers. (Sharma 126)

Hence, making sense of a homeland may ignite the imagination of nation in an individual/ community. But this recognition is robust when the certain 'homeland' is under threat from alien force(s). Identifying the British antagonists as the other, Azizun is more national in the macrocosmic sense of the term because nation here obliterates the mutual differences constantly at play within the communities in order to produce a trans-regional reference.

Like Azizun, Mandodari's approach to the idea of nation in Adalja's *Mandodari* is subject to the moment of crisis. Both of them are 'inspired' individuals and both grow politically charged at the face of national catastrophe. Though Mandodari is critical of Ravana's misrule in his kingdom and anguished with the future of her nation (Lanka), it is only at the reference to Lanka's destruction that Mandodari turns protective. She begs, prays and ultimately challenges Kaaldevata.

> KAALDEVATA: I have come to destroy this golden Lanka
>
> MANDODARI: O lord, be merciful. Be kind to us and spare us from your terrible anger.
>
> KAALDEVATA: The decision of Kaal is unalterable, Devi. The reign of Ravana and the power of his mighty kingdom are over.
>
> MANDODARI: Please don't say that, lord. The queen of this mighty empire bows at your feet. Please go away from here. ...
>
> KAALDEVATA: Lanka's destruction is destined.
>
> MANDODARI: But I shall not allow this to happen. This task of yours must remain unfulfilled. (Adalja 101)

Mandodari braves Kaaldevata '... your (Kaaldevata's) task will remain unfulfilled' (102) (*bracketing mine*) and the entire play revolves around a strategic fight between the two. Therefore Adalja draws the character of Mandodari in the light of those women who can even defy the authority of Kaal. Hence the intelligent reference to Anusuya and

Savitri in the play (Anusuya and Savitri being mythological examples of 'ordinary'(Adalja 102) women who defeated Kaal). Her defiance is also exemplary of a woman's rejection of the despotic patriarchal authority. She refuses to accept the decision of Kaal on Lanka. Even though she is akin to Azizun in putting on the role of a protector at the moment of national need, her experience of the nation is different. Azizun confronts nation's crisis at a point when the soldiers were revolting against the British misrule; but, for Mandodari, the situation turns more critical for she is pitted against both her husband who is the ruler of her country and the Kaaldevata who is bent on killing her husband and destroying his kingdom. In association with the soldiers, Azizun's objective is to go beyond the confines of the feminine stereotype and free her nation from the foreign political and cultural oppressions, while Mandodari has to stake her identity as a wife and free her 'land' from the tyranny resulting from her husband's over-ambition. Further, being the queen herself, she has to protect her nation from an imminent apocalypse. As reported in the play, Ravana is the king of 'three worlds', which entails that his kingdom transcends the boundaries of a single nation and unifies transnational political differences. But, Mandodari, though queen of the entire kingdom, reduces the actual 'national' to the ethnical and locates it in a specific homeland where her community shares common cultural elements. Hence she refers to her nation as 'my clan', 'my city', 'my people' and 'my land'(101-114). Notable here is Mandodari's passions in identifying with her country (homeland). She personalizes what generally is impersonally imagined.

In sync with Mandodari's approach to 'nation', is Anthony D. Smith's idea of associating nation with 'occupying' the 'homeland'. But he substitutes nation with *ethnies* and opines that they'need not have a public culture, only some common cultural elements – it could be language, religion, customs or shared institutions – whereas a common public culture is a key attribute of nations' (14). But differentiating nation and community in such terms invites problems of their own, especially when a poly-ethnic country like India is taken into account. Nation here emerges as a meta-whole consisting of an assortment of *ethnies*, which are individual wholes in themselves.

In India, where the terms *jati* and *desh*, are loosely used as alternatives for both nation and *ethnies*, the idea of homeland in terms of belonging to a 'human community' appears ambiguous. *Jati* refers to the ethnic identity of an individual, which often glosses over his political identity as an Indian. There are numerous examples of jati-based discriminations and movements that have painted the political canvas of the country grey, be it the anti-Bengali drives in Assam in the '60s or the anti-Bihari in Maharashtra in the recent past or the consistent discrimination faced by the North East Indians in other parts of the country. Hence, *jati* here refers to the deep and continuous cultural affinity of a person to a certain 'homeland', which is also part of a greater 'homeland', viz. the nation, to which his connection is relatively more 'symbolic'. The concept of 'homeland' is more curiously drawn in terms of *desh* for it is not just a colloquial translation of 'nation', but also a reference to particular regions in popular idiom and vernacular legends of the country. It is associated with a person's strong rootedness in a particular province, the socio-cultural, linguistic, ethnic and political specificity, which forms the *desh*/nation for him. This is so metaphorically enmeshed in a typical member of such a *desh* that it becomes an essential personality for him. India as a *desh* (held as a macrocosm) therefore is an integration of many smaller *desh*-es. Hence unlike Mandodari's consideration of Lanka in *Mandodari*, the concept of homeland as exclusively national may not seem plausible for a poly-ethnic land like India.

Smith also identifies the nation-*ethnie* divide with claims to 'public culture'. But in the process he never gives a proper definition of 'public culture', though he recognizes 'language, religion, customs or shared institutions' as cultural elements in the *ethnies*. If we then hold public culture as an assortment of such common characteristics that enable members of a nation to imagine themselves as a part of it, the difficulty in separating the nation/*ethnie* remains. The political imagination that constitutes a nation in terms of 'public culture' can produce an *ethnie* as well, for, each community has its own intra-communal structures to which are subordinated the shared experiences of that culture, be it in terms of language, religion, rituals, ethnicity, colour, race, history and memory, or be it by way of the political and administrative bodies that hold the entire edifice together. Therefore, to differentiate between nation and community/*ethnie*/*jati*/*desh*, there may emerge a language failure. But the nation – community debate may be temporarily resolved by positing the idea of 'nationhood' as 'an advanced stage in the ongoing process of political and social integration, reached through the gradual broadening of social communication between societies as they evolve into a community, then into a people, and finally into a nation.' (Dikshit 110) Nation and community therefore may coexist in the political imagination as stages in socio-political processes of integration, where social communication both recognized and delimited in terms of linguistic, cultural, racial, economic, historic and political kinship makes possible the evolution of community into nation. I understand the national social communication to be both 'recognized' and delimited' because conceptualizing nation necessitates both de-territorializing the communal and territorializing the national. Mandodari recognizes the importance of communal contingency for her 'land', but at the same time wishes for an integration of factions in order to experience a better national life. With repeated references to Lanka as 'Ravanasura's golden city' on one hand and 'my land', 'my city', and 'my people' on the other, she invokes a discrete division between the hypothetic existences of Ravana's Lanka which is marked with his high ambitions and innocuous means, and the Lanka in its own right which is not synonymous with an individual's aspiration. She lauds the collective communal identity over the 'three worlds' won by her husband. But on another occasion while speaking to Seeta before war, she desires sacrifice of factional difference:

> 'All these people scattered in different factions, forever fighting each other, could be united and could at last live happily in one kingdom under one emperor.

This is the dream I had, Seeta, that I hoped to see reflected in your eyes. We have a great opportunity to serve humanity, and prevent further hatred and bloodshed...'(Adalja 111)

Mandodari not only appeals for forfeiting differences between the enemy sections but also implores Seeta to sacrifice 'herself' to Ravana: "Surrender to Ravana, Seeta, and stop this war' (110). But in both the cases, Mandodari calls for the sacrifice of identity: national, communal and the personal, which, though interrelated, are mutually frustrating as well. Seeta, who has been uprooted from her 'home' amongst her own men, is expected to re-imagine the Lanka as her own land. Failure of social communication is obviously imminent. Seeta denies being the subject of Ravana's aspiration.

If Seeta's frustration is considered in the context of the partition of British-India, it can be argued that mereattempts toward social communications are not enough to argue for the birth of India, Pakistan or Bangladesh or any other postcolonial nation-state which has suffered the labor of 'partition'.The political partition of 'British India' into India and Pakistan in two wings of the East and the West (the East referring to present Bangladesh), is not merely a partition of a great land mass into three halves but also a strategy to compromise with the failure of social communication across religio-cultural differences, not to mention the politics involved in initiating such differences that resulted in the bloodshed of millions. However, Gyanendra Pandey points out in *Remembering Partition* that 'what all this has left behind is an extraordinary love–hate relationship: on the one hand deep resentment and animosity, and the most militant of nationalism – Pakistani against Indian, Indian against Pakistani, now backed up by nuclear weapons; on the other a considerable sense of nostalgia, frequently articulated in the view that this was a partition of siblings that should never have happened' (2). Partition therefore is also about sharing; sharing a common history, a common mythic past and ubiquitous 'shadow lines' that unite the common mass across the borders. Hence the birth of a nation-state like India encourages the co-existence of nationalism and communalism as antithetical forces. But, Jawaharlal Nehru, the first prime minister of independent India, spoke about 'nationalism' in a different light in his address to the Eleventh Conference of the Institute of Pacific Relations in 1953.

> What exactly is nationalism? I do not know; and it is extremely difficult to define. In the case of a country under foreign domination, it is easy to describe what nationalism is. It is anti-foreign power. But in a free country, what is nationalism? Certainly it is something positive, though opinions may vary. Even so, I think a large element of it is negative, and sometimes we find that nationalism, which is a healthy force in a country, a progressive force, a liberating force, becomes – may be after liberation – unhealthy, retrogressive, reactionary, or expansionist and looks with greedy eyes on other countries, as did those countries against which it fought for its freedom... All that is "nationalism'. (qtd. The Nation Form, 19)

If Nehru's definition of nationalism as 'anti-foreign power' is considered, its militant form also must be directed towards the 'foreign power'. But as Gyanendra Pandey observes in *Remembering Partition* (2001), militant form of nationalism is adverse to the 'interests' of nation (Pandey 2), because it essentially aims at building meta-narratives that promote singularity of culture, history, language, religion and politics and in the process seek to obliterate the existing socio-cultural uniqueness, the linguistic differences and the incoherence in religious and racial identities.

In *Azizun Nisa*, Tripurari Sharma tries to provide a definition to 'militant nationalism' in exposing the nationalists' attempts toward obliterating contradictory voices in producing their own narrative of national struggles. Azizun's association with nationalism is correlated with her imagining the nation as an essence which erases any possible inconsistency. She is not merely critical of the factions who do not support the mutiny of the soldiers, but also justifies the mass murder, bloodshed and terror unleashed by the Indian soldiers in the name of nationalism. Mohd. Ali is criticised for being a non-participant in the final gory attempt of the Indian soldiers to defeat the Britishers. Ali Khan too is denounced for betraying his fellow countrymen and siding with the British on the pretext of becoming 'friendly with whoever is in power' (Sharma 164). Even when the catholicity of Azizun's art is questioned, her answer is evocative of her commitments –

> ZUBAIDA: … A dedicated artiste should close all the curtains and till the milieu changes for the better, engross herself with the composition of new songs.

> AZIZUN: A bloodbath may rage outside but the ink must flow inside! (151)

Art therefore must cater to the national cause for Azizun. Again, when Zubaida questions Azizun's vulnerable participation in matters of rebellion, Sarwar puts forward a narrative of nationalist education so that disparate voices may be neutralised.

> SARWAR: Everyone is fighting one's battle, Zubaida Bi, with one's own share of the poison. Even my mother can't be kept separate because the fight is between the pure and the defiled; the fresh and the stale; between man and man. And it's right that it should be so because she's gone where all must go. The right and the wrong lead to the same result, meet the same end. (151)

But Azizun, Sarwar and the other nationalists view nationalism in a context where the 'nation' is under the political control of foreign power. With a change in the political identity of the citizens, the narratives of nationalism may undergo change too, for, both 'nation' and 'identity' is re-imagined. Hence, 'identity' not only as a socio-cultural, political product but also as a 'personal' means of integration (and disintegration) must be brought into more critical consideration, more so, in the light of women's relation to the national.

National Identity, Woman and War

> We have an *identity* because we *identify* with figures or representations which are made available to us. The concept of identity implies that there is a constitutive linkage between forms of *subjectivity*, i.e. the ways in which we conceive of ourselves, and forms of social *objectivity*, the patterns of social life within which we exist.(Poole 45)

It is 'identity' which relates self to society, because different facets of an individual's identity are 'constituted in and through particular forms of social life' (45). But 'identity' as such is dynamic in nature which holds the tension between self and society both in 'crisis' as well as in relief, for it is subject to a person's social situation at a given point in time on the one hand and on the other is conceived only in his/her *commitment* to the nuances of social life, which prerequisites sacrifice of the personal for social. However, John Locke in his famous discussion in *An Essay Concerning Human Understanding* considered the 'person' to be a legal concept for his legal accountability is associated with another individual existing prior to him. In sync with Locke, hundred years later, Imanuel Kant agreed that a person to be so must remain morally and legally responsible. For Kant, a person can only be conceived in terms of reason, because mere human aspects of a person are incapable of justifying the moral realm. A person therefore as such has no value unless and until he is 'the subject of morally practical reason' (47). Since moral and legal responsibility is crucial to the existence of a person, Ross Poole argues that 'being a person is only *one* of the forms taken by the self, and that there are *other* modes of identity, other ways of saying 'I'' (48).

Hegel, however, identifies personhood with forms of social life. He holds that Locke and Kant were right in connecting the legal and moral realms with the existence of a person but got the connection in the wrong way round. For Hegel, a person practices law and morality not because he is a 'person' but it is because of these practices that he becomes one. Hence *becoming* person is about making conscious rational decisions rather than existing unintelligibly as mere humans. However, this consciousness is not initiated by isolated self-awareness but by the social situatedness of a person which is embodied in the assortment of legal and moral institutions and practices. In the light of above discussion if we consider the national identity of a person, it can be claimed that it refers to a person's commitment to a *certain* set of legal and moral codes, unique or fundamental to that nation. But how does consciousness lead to the practice of nation in order to acquire national identity? Since national identity 'underlies all our other identities' (Poole 67), it must enjoy privilege over them. This prioritization asks for a greater submission to the national than any other regional, communal or contingent structures. Hence national identity claims the *sacrifice* of the personal before the communal and henceforth communal to the national. Such sacrifices are embodied in a nation's history, tradition, myths, language, culture, politics and the 'spirit'. The sacrifice of self, therefore is not made in terms of unconditional surrendering of the personal but depersonalizing oneself in order to achieve a greater sense of 'political' identity. Thus achieved, national identity unifies the historical, cultural, linguistic, communal and regional differences of the masses, along with safeguarding political, religious, social and legal rights of the individuals. To these, is attached the sense of belongingness not just in terms of the political individual's claims to the nation, but also the nation's claims over its people. The national identity therefore brings together three essential components of citizenship, 'membership, rights and participation', which Richard Bellamy defines as 'a condition of civic equality' that 'not only secures equal rights to the enjoyment of the collective goods provided by the political association but also involves equal duties to promote and sustain them – including the good of democratic citizenship itself.' (17). But sheltered in overlapping discourses of freedom, autonomy, democracy, postcoloniality, internationality, globalization, women, gays, lesbians etc. the concept of citizenship is widely contested.

The anti-colonial nationalist struggles for independence in the third world countries promised sovereign, equal and autonomous citizenship, but after independence, politically motivated democratic citizenship grew around compromises between contradictory tendencies of 'universalism and particularism, freedom and order, individual rights and collective responsibilities, identity and difference, nation and individual' (Davis and Werbner 2). Since compromise in any form presupposes a hegemonic relation between unequals, 'democratic citizenship' with respect to women, whose place in history toggled between 'subjectified and subject-making (non)citizens' (5), opened up few aporias.

The anti-colonial struggles of the now postcolonial nation states invoked the stereotypical triad of woman–nation–home, equating the woman with a domestic territory which must be preserved from outside aggression. From either side this equation was based on objectifying women as possession, though nationalist narratives framed the strategy of controlling in terms of protection. Cherrie Moraga in reference to the Chicanos writes:

> Chicanos are an occupied nation within a nation, and women and women's sexuality are occupied within the Chicano nation. If women's bodies and those of men and women who transgress their gender roles have been historically regarded as territories to be conquered, they are also territories to be liberated. Feminism has taught us this. The nationalism I seek is one that decolonizes the brown and female body as it decolonizes the brown and female earth. (Moraga 150)

In the same light, Indian nationalism too associated nation with women, forming a gendered narrative of nation which invariably considered nationalism masculine. Speaking on the nature of Indian nationalism, Partha Chatterjee argued that woman was equated with home: the unpolitical, spiritual, chaste and private space which was to be preserved from the threats of colonial exploitation. Women in the Indian nationalist struggle accepted such gendered association which was destined to result in the reinforcement of patriarchy as the face of Indian anti-colonial movement for Independence. Chatterjee therefore remarks:

> Women from the new middle class in nineteenth-century India thus became active agents in the nationalist project – complicit in the framing of its hegemonic strategies as much as they were resistant to them because of their subordination under the new forms of patriarchy. (148)

What holds true for the Chicano and the Indian nationalist struggles in relation to women, nation and nationalism, is almost echoed in other anti-colonial nationalist struggles as well, though their geo-spatial, cultural politics were conditioned by their unique associations. One of the noted postcolonial critics, Elleke Boehmer, therefore argued, that man has a *metonymic* presence in relation to the national while women are mere *metaphors* implicitly representing national values and territories (229). Such symbolic presence is further explored by Nira Yuval-Davis and she connects women and nation in terms of reproduction. She argues that in being the biological producers of national population, women are also the cultural reproducers for they embody the collective that forms the matrix which represents the 'essence' of a country. It is this 'essence' which the colonial forces are keen to exploit. Hence women undergo rigorous monitoring in terms of their dress codes, social behavior, roles and perceptions by nationalist fundamentalists. Yuval-Davis also argues that women are discriminated even in their claims to citizenship, for legislative processes have always dealt with women's issues, rights and duties in separate terms. Moving beyond the legal issues, Yuval-Davis explores women's relation to nation in crisis such as the war. For her, wars have always been gendered. Be it a civil or an international war, women are the worst affected by war 'machineries'. The invading armies among other strategies use rape as one of the worst weapons to not merely unleash terror upon the civilians but also to deflate the native army ideologically for most of the nations equate women to motherland (130). However the accounts of material conditions of war zones show that not just the invading but also the national armies 'feed' on women, which almost always go unacknowledged by any legislation.

Narratives of war-time rapes and women's engagement with partition through theatre in India are best found in Kirti Jain's *Aur Kitne Tukde* (2001). Directed by Jain, the play is a reworking of Urvashi Butalia's book, *The Other Side of Silence* which chronicles the experiences of women during the partition of India. The play presents four women, Sadia, Vimla, Zahida and Harnam from different cultural orientations similar in their experience of violence during partition. In *Rehearsing the Partition* (2006), Jish Menon points out that 'Through an analysis of Kirti Jain's 2001 theatre production of *Aur Kitne Tukde*, I consider how Hindus, Muslims and Sikhs appropriate colonialist and nationalist ideologies surrounding the notion of 'woman' as repository of cultural value. The women in Jain's play are not prior subjects who experience violence but rather the experience of violence makes (and unmakes) them as gendered, ethnic, and national subjects. I argue that they come into subjecthood after a violent objectification and are reconstituted by their experience of national and sexual violence'(29-47).

But women playwright-directors in India have not been typical in their representation of women's relation to war. Modern Indian women theatre practitioners like Tripurari Sharma, Varsha Adalja, and Poile Sengupta instead of representing women as victims of war, rework popular events and characters from history and mythology to betray women's active participation in instrumentalising war and maneuver circumstances to influence the outcome of war. Hence Azizun emerges as a crafty 'executor' in the 1857 mutiny and Mandodari appearsto be a strategist in war whileShoorpanakha in *Thus Spoke Shoorpanakha, so said Shakuni*, concoct a situation where wrongs done to her by history is avenged.

War has traditionally been seen as inter or intra state crisis which results in mass destruction, large scale devastation and heavy economic, political and anatomical losses. History has seen wars being fought along the fault lines of territorial possessions, wealth, power, culture, ethnicity and civilization, which has constantly reframed the world order. With reference to Michael Dibdin's novel, *Dead Lagoon*, Samuel P. Huntington quotes in *The Clash of Civilizations and the Remaking of World Order,* 'There can be no true friends without true enemies. Unless we hate what we are not, we cannot love what we are...Those who deny them deny their family, their heritage, their culture, their birthright, their very selves!' (20) Huntington identifies 'the tendency to think in terms of two worlds', recurring 'throughout human history' to be one of the fundamental causes of war.

> 'People are always tempted to divide people into us and them, the in-group and the other, our civilization and those barbarians. Scholars have analyzed the world in terms of the Orient and the Occident, North and South, center and periphery. Muslims have traditionally divided the world into *Dar al-Islam* and *Dar al-Harb*, the abode of peace and the abode of war. This distinction was reflected, and in a sense reversed, at the end of the Cold War by American scholars who divided the world into 'zones of peace' and 'zones of turmoil'. The former included the West and Japan with about 15 percent of the world's population, the latter everyone else.' (32)

In *Azizun Nisa: A Tale from the Year* 1857, Tripurari Sharma has conceived war in similar light. The play is built around the 1857 *sepoy* mutiny which essentially had its inception in the absolute cultural separation between the 'native' Indians and the 'alien' British who 'lacked' the authentic knowledge of the religio-cultural structure of common Indian thought. She allows little space for the British voice and almost frames the entire narrative from Indian perspectives. But even in this asymmetrical framework she manages to present the disjunctions that amplified the separation between the two camps. In the introductory part of the play, Shamsuddin is seen disturbed with the circumstances. In response to the Sentry's enquiry regarding his Namaaz, Shamsuddin says, 'When and where namaaz should be read does not need the permission of any foreigner; nor is any sermon on religion necessary' (Sharma 123). That the British didn't 'honour and respect' the Indian religious practices and moreover used them as instruments of oppression against fellow countrymen initiated the Indian soldiers against them. Hence the mutiny emerged as a fight between Indian 'religiosity' and British 'political' administration, where religion appeared as the fabric that constitute the very identity of the Indian soldiers and administration as one which was not only usurped by the 'foreigners' but also an alien form that aimed absolute separation between religion and administrative structures. Disenchanted with his job in the army, Shamsuddin vents his disgust thus:

> No...there can be nothing right or wrong for a soldier; there is only the command...and to follow the command. I did the same ... they put the rifle in my hands. They gave me cartridges... I tore the cartridge covers with my teeth – put them in the gun and fired – night and day, morning and evening... did the same every time, everywhere ... I went on fighting, went on winning ... but lost each and every fight! My duty has become my sin now ... the cartridges that I tore with my teeth – those had grease from the meat prohibited by my religion ... That is what has happened. That's my reward for being dutiful ...

the test for my loyalty. And that which has alienated me from my God ... separated me from Him. I have eaten their salt. Licked it. Now it's corroding my entire being ... tear this skin off my body ... separate it from me. (124 – 125)

Tripurari Sharma projects Shamsuddin's anguish as evocative of the resentment among the Indian soldiers and Indians at large. While *Azizun Nisa* portrays war as a result of the ever-widening gulf between the British and the Indians, war in *Mandodari* is fought at multiple levels. It is not merely a war fought in the battle fields, but also a fight between pride and time (Kaal). Varsha Adalja gives time a visible presence in the play in the form of Kaaldevata, who is made to enter into a strategic game with Mandodari. The play can also be read as a narrative of the volatility of power in being pitted against the changeless authority of time. Right from the commencement of the play to its development into a tragedy for Ravana, power is invoked, referred to, suggested and misused as a means of political and personal oppression. Throughout the play, both Ravana and Mandodari make repeated references to the former's immense powers which made him the 'King of three worlds', its misuse in abducting Seeta, and the resultant war that entails his tragic end. Hence power and its misuse emerge as mitochondrial to war. In a series of lectures titled *Society Must be Defended*, Michelle Foucault hypothetically equates war with power andproposes that 'Power is war, the continuation of war by other means' (15) and inverting Clausewitz's proposition, 'War is merely the continuation of politics by other means' (Carl von Clausewitz), he suggests, 'politics is the continuation of war by other means' (Foucault 15). War, to Foucault, therefore is a permanent affair. He argues:

War is the motor behind institutions and order. In the smallest of its cogs, peace is waging a secret war. To put it another way, we have to interpret the war that is going on beneath peace; peace itself is a coded war.

We are therefore at war with one another; a battlefront runs through the whole of society continuously and permanently, and it is this battlefront that puts us all on one side or the other. There is no such thing as a neutral subject. (51)

The 'golden city' of Lanka stands not just as a symbol of ambitious conquests, but also a home to permanent conflicts, confusions, anguish and suppression all amounting to war. In the very introduction to the play, Adalja sets the tone when Mandodari speaks on the state of affairs in Lanka: 'Having come here once, it is impossible to leave the kingdom of Lankesh' (Adalja 100). That submission to the king's desires is the only alternative for any one in Lanka, is appropriated throughout the play. Mandodari's repeated attempts to explain the inevitable consequences of his actions, is ignored by Ravana, while Bibhisana's advices only turns him out of the kingdom.

RAVANA: Seeta dwells in my heart, Bibhisana.

Bibhisana: A King's personal prestige or insult has no importance in the matter of the kingdom's welfare.

RAVANA: Bibhisana, take care.

Bibhasana: When the wellbeing of a kingdom is threatened due to the rash act of a king, then the king is failing in his duty both as a king and a citizen.

RAVANA: Lankapati's city is golden; your Rama's city is made of clay.

BIBHISANA: People's welfare cannot be measured in terms of gold and clay. Safety, prosperity, unity, morality – these form the basis of a true nation.

RAVANA: You wicked fellow, get out of my sight right now. (108)

The play also unveils the inner recesses of Mandodari's anguished mind which betrays her qualms and her pains in being the wife of a lustful king. In an intense soliloquy, Mandodari discloses her innermost thoughts which hide her feminine desires, frustrations and uncertainties that shroud her status as a queen and a wife.

VOICE: Mandodari, are you jealous of Seeta?

MANDODARI: Why should I be jealous of Seeta?

VOICE: That's an untruth, Mandodari. You are jealous of the love Seeta and her husband share. They share their joys and sorrows; they wander in the forest together; they are ready to die for each other. You have not experienced such deep love, have you.?

MANDODARI: What do I lack? I have beautiful palaces, diamonds, ornaments ... I am very happy.

VOICE: No, you're not happy. Happiness does not come with palaces. ...

MANDODARI: Ah, Seeta, Seeta! Darkness has fallen upon this city since she came here. ... she is the cause of all this trouble my husband, my family, my people, and my city are facing. ...

MANDODARI: Lankesh has immense powers and divine weapons. If he wins the war and Rama is killed, then he will marry Seeta. She will become his queen in this palace and I will become her attendant ...

VOICE: What if Ravana is killed?

MANDODARI: Then too my future is bleak. Perhaps I shall then wander like a mad woman among the ashes of the burnt city ... or perhaps I shall become a sati and throw myself into the pyre of my dead husband. (112)

Adalja suggests Mandodari's plight as synonymous with Lanka's, which has also been reduced to a non-entity before the frenzied masculine desires of the king. Such phallic lack is mirrored in every Lankan, who is compelled to surrender her/his voice before Ravana's. Such a socio-political edifice, therefore invariably situates Mandodari and Seeta in the same frame. While Mandodari protests Seeta's abduction saying 'Kidnapping a helpless lady cannot be an act of valour. I don't find any bravery in it.'(103), she is herself confounded to the tyranny her husband wields. Ravana seeks to win Seeta's consent –'... Look at me, Seeta. The beautiful queen Mandodari will be your attendant. All my riches will be yours. Come to me, Seeta' (105).Feminist suggestions in presenting the dynamics of a society which revolves around the patriarchal institutions of machismo may be easily assumed. However, as exponents of women's theatre which is critical of the socio-patriarchal structures but avoid demonizing the 'male', both Sharma and Adalja seek to represent nation and war as polyphonic political institutions which affect women as well as men. But, neither of the playwrights surrenders women's perspective. As much as *Azizun Nisa: A Tale from the Year, 1857*, is about the failure of *Sepoy* mutiny, it draws Azizun Nisa, as a woman who enthusiastically transforms herself from a courtesan to a soldier. Sharma has been keen not to magnify the gender question but focus exclusively on Azizun's 'amateurish' decision to participate in an armed rebellion of which she had no previous experience. She identifies herself more as a courtesan than a woman. When accused of prostitution she asserts herself as a dancer: '... I'm a dancer. I'm an artiste. I do not wear the veil but I'm not a public woman. People in the city ... acknowledge me as a courtesan, a poet-lyricist. I'm not in the flesh trade...' (Sharma 133).

When Azizun is questioned of her bravery, her response is not addressed from her biology but 'training'.

'Zubaida: How can you laugh, Azizun? Aren't you ever afraid?

AZIZUN: The tactics of living by myself in the middle of the bazaar; the combination of a little hard-heartedness and a little recklessness! ... I swear by my God, had I weapon in my hand then with one swing I would have stopped that man's inauspicious steps ... then whatever happened, I wouldn't have cared! ... That's the only lack in his training ... but this gives one a sense of identity, doesn't ... self-esteem ... an elegant style! Can make one proud, truly. Whether it is the darkest night or the deepest forest, the step wouldn't falter.' (135).

Azizun denies and defies being reduced to her anatomy. But Sharma is also aware that such defiance cannot be typical to the society. Hence she introduces a character like Zubaida who appears as a foil to Azizun.

ZUBAIDA: This is a battle among men so let them fight it out. You are both ignorant and incapable of taking part.(151)

For Zubaida, battle is a man's affair and Azizun should not have participated in it. She criticizes Azizun's attempts to harm the 'fixed' gender roles. Mohd. Ali too, questions Azizun's interest in war, 'The matter is not of your interest. ... We're preparing for a battle. ... You might disapprove of my manner, but what is a woman's interest in matters of war?'(143) and Ali Khan humbles her in a sword encounter, 'I've never tasted defeat. You're a woman. So I shan't fight anymore. Get up and pick up your sword.'(165) But this doesn't weaken Azizun's spirits and she becomes more desperate to prove her prowess as a soldier.

> AZIZUN: Yes, I must complete what I've set out to do. I'm not a mere woman. He should have treated me like a soldier. Fought and killed me. I'm not afraid to die. But no, in his eyes I remained a mere woman. He thought I was a coward. There's more to be done to be his match. I must become so strong and tough that one wouldn't know that one was facing a woman. Then there wouldn't be any need to show pity. (166)

Hence Azizun seeks to de-categorise herself as a woman, for 'woman' as 'construct' inspires patriarchal definitions which hinder her movement beyond the socially ordained stratifications. In her role-play as *sipahi* she not only challenges the gendered perception towards soldiery but also contributes towards an alternative narrative of women's participation in the politico-national discourse. In *Mandodari,* Adalja too questions the gender codifications with Mandodari challenging Kaaldevata in a self-devised game of pawns. Kaaldevata is drawn as the custodian of patriarchal values which essentially abnegates the position of woman in affairs of state and war. Kaal arrives in Mandodari's palace and announces the destruction of Lanka. He presupposes Mandodari's unconditional surrender to the impending apocalypse. But Mandodari's challenge somewhat dislodges Kaaldevata, and he immediately retorts to the traditional masculine approach towards women as inferiors –

> MANDODARI: Stop, O Kaaldevata. I invite you to accept my challenge that your task will remain unfulfilled.

> KAALDEVATA: A challenge? To Kaalpurush? Foolish Lady, are you in your senses? I can demolish the portals of magnificent palaces with one breath.

I can devastate glorious civilizations with a single stroke. I can dry oceans and send mountain peaks tumbling into the valleys. I make the earth tremble in fear. Is the might of Kaal being challenged by an ordinary woman? (102)

Adalja therefore makes patriarchy seem vulnerable before Mandodari's bold defiance. The latter reveals her identity as a strategist in war and the play further unfolds as a 'game' played between Kaldevata and Mandodari where even Ravana, the height of patriarchal depravity, and Rama, the repository of values, are interplayed as mere pawns.

'You may not know that I have helped Ravanasur many times with battle strategy. I have devised this game with such designs in mind.'(102)

Though Azizun and Mandodari share experience of being subordinated to patriarchal insolence both of them seek to instrumentalise the 'patriarchal machineries of war. Mandodari protests against Ravana for using Seeta as a hock in his battle, but herself uses Seeta as a 'move' in her game of destruction with the Kaaldevata.

RAVANA: Your Rama killed Khara and Dushana. He cut off Shoorpanakha's nose. Do you ask me to bow to this man? His wife fell into my hands like a ripe fruit. Why should I not take her?

MANDODARI: Lankesh, a woman is not an object to be used to settle enmity nor a victim of lust. ... (105)

But when the occasion arrives, Mandodari pawns Seeta, requesting her to surrender herself to Ravana. Mandodari's narrative on woman at this juncture, while she tries to appease Seeta into sacrificing herself to the lust of Ravana, is enmeshed with traditional patriarchal indoctrinations, which make Seeta and Mandodari share similar quandaries.

> MANDODARI: Here woman is an object of pleasure... a mere plaything to be used like a piece of linen that can be thrown away when it is soiled. To have power over womanis the right of man.

> SEETA: Do women get no respect in asura culture? Among Aryans, woman is worshipped as a goddess.

> MANDODARI: O Seeta, the daughter – in – law of the Suryavamshis, don't you think there is ambiguity in the treatment of women as goddesses? When the victorious kings confiscate kingdoms, don't they also take the women folk of the defeated kings? The gods keep apsaras for enjoyment. Your father – in – law has several queens. ...

> MANDODARI: If Ravana gets you, he will not fight and many lives will be saved. (110)

Hence Adalja represents Mandodari as capable of maneuvering patriarchal norms to her own ends. She is critical of the patriarchal praxis but she also uses the same for avoiding the destruction of her land on the other. But in the process, she appears vulnerable as well. 'I shall make myself the pawn in my game now, O Lord' (109), says Mandodari to Kaaldevata. However, all her moves apparently fail and Kaaldevata proclaims his own victory. He acknowledges Mandodari's love for her country and blesses her-'May you always be honoured as a great sati.'(114). But in his blessing, he secretly harbours the paradox that women's attempt to participate in the 'masculine' endeavours of warfare and providing strategic and martial protection to the family and country at large, in place of earning socio-political importance, reduces herto the stereotypical category of 'sati'. The image of 'sati' has always been associated with the epitomization of women's sacrifice and commitment to the husband and his clan. Mandodari is therefore drawn into revealing her real intentions of killing her husband in order to seek redemption for her clan. She had devised the game of 'pawns' only to ensure that death is wrought on Ravana. Hence, as a contriver, she has undone the conventional 'expectations' of a woman. Instead of being elevated to the status of a sati, she has longed for the death of her lustful husband, and thereby be fooled Kaaldevata.

> MANDODARI: ... I was waiting for my lord's death.

> KAALDEVATA: What are you saying, Mandodari?

> MANDODARI: How is it that you are omniscient yet did not know my thoughts? Well, to read a woman's heart one has to be a woman perhaps! How would you understand the agony of being the wife of such a lustful yet blind man?

> KAALDEVATA: I don't understand you.

> MANDODARI: Through Seeta's abduction and the ensuing war, I sought redemption of my clan. The arrow that killed Ravana, actually released his soul and gave the egoistic man his salvation. Though I am widowed now, I am a happy woman. I have succeeded in what I set out to do, ha, ha, ha. (114)

Mandodari's maneuvering of Seeta, as a pawn in war is echoed in *Azizun Nisa* as well. Azizun engineers the idea of killing unguarded women and children in the women's quarters after having suffered defeat elsewhere. She holds them as pawns in the battle between *sepahis* and the British soldiers heading towards them. Like Mandodari, she defies being perceived as a victim in war but conversely uses British women as wagers whose death would demoralize their army. Hence, nationalism takes the shape of ruthless militancy in the play, but Azizun and her colleagues execute the plan justifying war.

> AZIZUN: Let them come. The huge army comes trampling across our homeland intending to rescue a few helpless women and children. How impatient must they be for this victory – to free them from the trap of the wicked. They'll hug them – kiss them – wipe their tears and assure them that they are completely safe. The smile of relief on those arrogant faces ... no they do not deserve that. Those who have no courage, why should their emotions win? In spite of their utmost efforts, they should taste only defeat at Kanpur ... their calmness and pace should be snatched ... their intentions should meet with only disappointment ... Let them not find that for which they come. Let all be finished. That would be a defeat to stun them and make them regret that they ever came here and that if they hadn't, perhaps they'd still be alive. ...
>
> AZIZUN: This is a war ... and in a war, all must be ready to die. The difference lies in who gets into whose hands. (Sharma 175-178)

Though Zubaida and Mohd. Ali protest such large scale killing of 'innocent women', Hussaini and Adila help Azizun frame the plan and Sarwar becomes the instrument of execution. Hence, through Azizun, Sharma portrays a woman whois either devoid of the feminine notion of 'natural caregivers' or can suspend her womanhood in order to achieve success in war. She dispassionately unleashes terror on British women, considering them not as gendered victims of war but as the mere 'other' who are better sacrificed in order to preserve 'liberty' for the 'self'. Therefore, both Tripurari Sharma and Varsha Adalja present women characters as victims on one hand and perpetrators of violence on the other, a propos their respective locations during war. Seeta in *Mandodari* and the British women in *A Tale from the Year 1857: Azizun Nisa* suffer only due to their vulnerable locations in the entire course of events, while Mandodari and Azizun successfully manipulate war and associated operations because of the specific contingencies which inspire and condition their approach to war. However this does not discount the personal impulse of both the characters, which resisted the social compulsions of their sex.

Therefore both *Mandodari* and *Azizun Nisa* emerge as important productions which throw considerable light on the position of women playwrights and directors with regard to nation and war. Since the idea of nation can never be engaged in isolation from its history, culture, myth, language, religion and memory, women theatre directors try to locate their plays amidst the intersections of these cultural elements. Adalja presents Mandodari debunking the myth of Ramanyana which is primarily available as an epic. In almost all its written versions, the epic has maintained silence over Mandodari; for, an epic is chiefly about a grand action concerning two extra-ordinary individuals/families/clans etc, where seemingly insignificant voices find themselves overshadowed by the meta-narratives. Adalja's attempt to present the 'myth' through such a character which has been historically kept silent, therefore is appreciative of women's immutable existence amidst the epic battles which redefined the concepts of nation, nationality, power and woman. Likewise, Tripurari Sharma makes Azizun Nisa more alive in history, for amidst soldiers, she emerges as a soldier. Azizun brings into practice her nationalist imagination at a time when nation itself hasn't politically materialized.

But when state sponsored militant nationalism is brought into practice, it not only tries to produce a prejudiced meta-narrative of national history but also denies any alternate view. During the first production of the play, in the National School of Drama, Delhi, in 1999, *Azizun Nisa* met with severe criticisms from 'nationalists' who argued that it abuses history and showcases Indians involved in innocent bloodsheds (of British women and children). For them, such presentation endangers the image of Indian nationalism which has all through been projected as tolerant and non–violent. Sharma even received letters of disagreement with her presentation of women as actively participating in public bloodshed. But in an interview to this author, at NSD, Delhi, Tripurari Sharma said that her research and the stories about Azizun still popularly heard in Kanpur, supplement her portrayal in history even though not entirely non-fictitious. Hence, Sharma confronted 'militant nationalism' in her production of the play, following which the play had to be revised before its next production in India in 2007. But intriguingly the play earned much appreciation when it was produced in Pakistan under the patronage of Pir Zada foundations (Sharma Interview). The performance history of the play therefore exposes the nationalist narratives that not only claim to foil attempts toward unconditional introspection into history of Indian national struggle, but also promotes censoring the presentation of 'authentic history' in order to produce an 'acceptable' rhetoric.

Therefore in engaging with nation and war, contemporary Indian women theatre practitioners avoid taking any essential stand inrepresenting women as victims or victimisers. Instead of reducing women to any particular narrative definition, they trace the individual approaches of women to 'nation' and 'war' in their contingencies. Hence, nation as a political institution and war as either 'politics' or 'political crisis', emerge in the theatres of Indian women playwright-directors, not as essential forces that annihilate the 'independent' existence of women as citizens of a state but as notions which surely run the risk of being usurped by hetero–normative patriarchal nationalist indoctrination, if they are isolated from their contexts.

CHAPTER

Women, Class, Caste: Rudali and Listen Shefali

In his essay *The Future Results of British Rule in India,* published in the New York Daily Tribune, 8 August, 1853, Karl Marx defined India as 'a country not only divided between Mahommedan and Hindoo, but between tribe and tribe, between caste and caste; a society whose framework was based on a sort of equilibrium, resulting from a general repulsion and constitutional exclusiveness between all its members'(Marx) and argued that modern Indian society may progress only under the aegis of 'unity, imposed by the British sword' (Marx). But after its independence in 1947, India as a nation-state has progressed by acknowledging and confronting the fissures inherent in its socio-cultural, political and religious structures. Committed to its interventionist nature, theatre too has been an equal participant in the process of engaging with the social and cultural crevices. In this chapter, I explore Indian women's theatre's rendezvous with 'class' and 'caste' as two fundamental categories, which has been instrumental in the continuance of socio-cultural, economic, political, religious, ethnic and gender difference.

I deliberately choose two women authored texts, Kusum Kumar's *Listen Shefali* (composed in 1975 in Varanasi, where Kumar participated in a Sahitya Academy workshop, and published in 1978) and Usha Ganguli's *Rudali (1992),* an adaptation into dramatic form of Mahasweta Devi's novella *Rudali.* For, both the plays explore the 'protest' motif against caste/ class based gender subordination in modern Indian society. While *Listen Shefali* locates a young dalit woman, Shefali, amidst the hypocrisies of a society where electoral politics and position in the caste/class structure form an invisible network of woman subordination, *Rudali* gives a brilliant account of Sanichari whose life exemplifies the struggle of a lower class/ caste woman against the social, cultural and economic oppressions. However, neither of the plays tries to evoke sympathy for women and therefore situates the characters in real material grounds, amidst the variety of relations, experiences, struggles, fulfillments and frustrations. Hence, both Kumar and Ganguli, though non-Dalit themselves, have substantially represented the Dalit issue, challenging the hetero-patriarchal and political nature of class-caste nexus and at the same time reasserting the exclusivity of Dalit women's experiences and uniqueness of their engagement with patriarchy, politics and society at large. Therefore, the plays can be claimed by 'Dalit theatre' as well, though the emergence of Dalit literature in post-independence India was a direct result of distrust on the *savarna* writers who were critiqued for misrepresenting the Dalits. It was strongly believed that only the writers who had the living experience in Dalit caste-class subordination can convincingly portray Dalit life and experiences. Such belief was stimulated by two major movements in Maharashtra in the early 1970s – the Dalit Panthers, launched in July, 1972 and the Dalit Literary Movement (dating back to 11th Century, when the first Vachana poet, Chennaiah, a cobbler by profession and a 12th Century Dalit poet, Kalavve, challenged the upper caste intelligentsia). 'These movements, surfaced among the lower castes in social and literary affairs in India… represent a new level of pride, militancy and sophisticated creativity' (Jalote 33). Hence Dalit literature claimed to produce public consciousness in engaging with the issues of 'persistent enslavement of 'Harijans' by the upper-castes in villages, the assaults on dalit women, police brutality and complicity with the upper-castes in facilitating land seizures, and other forms of social boycott, such as the denial of water from public wells, and the refusal of teachers to teach Harijan students' (Bhatia 85). With the growing influence of such literary developments in the mid-1970s, the Pune based Dalit Rangbhumi (Dalit Theatre) 'staged its first Dalit play in 1979' (Jalote 34). However, Dalit oriented theatre is already seen in Avinash Dolus's *The Village without a Face,* where Mahars resist being forced to live on scavenging and claim to have rights to education, practice their religion in temples and gain economic freedom. Erin B Mee identifies Datta Bhagat's play *Wata-Palwata* (1987) (translated into English by Matya Pandit as *Routes and Escape Routes), as the 'the first modern play to reach a large and diverse audience' (Mee 4). Moreover, *Avart* (Whirlpool, 1978) directed by Satya Dev Dubey and Amol Palekar, is a play that makes use of the traditional Mahar art-forms such as the *tamasha* and *dindi.* Having its inception and growth in Maharashtra, the Dalit theatre travelled other parts of the country, viz. Delhi, U.P, Madhya Pradesh, Andhra Pradesh, Karnataka, Tamil Nadu, Kerala and Goa, with similar popularity, where the questions of caste discrimination continued thronging the social circles.

However, limiting Dalit literature only to the works of Dalit-born writers would be a misnomer, because caste discrimination as a major theme recurs in the works of non-Dalit writers as well. Vijay Tendulkar's *Kanyadaan* (1983) is a vehement protest against the Hindu marriage codes mentioned in *Manusmriti,* an ancient text which 'summarizes socio-religious regulatory practices' (Bhatia 86). The latter strictly prohibits inter-caste marriage, while the former revolves around a plot where the female protagonist chooses to marry a low born Dalit writer. In addition to the dissent against the socially codified marriage rights, Tendulkar is also eloquent in exposing the status of 'upper caste women' in the ancient Indian society, for they remain unspoken of in *Manusmriti*. For Aparna Dharwadker, using 'caste as theme and a young Dalit writer as antihero, *Kanyadaan* inevitably evokes the twentieth century history of the struggle over the practice of untouchability, as well as the more immediate phases of the Dalit movement in Maharashtra and the nation as a whole'(289). This inter-caste marriage motif, which was increasingly coming into regular practice in the mid and late 1980's, is further explored by Girish Karnad in *Tale-Danda* (1990), where an untouchable boy is married to a Brahmin woman. The play draws parallel between contemporary socio-religious and political condition and a 12th Century A.D. development during the Bhakti movement in Kalyani, where mystics, philosophers, social revolutionaries and poets rejected all forms of idolatry and uneven practices (of sex and caste among others) and upheld social, cultural and political equality. However, the play dramatizes the end of the movement when it collapses in bloodshed following the marriage. Apart from Tendulkar and Karnad, a host of plays engaging with the caste issues were produced, especially against the backdrop of the 'Mandir', 'Mandal' debates in the early 1990s which triggered Hindu-Muslim riots and asserted the implementation of Mandal Commission recommendations. Notable among them is the adaptation of Mannu Bhandari's novel *Mahabhoj* into a play where 'a young fearless leader of the lower castes in a village is murdered by the gangsters of the local leaders of the party in power' and Rahul Katyayana's *Singh Vijaya* (1991) which revolves around the successful marriage between a Dalit Physics teacher in Allahabad University and a Brahmin girl. Politically, the play suggests the flourish of a modern democratic society built on caste parity in place of caste discrimination. However, it must be noted that almost all of the above mentioned plays deal with caste as a meta-issue and almost isolates it from the questions of gender. But Kumar's *Listen Shefali* is unique in intertwining caste and gender as two equally essential co-ordinates of Shefali's experiences. Though caste looms large in the play, Shefali is never free from her 'woman consciousness' and the play goes on to suggest that Shefali's caste experience is unique in being a *woman* from the lower caste.

Kumar draws Shefali as an 'angry young woman', who has been a non-conformist throughout. Right from her childhood, Shefali has protested against the sanctioned generosity of the upper castes. Mediated through the politics of 'privileging' the lower caste 'sub humans' the so-called 'welfare' politics of the state which provides for the dalits on one hand and perpetuates the discrimination based on the caste system on the other, has corroded Shefali's dignity to the extent of usurping her personal identity. Though caste consciousness, referred to as a 'disease' (Mukherjee, 195) by Bakul, Shefali's wooer for marriage, is discouraged both in the family and society at large, has motivated Shefali into rebelling against such subtle politics of self-effacement.

> SHEFALI: ... Right from childhood, in the society, at every stage I found generosity surrounding me. We just had to accept it saying 'yes sir!'... In school, food, clothing, books were given generously ... in fact, given free ... we just had to declare that we were Harijans. So, we three sisters wanted to remain 'janharis' in school...
>
> In school, they distributed books and sometimes wool and cloth for uniform. We three sisters never accepted such generosity ... why should we say that we are Harijans? The 'jahari' girls, are they better than us? They bring broken pens and pencils and borrow from us to write ... at such times they need our help ... the more I think of this, the sadder I feel about it...

The rebel in Shefali, later rejects the prospect of marrying Bakul, the son of Satyadev Dikshit, a politician turned social worker, to protest against being made a political tool for showcasing upper caste generosity. However, her refusal of such a 'reformist' solution to the 'unfortunate' reality of being a dalit woman comes only at her discovery of a strategic 'love game' played against her by Bakul and his father. Unfolding in six scenes, the play is set in two intriguingly opposite frames, the ghats of Yamuna and Shefali's home, which 'strategically links her (Shefali's) household and the tensions therein, including her quarrels with her mother, to the caste prejudices that play out in the public sphere and become an important part of Shefali's emotional and intellectual experience' (Bhatia 91). This public-private linkage is brought into more critical relief as the three distinct family units in the play are held in tension with each other: a fatherless conflicted family of Shefali where her sisters and her mother engage heterogeneously with ideas of self-respect, poverty, caste, reformation and the society at large; the upper caste family of Bakul, which thrives in compromise with the political ambitions and a 'self-identified family' of Manan and Geru, where they share no filial connections but are strongly bound through mutual experiences of poverty and 'business'. Kumar's choice of such a complex framework to present the theme of protest against politics of caste structure, leads her to deviate from the 'realistic 'psychodramas' practiced by canonical male urban playwrights that take place in middle class settings and homes' (91).

The fractured setting of the play, namely the ghat, Shefali's house and the shiva temple, provides a background to the 'protest' which Aditya Agnihotri conceptualizes as projecting 'a multiple experience, agitating, energizing, ennobling and yet delighting all at the same time' (26). The strategy is to not merely challenge the status quo but also ''agitate' against it', in order to achieve 'social and political revolution' (27). In almost all her plays, *Dilli Ooncha Sunti Hai, Om Kranti Kranti, Sanskar ko Namaskar, Ravan Lila* and *Pavan Chaturvedi ki Diary*, Kumar has explored the themes of protest in social issues like the caste system, the exploitation of both the dalits and non-dalit working classes, and asserted the preservation of 'dignity and selfhood' (Mukherjee 119).However, Kumar's theatrical engagements with such remonstrations were not isolated phenomena, for almost the whole of 1970s was fraught with protests both in the political and cultural fields and theatre activists responded alike. Tripurari Sharma may be mentioned here, for, her entire theatrical career has revolved around voicing resistance against socio-cultural discriminations. Through the productions of her group, *Alirappu*, she has engaged with 'issues pertaining to domestic rights, legal rights and literacy' (Bhatia 89). Negotiating similar issues were other major organizations like Jagori, Stree Mukti Sangathan, and Theatre Union (formed by Maya Krishna Rao, Anuradha Kapur and Rati Bartholomew in collaboration). Women's issues were increasingly being discussed and protests against atrocities on women were brought forth in the public domain through theatre. Dina Mehta's *Brides are Not for Burning* deal with dowry deaths as encountered by Indian women irrespective of their class positions. *Dafa 180*, a Theatre Union production addresses the persistence of rape as sexual violence against women even after the new legislation of 180 secured women's rights against being physically harassed in police custody and prison. Themes of such social protests have continued to be broached by Mala Hashmi's theatre group *Janam*, Shamsul Islam's *Nishant* and *AavhaanNatyaManch* (89). However, Kumar's theatre practice is unique in its own terms because according to Tutun Mukherjee, 'she is one of the few women dramatists writing essentially for the stage' (119), while most of her contemporaries preferred streets or other open spaces as the railway platforms, ghettos, *bastis* etc, where they could directly encounter the common public.

In *Listen Shefali*, caste distinction is not just thematically conceived but also dramaturgically meditated. The *Yamuna ghat* is symbolically divided into two with a bamboo partition, separating Maman and Shefali. Such social fissures have retained their moorage in almost all walks of modern Indian life, though they have undergone multiple social, cultural or political reformations. Kumar therefore has chosen a semi-urban milieu, where characters are caught in diverse sociological fractures. While faith in palmistry represents the ardor to remain arrested in the superstitious past, Maman's deft use of the same art to meet the pecuniary needs opens a window to the nature of micro-economic professionalism.

According to Jalote, 'In most Indian villages Untouchable living quarters, wells, and temples are still separate from those of the upper caste Hindus. Though an untouchable or a socially backward person who enters the modern sector of Indian society as teacher, government servant, or factory workers is free from earlier social disabilities, the subtle discrimination is still felt by the uneducated untouchables' (38). But for Kumar, caste has an all-pervading presence, for it cuts across the boundaries of class, education, individual efficiency, faith, religion and politics. Shefali is an English educated woman who is reported to be once employed as the teacher of Satyadev Dikshit to teach him English. Shefali's competence in English, therefore opens up a new vista in understanding the complex relation between English education and dalit experience in Modern India. Proficiency in English promises the possibility of a range of economic opportunities and empowerment, but Kumar's contention is that acquisition of such economic power does not guarantee an escape from caste experiences. Shefali's employment as a teacher of an influential politician momentarily 'upsets the balance of power, yet it is one that is quickly squashed when Shefali becomes, for the politician (and his son), a means for simply advancing his political career through her marriage to Bakul and thereby projecting himself as someone who serves the national interests through caste integration' (Bhatia 94). Traditional politics placed marriage in relation to caste in the sense of strictly preserving the caste 'purity', in order to ensure the growth and continuance of well-bound community structures. Moreover, if a woman marries within her own caste, it ensures the continuity of the traditional occupations. Upper castes are chiefly conscious of sustaining their 'purity' and their racial 'uniqueness', for, the material aspects of the society is more at stake for them. Hence, marriage has been no less than a political strategy both in the traditional and modern sense. Kumar's use of the marriage motif in the play, where getting Shefali married to Bokul is drawn as a political move, therefore brings the entire Gandhian politics regarding inter-caste marriage on floor. In the introduction to *The Doctor and the Saints* (2014), the annotated critical edition of B. R.

Ambedkar's *Annihilation of Caste*, Arundhati Roy argues that 'Gandhi 'deceived' people' (41) on the issue of caste. She quotes Mahatma Gandhi writing in *Navajivan* in 1921:

> Caste is another name for control. Caste puts a limit in enjoyment. Caste does not allow a person to transgress caste limits in pursuit of his enjoyment. That is the meaning of such caste restrictions as inter-dining and inter-marriage... These being my views I am opposed to all those who are out to destroy the Caste system. (41)

However, towards the end of his life, Gandhi tried to make amends saying that he 'no longer objected to inter-dining and intermarriage between castes' (41). But as Roy argues, 'Gandhi never decisively and categorically renounced his belief in chaturvarna, the system of four varnas' (42), though there has been some anecdotes from his ardent followers that Gandhi did attend a number of inter caste weddings. Hence the attempt to project Shefali and Bokul's marriage as an inter-caste wedding secretly harbors the political motives of Dikshit, rather than playing against the caste system as a whole. Pertinent here is to mention Kumar's deft use of Maman's invocation of Gandhi as a background for the debates on such a marriage:

Gandhi baba Gandhi baba aaja

Gandhi baba Gandhi baba aaja (Kumar 197)

Such invocation not only makes us read Maman as a Gandhian in his sympathy for the plight of the Dalits, but also lends a critique of the Gandhian ideology which believed in minor reforms and adjustments in place of dissolving the entire caste system as a whole. This, however, is ironically heightened by the dramaturgical presentation of the separation between the real material conditions of the Dalits and the Gandhian ideology, by dividing the stage into two halves with bamboo lines, one for Maman, who hails from the Upper Caste and the other which allows Shefali's stay and voice. The separation also points towards Kumar's critique of Gandhi's attempt to set an outsider's perspective on the Dalits and consider them to be mere 'objects of pity and sympathy' (Bhatia 93).

Bakul, however, voices the upper class bounty in giving the marriage proposal to Shefali:

> All will be doubly generous and considerate. It's not a joke to be the wife of Bakul! To be the daughter-in-law of Sri Sri Satyameva Dikshit is even more remarkable. ... (Kumar 195)

However, vexed with Shefali's rejection of the proposal, Bakul blames her ego for her mistrust:

> Shefali, I think your situation was never a problem. You ... just within yourself ... right from your childhood to this day, thoughts and ideas have become entangled ... and they have become increasingly complex ... Tell me what is that you know? Except knowing yourself, what do you know of others or care to know? Sometimes I wonder if your veins are filled with bloated ego instead of blood ... Where will you go with such an enormous ego? How will you ever understand anyone else.' (196-7)

Blaming Shefali for her own mistrust is symptomatic of the general political strategy of blaming the lower castes of being 'hyper-sensitive' to their socio-cultural marginality. Such 'strategy', propagated through cultural artifact, is constitutive of counter-narratives to the discourse of caste(ism). Getting wedded to Bakul would again reinstate the notion of Upper caste charity, which Shefali has always vehemently resisted.

I should have known… if nothing else, the favours you bestowed on me, I should have known about this … your kisses, your firm embrace, awash in the wilderness of love… all those were merely showers of your generosity… How could I guess that this was your way to show your generosity? Had I known earlier, I'd have thanked you suitably! … Don't lie anymore Bakul! I know only to love…I used to love …you are doing accounting now … you and your people. I am a Harijan girl from a poor family… you love me… want to marry me…so I must be grateful… I must be thankful to you… Thank you very much. Thank you very much indeed! (197)

Her resistance echoes the Ambedkerite confrontation of Gandhian politics in oversimplifying the means to resolution of prevalent caste discriminations. Though Ambedkar himself supported inter-dining and inter-caste marriages, he disagreed to believe that 'caste equality' can sometimes be the resultant of such practices some day. For him, resolution of caste bigotry is possible only through the rejection of *shastra*, which he deems responsible for the faith in and continuance of caste system. In his posthumously published lecture *Annihilation of Caste,* Ambedkar strongly recommends the dissolution of Shastra to bring about caste equity:

Criticising and ridiculing people for not inter-dining or inter-marrying or occasionally holding inter-caste dinners and celebrating inter-caste marriages, is a futile method of achieving the desired end. … To agitate for and to organise inter-caste dinners and inter-caste marriages is like forced feeding brought about by artificial means. Make every man and woman free from the thraldom of the Shastras, cleanse their minds of the pernicious notions founded on the Shastras, and he or she will inter-dine and inter-marry, without your telling him or her to do so (Ambedkar "Inter-caste marriage")

Umbrage against the *Shastras* and their practice corresponds with Ambedkar's resistance to the Gandhian politics of patronizing and homogenizing the multiple Dalit groups under the name of 'Harijans'. In his struggle to eradicate untouchability and at the same time to continue with the caste system as an 'essential element' in the Indian society, Gandhi sought to rebaptise the Untouchables by fusing four thousand separate castes into the easily discernible *chaturvarna* system. The name 'Harijan' ('Children of God' (Roy 129)) in itself carried the political motive of firmly associating the untouchables with Hinduism especially against the backdrop of increasing threats of mass conversion into other religions, from the Dalit intelligentsia. To supplement such a political move, Gandhi founded a newspaper, 'Harijan' and started the Harijan Sevak Sangh and emphasized that the Sangh be constituted of Upper caste Hindus only. Ambedkar, who was critical of such political measures forwarded by Gandhi and Congress Party, considered these as 'Congress's plan to 'kill Untouchables by kindness'' (129).

Kumar invokes the Ambedkarite line of critique in Shefali's gripe against being bestowed with the 'benefits' of belonging to the lower caste. This, though in sync with the lower caste rejection of the reservation politics in modern India, cannot be considered essential to the understanding of the Dalits in general. Kumar is alert in presenting Shefali's resistance as unique in its own terms. Shefali's rejection of charity right from her school days and resolute assertion of selfhood is frequently berated by her mother. When Shefali refuses to marry Bakul, her mother convinces her younger sister to give her consent to the marriage proposal (from Bakul). Hence, dramatizing multiple Dalit identities, their existence and their attempts to metamorphose the social, material conditions, provided a strong critique of the 'universal Dalit selfhood', which in itself was a deviation from the canonical Dalit literature.

Shefali's mother, apart from being a foil to her rebellious daughter, is also a 'pragmatic' woman for whom caste/ class considerations has always been the foremost. Kumar's contention therefore is to suggest that in the modern Indian society, caste and class correspond with each other in forming the general social perspectives. According to Andre Bettile, it is at this intersection of caste and class where power plays an important role, in creating social stratifications. The voice of Shefali's mother, is that of a working class lower caste woman, for whom charity sanctioned by the government, however political it may be, is welcome relief, and a marriage proposal from an 'Upper caste' politician is an opportunity to move beyond the caste/ class hindrances. Conditioned by her poverty, Shefali's mother seems inconsiderate about her daughter's perceptions on marriage.

> That gentleman came to our house twice, only to settle your marriage. We're poor people… what else do we need? For the last so many years you have been meeting his son … now marry him and be the respectable daughter-in-law of a well to do family. Once you go, we'll stop Kiran's education. She can work for sometime… you just set your life right, Shefali. They are asking for this marriage. (Kumar 209)

But Shefali's high sense of self-worth propels her to frustrate the Dikshit father/son duo's strategy of gaining political mileage from the marriage:

> SHEFALI: … I know why they want this marriage, at this moment … right now … both father and son, want to announce to the world that they have contributed towards the upliftment of a Harijan girl. They want recognition on this basis … for this they want to hear slogans of *zindabad*…. I will merely be a means for their self-advertisements. (209)

Shefali's defiance against being constructed in the image of an essential dalit lower class woman corresponds with her assertion of being equal not only in terms of caste but also gender.

> SHEFALI: Who is asking for equality? I am equal ...
> if I had to compromise for their favour and pity,
> you would have performed my marriage long ago.
> Mother, why shouldn't I think that we are something
> more than just seekers of their pity? (210)

Shefali's belief and practice of 'equality' throws into question the traditional 'performance' of marriage as an institution that brings together man and woman in an 'unequal' relationship which conspires to mar the 'I' of the woman who is thence seen only in a derivative relationship to her husband. Kumar's sense of dramatic composition invites more critical appreciation here because the debates between the mother and daughter which also exemplifies the debate between tradition and modernity, is followed by a brilliant episode of *aarathi*, where Shefali is caught between the steadfastness of faith and doubt. The performance of *aarathi* holds as a prerequisite an absolute submission, which Shefali has never known. But this does not account for momentary lapses which preserve the scope for the eclipse of the consciously meditated dispositions through 'performative' customs. Shefali finds a girl piously performing the rites of *aarati* for *tulsi*, the epitome of dedication and love according to the Hindu mythology. She consciously argues that 'such examples make me (her) uncomfortable' (213) (bracketing mine), but she is irresistibly drawn towards joining the performance. Relevant here is to note Kumar's stage directions –

> *The girl sings aarathi. Shefali turns around and looks at her,*
> *and becomes calm. She goes to the girl, sits down looking*
> *at the girl in a confused state of mind. The girl extends the*
> *aarathi plate towards Shefali as she sings. Shefali keeps*
> *staring at the girl then takes the plate and slowly does*

aarathi. Shefali stares at the girl who continues singing, puts
the plate down and folds her hands with reverence. (213)

Such *jeu de theatre* (stage direction), which projects the compulsion
to surrender 'performance' before regular practice, can also be read
as an intelligent suggestion to the title of the play, 'Listen Shefali!',
which implies that though Shefali would assert her voice, she would
conversely be encouraged to listen rather than speak. Shefali therefore
would become the symbol of an individual's futile struggles against
the pervading social indifference. And it is this recognition that
adequately answers Shefali's silence at the end of the play when her
mother marries off Kiran to Bakul.

> one fails to understand why at the end of the play,
> the same Shefali – in spite of all her pain, guilt
> and anger – silently accepts and even blesses the
> surreptitious marriage of her younger sister, Kiran,
> with her lover, Bakul. It seems as if Shefali's struggle is
> a small and limited struggle against her own personal
> exploitation. Rather than fight and protest against
> her exploiters and their stratagems, she escapes into a
> self-destructive silence in the final, decisive moments.
> The play ends in darkness, hopelessness and defeat as
> Shefali is left all alone. (Subramanyam 87)

But instead of exploring Kumar's intention in presenting Shefali's
silence at the end, we may rather understand it as providing a more
pragmatic perspective, because the silence here is not unraveling
stoic acceptance but a painful recognition of the fact that 'caste'as
an instrument of discrimination is sustained both by the upper and
the lower castes. Kumar has been strategic enough in presenting a
fatherless family of Shefali, for, with no father, Shefali and her sister
arre apparently 'free' from masculine authoritarian voice that would
essentially bind them to a singular perspective. But the mother's
anguished voice not only lends an alternative but also supplements the

absent masculine voice. Therefore, Shefali and her mother perceive the world from two different perspectives. Shefali believes in essential equality between members of a society and therefore rejects all sorts of donations, assistances and political 'gifts'. But for her mother, there is no inherent equality existing in the social scheme of things. A political system therefore has emerged that believes in sanctioning endowments in place of empowerment and opportunities –such as training, education, job or marriage – actas mere keys to redefine 'equality'. Therefore Shefali's mother, at Miss Sahib's bequests, educated her daughters and earned a job for Shefali at the Dikshits. The marriage therefore provides her with an opportunity to free herself and her daughters from the confines of a strictly defined lower class, though 'neo-liberals' would argue that such endowments would only 'underclass' them. For, as Neo-liberals see it, the recent policies of striking equality by including individuals in social mainstreams through minimum endowment of capabilities and opportunities, 'have played an important part in increasing inequality via their role in the creation of an "underclass"' (Crompton 138). However, the 'underclass' is not to be seen as a mere stratification, because, as Rosemary Crompton says, 'The notion of the 'underclass' proved to be a highly contentious concept, and it has been argued that the term has been developed not in order to describe an objective phenomenon or a set of social relationships but, rather, as a stigmatizing label which effectively 'blames the victims' for their misfortunes' (138). However, the 'underclass' is not entirely a twentieth century concept developed in the wake of crude market orientations of the capitalist society, because Marx mentioned a similar category from the nineteenth century, defining it as the 'lumpen proletariat'. 'In the most general terms, the concept describes those in persistent poverty, who are not able, for whatever reason, to gain a living within the dominant processes of production, distribution and exchange' (139). Shefali's silence and acceptance of Kiran and Bakul's marriage by blessing the couple at the end, therefore may be interpreted as her recognition of their (Shefali's family) 'underclass' status which needs to be negotiated first, and only then caste revolution may ensue. This, further marks

Kumar's departure from the dalit canon as well, for, she dislocates the established debates on caste subordination, and repositions it at the intersection of caste and class, an exposition of which is also found in Usha Ganguli's *Rudali*. While Kumar is more concerned with the caste existence and class comes as a catalyst which enhances the social experiences of subordination, Ganguli makes class the fulcrum on which the intensity of caste experiences is hinged. However, in both the plays women's experiences are central to the comprehension of class and caste.

Adapted from Mahasweta Devi's novella of the same name, Usha Ganguli's *Rudali* speaks of a metamorphosis in Sanichari's (the protagonist) world from 'compulsory heterosexuality' to a woman oriented existence, which Adrienne Rich would call 'lesbian continuum'. Though Ganguli shifts from Devi's ultra-left concerns with class in projecting a more gendered condition, class not merely remains a major concern, but also brings caste into the same fold. In fact, Ganguli portrays Sanichari as a low caste, poor village woman, who is primarily concerned with her daily existence amongst abject poverty in the first four scenes of the play, but in the last six scenes, she builds Sanichari's character in a more 'humanistic' light, who enjoys Bikhni's warm company and a better economic solvency. Hence, Ganguli divides the play into two equal halves – scenes i to iv, showing compulsory heterosexuality simultaneously internalized, resisted and subverted, and scenes vi to xii, a surer stay in the woman's world, while scene v is the pivot which propels the thematic shift in the play.

Both Mahasweta Devi and Usha Ganguli harp on the theme of protest in *Rudali*, but concurrently reject the texts being termed 'feminist'. For Devi, class elides the gender concerns of her text for being a leftist activist herself she has never bothered about the gender difference among men and women when it comes to the struggle for survival. In an interview with the *Seagull Theatre Quarterly* in January 1994, Mahasweta Devi vehemently argues-

For you it may be important that this story is written by a woman, another woman has adapted it into a play, and yet another adapted it into a film. But I think that a writer has written the story, a director has adapted it into a play and another directed the film. It is not very important to me whether it was done by woman or not. . . I write as a writer, not as a woman. . . When I write I never think of myself as a woman. I have written a story called *Chotty Munda and His Arrow* which is about a tribal woman. *Aranyer Adhikar* is about male tribals. So what? These are stories of people's struggles, their confrontation with the system. . . I look at the class, not at the gender problem. Take a story like *Ganesh Mahima* – it is about a woman. But I have written it from the class point of view. In *Rudali* you have a character like Dulan who knows how to use the system. In my stories men and women alike belong to different classes. (Katyal 5, 6)

Unlike Devi, Usha Ganguli is seriously concerned about women's status, struggle and liberation, but like most of the women activists, creative writers and theatre practitioners in India, Ganguli too shies away from being labeled a feminist. Explaining her position, she says, 'I feel that I differ from the way people tend to use the term feminism. This term has nowadays become a fashionable one, and I don't believe in a particular brand of feminism. Therefore I don't want the play [*Rudali*] to be labeled as feminist. On the other hand I believe in the liberation of women and their freedom, and I'm trying my best as a person, as a teacher and as a theatre worker, to work towards that.'(5) Deviating from the traditional feminist approach, Ganguli therefore focuses on the exclusivity of women's experiences, even when they are positioned in a particular class/ caste structure. Speaking about *Rudali*, Ganguli says,

Sanichari and Bikhni don't appeal to me simply because they belong to a different class. There is something very human in them, and that breaks the class barrier. Everybody is able to communicate with them, their struggle breaks everybody's struggle . . .I strongly believe that Rudali is a woman's text. I believe that the Indian woman, whether it's Sanichari or someone from the middle or upper class, is highly exploited in our society. Somehow in *Rudali* I see Sanichari protesting against society on the whole. Somebody told me that *Rudali* is a play about a village. I don't agree. It is not about a particular village or a city or even about a particular character, but about all of us. Sanichari represents women in general. It is the humanistic element that makes it acceptable to all of us. (6)

Though Ganguli initially sounds critical in her appraisal of the play, the sweeping generalization intended at, in the phrase 'all of us' turns the scheme of things problematic because it bluntly frustrates both the architectural and the thematic balance of the play. However, according to Anjum Katyal, 'The easy term 'all of us' with its humanist, universalizing, all-embracing connotations in fact disguises an opposite significance. It signifies something closer to 'those like us'. In other words it is exclusive rather than inclusive, and presupposes a consonance of values, tastes, and ideas which in turn presupposes the specifics of class and social background'. (6) But whatever be the case, *Rudali* as a play merits the consideration of class/ caste/ gender nexus in its exposition of the three, both in their aesthetic and material conditions.

Produced for the first time in December, 1992, by Usha Ganguli's Hindi theatre group, *Rangakarmee* in Calcutta, the play has received popular attention from the theatre going public irrespective of their linguistic diversity. In fact, *Rudali* has succeeded in establishing that theatre has a language of its own. However, it must also be mentioned that the production history of the play marks a radical departure from the conventional theatre practice in Calcutta. Rangakarmee's preference to 'explore and expand the boundaries of the realistic/ naturalistic theatre' (13), the growth of a new audience, which was a cross-section of all Hindi speaking people of Calcutta and beyond' (14) and a long history of 'left/ class consciousness' in the state may adequately account for the acceptance of such a play which draws from a specific socio-cultural and political region of the country. Committed to proscenium theatre and aware of the urban audience, Ganguli has intelligently adapted Mahasweta Devi's story line without suspending her original voice which preserves the fundamental difference of class and gender in the novella and the play. She uses adroit stage directions in order to slip into the story and out, thereby maintaining a healthy balance between the original and the adapted versions.

The stage direction, at the outset, is suggestive of Sanichari's socio-economic condition:

> Before the stage lightens we hear the chakki – an aural-cum-visual metaphor for Sanichari's existence in poverty and labour. The set is designed carefully to take forward the metaphor with a few well-placed props. On stage are Sanichari (grinding wheat), her dying son Budhua on a charpoy, her physically feeble but sharp-tounged old mother-in-law Somri wrapped in a quilt, and her little grandson Haroa lying under the charpoy playing with a toy. (Katyal 30)

Situating the class position, Ganguli directly plunges into the intra-family tensions with Somri cursing Sanichari for not having readied her food. She immediately introduces the name of Parbatia through a dialogue between Sanichari and her mother-in-law, exposing the on-going same-sex battle in the house hold and at once suggesting the socio-cultural situation which prefixes the gender roles. Sanichari is caught in the domestic chores, while Parbatia 'enjoys' her life in the market and hates staying at home, doing the daily works. Mahasweta Devi draws Budhua in the light of a sick but supportive son, while Ganguli projects him as a docile, non-committal man having has a vague 'non-productive' presence in the family. But Budhua still continues to be the keel on whom the women characters of the house remain attached to. At the end of the first scene, Parbatia makes it clear that she will stay with the house till Budhua is alive – 'The moment he dies, I'm leaving'(Mee,120), and immediately after the death of Budhua, she runs away. Therefore, the playwright-director hints at a woman intensive family structure where the male existence however vague it may seem is nonetheless recognized as a compulsory force in the 'ordinary' scheme of things.

Apart from the heterosexual arrangement in the social nucleus, Ganguli has also focused largely on the portrayal of women from three different age groups – united by their class positions, but unique in their struggles for survival. While Somri is parasitic in her old age, Sanichari finds herself arrested in misery, poverty and responsibility, but for Parbatia, 'callous selfishness' (Katyal 33) has made her irresponsible and uphold her personal 'liberty' over everything. On interviewing Usha Ganguli, Anjum Katyal found the playwright insisting the fact that in drawing Parbatia she has followed the original text to its highest extent: 'When I visualize a character I don't put any value judgment. When I spoke to Mahasweta Devi, she requested me not to portray Parbatia as someone bad, but as someone who was merely trying to survive. . . [My treatment of Parbatia] is all in the story. (33). But as we shuffle through the pages of the play, we find that in her attempts to make the character appear more 'real', Ganguli have grossly deviated from the novella; one such instance is when Parbatia steals the paltry household savings and runs away at the face of Budhua's death. In Parbatia, therefore is 'a strong anti-Sanichari character/ relationship to balance the strong Sanichari-Bikhni alignment that marks the rest of the play'(34). Hence, in presenting the women characters as different from each other, and securing them individual niches Ganguli successfully refutes the feminist notions of essentialising inherent differences among women.

We come across strong caste/ class couple for the first time in the play when Budhua dies, and Sanichari calls for an upper caste Vaid, who betrays extreme adversity towards the lower class/ caste. Finding Budhua already dead, the Vaid turns impatient for his fee and begins condescending the lower castes. His inconsiderateness in allowing the Sanichari time for coping with the shock of losing her only son marks the extreme insensitivity of the upper class/ caste for their lower counterparts. The Vaid's severe steadfastness in procuring money can be correlated with the Upper Caste's strategy of scavenging on the poor and the lower castes. At the death of Sanichari's husband, she was forced to perform two ceremonies. Since her husband died in the Tohri village, the Brahmins from the village asked for *panda* – the custom of making offerings to a particular section of the Brahmins when someone dies. She had to pay a rupee and a quarter along with *sattu* and sand. But after returning to Tahad village, Brahmins from the village asked her to perform the ritual again, arguing that Tohri Brahmins were unaware of their rituals. She had to feed curds and *chivda* to all villagers and in the process take loans from the village strongman, Ramavatar. Sanichari rightly doubts the upper caste-class associations for perpetrating lower-caste subordinations:

> Who knows … the thakurs and Brahmins are all in this together. They control everything. It took me five years to pay off my debt to the thakur. (Ganguli 140)

But Sanichari arrives at such a consciousness much later. When in an instance, Haroa comes complaining about being mistreated by Lachman Singh's son, she advices him to unquestioningly accept it as part of their material conditions of in the lower class. Ganguli therefore creates the opportunity to harp on the traditional master-slave narrative through this episode. But she does not stop to critique the ideological acceptance of the upper class/ caste subordination in producing the 'normal' sociological structure that blames the poor man's fate as responsible for its perpetuation.

> HAROA: Lachman Singh's son thrashes me with his shoe....
>
> SANICHARI: That's a poor man's fate, Beta – the kicks of his master. Go on Beta, go to work. (127)

The conversation also hints towards the hereditary nature of class/ caste oppressions. Lachman Singh was already unpopular for exploiting the poor and now his son follows him suit. In a Marxist appraisal of the situation, Sanichari might appear to be a victim of 'false consciousness' who believes on a social structure where upper class as 'masters' have the right to subjugate the lower into physical torments but we understand that her life amidst a strong orthodox social condition, never provided the scope for any alternate perspective.

However, her perceptions undergo enough changes with Bikhni entering the frame. In a cinematically developed scene when Bikhni and Sanichari almost bump into each other, Sanichari experiences for the first time being 'looked at' with concern.

> BIKHNI: You look as if you've been out since morning, and I bet you haven't eaten a thing all day. (137)

Ganguli builds up the plot in such a way that both Bikhni and Sanichari approach each other when almost free from all previous family associations. 'At this point, she (Sanichari) is a woman shorn of all roles – no-one's daughter, wife, mother, mother-in-law or grandmother. She is free of all other ties and relationships, as is Bikhni, who has been abandoned by her son, and has left home with no plans and nowhere to go.' (Katyal 19). Both of them therefore are liberated from the confines of fixed gender roles that family enforces in a hetero-social framework. Both equally abandoned offer tender companionship to each other. Ganguli probably suggests a 'lesbian' relation which is not reduced to the body but accounts for an emotional and social dependence. In an emotionally charged scene, Bikhni comb and groom Sanichari's hair with utmost care and warmth. As they affectionately caress each other, an emotional turmoil brings out Sanichari's securely hidden grievances. She confides thus to Bikhni:

...My son died, my daughter-in-law ran off...I brought up my grandson, looked after him till he was a young man, and then he went off with the no-good magic-men. . . My whole life has been spent working, working. . . No, I never had the time to weep. They all died, one by one. My in-laws, my brother-in-law and his wife, my husband, my son. I didn't shed a single tear. They call me a *daain* — say it's as if I was born just to devour others. (Ganguli 138-139)

Behaving as one's most intimate would, Bikhni consoles and comforts Sanchari. In her attempts to provide child-like consolation to Sanichari, Bikhni betrays herself as Sanichari's partner who will not only show emotional care but also provide economic support.

Which son of a bitch dares call you a *daain*? I'll scratch his eyes out! Don't worry, Sanichari, you'll see, everything will turn out fine. I'll get hold of some fertilizer from the government office and start growing vegetables once again, and I'll sell them myself in the market. (139)

In her innocent attempts to help her friend economically, Bikhni 'unknowingly' plays the traditional masculine role in a 'homo-sexual' couple. Pertinent here is to note that Ganguli has all throughout the play projected the market as 'open' for both the genders. In presenting the public space as non-exclusive for men, where women can actively participate in the economic cycle, Ganguli lends a different perspective to the evolution of the traditional Indian society.

The woman exclusive activity invoked in this scene is further explored in the play as Sanichari and Bikhni engage as Rudalis in the profession of crying at 'rich house-holds'. Dulan explains them their job:

Only the families of the poor mourn their dead. The rich house-holds have to hire mourners. *Arre*, if you mourn for them you'll get money, grain, and the day after the *kriya* you'll even get clothes and a good meal. (145)

It is Dulan, who is the only male character properly developed in both the novella and the play. It is he who gives timely advices to Sanichari throughout her hapless existence before meeting Bikhni and after. Presenting a close bond between him, Sanichari and few fellow villagers of the same class, Ganguli suggests a community life between them. But, beyond this, Dulan is a crude bargainer. He advocates and practices 'professionalism' for survival:

This is crying for money, crying as a business,. Just do it the way you would grind wheat or carry bricks for the sake of daily wage. . . Sanichari – I want my share of your earnings from my job I arrange for you. (145-146)

While both Sanichari and Bikhni get seasoned as Rudalis, Dulan continues maneuvering and schematizing the socio-economic conditions of individuals only to serve personal purposes. Later in the penultimate scene of the play, in order to cater to the need of a group of Rudalis, Sanichari goes to the whore's quarter to raise her group. Addressing Parbatia as 'bahu' even though she retains all past malice against her, portrays Sanichari's growth into a shrewd business woman. Sanichari therefore becomes part of such a class system where a 'proletariat revolution' may seem impossible but the market economy is also not inaccessible.

Ganguli sounds critical of the Upper Class/ Caste hypocrisies. The death sequences 'celebrated' in the play is coupled with criticism of the Upper Class pretence on the one hand and the lower class opportunism on the other. But the visit to Sanichari's house by Nathuni Singh's middle wife merits a special mention here, for it opens up new vistas of understanding the nuances of the upper class social structure. Thakurain is propelled to invite Sanichari and her team, because she wants to leave her mark amongst the others members of the Thakur family in performing the funeral rites for her father. In her attempt to justify her position, she betrays the reality of the Thakur household, wherein even the Thakurain is mistreated for being unable to bear a son.

> THAKURAIN: What authority would I have? Have
> I produced a son and heir for the family? I gave birth
> to a daughter, that was my big crime. When my
> mother-in-law died, thirty thousand *rupees* were spent
> on her *kriya*. Half of that money was given y my
> father, but even after that they treated me badly. I
> refuse to stay there any longer. I'll go to my father's
> house, and I'll organize such a magnificent *kriya* for
> him that the whole community will talk of nothing
> else... (157)

Usha Ganguli's contention therefore may have been to show that though class/ caste experiences may condition the subordination of women, few aspects of gender domination such as the potential to bear a child (son), remains same across classes. However, both Kusum Kumar and Usha Ganguli have recognized the fact that lower class/ caste women may enjoy more social/ political/ economic liberty than the upper class women. Satya Dev Dikshit's household in *Listen Shefali* remains silent about the absence of women and projects a motherless family. Shefali, we see, is somewhat liberated from the domestic chores and goes to the extent of taking up a teaching post at the Dikshits. Even in *Rudali*, Sanichari and Bikhni are free to take up their professions and they create exclusive economic groups of women. Though Bikhni dies before the end of the play, Sanichari, with her newly acquired business skill of manipulating the market for her personal needs, still continue the struggle. However, the play ends with Sanichari scratching the earth and discovering a coin.

Samar Chatterjee rightly suggests that here, 'Earth symbolizes life, but money has become part of it.' (Katyal 26)

Both *Listen Shefali* and *Rudali*, therefore, are unique in projecting the socio-cultural flux on which rest the considerations of class, caste and gender. Therefore, the women theatre practitioners in India deny projecting any essential conclusion while negotiating with women's position amidst the class – caste alliance in modern Indian society.

CHAPTER

Women, Body, Abuse: Lights Out and Getting Away with Murder

Engaging with the complex notions of 'body' and 'abuse' has been one of the regular features of Indian women's theatre from the 1970s to the new millennium. One of the prime reasons behind the sustenance of such engagement is that the very 'doing' of theatre itself enables the discussion on 'body'. Colette Conroy in her book *theatre and the body* observes that theatre facilitates thinking on body at least in four different ways. Making and watching theatre is directly connected with the actors playing roles of different characters on stage. A particularly trained body of an actor under specific directorial convention, projects itself on stage in a way that would affect the audience differently than it would under different conventions. Again, certain forms of theatre allow the exploration and interrogation of body as a 'site' of power, which immediately and inevitably suggests volatility. The body of the actor synthesizes performance and culture and therefore allows the 'spectating body' (audience) (Conroy 6) to analyse the 'working of power upon the body in culture' (5). Finally, Conroy argues that theatre allows the distinction between an ideal body and the real physical bodies; the ideal body being that dispassionate medium *communiqué* which performs any 'character' on stage without interfering in the audience's process of analysis, while the real bodies are 'physical objects that vary hugely from each other'(6).The interaction of the audience and theatre therefore enables the exploration of the potential and the real body as well as the reconsideration of the real through the potential body. Buoyant with the opportunities of pushing 'the extremes of cultural imagination' theatre provides 'space, structure and context for the contemplation of actual and potential' (Nevitt 6). Exploring such possibilities in theatre, however, must involve the audience, both as individuals and as participants in the social collective. This chapter explores Indian women playwrights' (and directors') engagement with theatre's nuanced relation with women's body on stage and 'violence', a term, which I critically differentiate from and interpret as abuse.

ManjulaPadmanabhan's *Lights Out* and Dina Mehta's *Getting Away with Murder,* the plays I choose for this chapter, were first performed in 1986 and 1990 respectively. Though a number of plays composed in the 1990s and 2000s thematically address the issues of body and violence, my choice of these two plays primarily rests on the fact that they were composed in the 1980s. What is the contribution of 1980s to 'Women's theatre'? The question does not entail easy answers. For, it can only be explored inthe role theatre played in producing the 'enormous cultural significance' (Mangai 29) of women's movements that began in the late 1970s.

The women's trade unions, founded by the Gandhian socialists in 1970s, failed to produce serious discussions on women's issues. But the women's groups which emerged as wings of Left political parties around 1975 initiated feminist debates and associated feminism with other social movements of the time. As discussed at length in the introduction of this book, the repealing of Emergency in 1977, encouraged the formation of a number of women's groups (notable are *Saheli* and *Salehi*), who largely addressed the educated, urban middle class on issues such as rape, dowry deaths, wife-beating, bride-burning, mothering, housekeeping etc. These women's groups, along with taking to the streets against sexual and cultural oppression on women, organized workshops and produced theatre performances for raising consciousness among women. Inspired by Badal Sircar's 'third theatre', some of the groups 'took to organizing theatre and art groups from amongst their staff. These groups would develop a set of plays and skits which would then be performed during campaigns and protests.' (Mangai 30) One such example is RUWSEC, a women's group in the 1980s, in Chenglapattu, Tamil Nadu, who used theatre skills of its members to put across a non-literate dalit women audience, matters of labour, health and violence women suffer within the family. Conversely, theatre groups like Tripurari Sharma's "Alarippu" performed regularly in public squares, railway platforms, ghettos and *bastis* in order to disseminate women's 'concerns' amongst the public. But before Alarippu was formed in 1983, Maya Krishna Rao collaborated with Anuradha Kapur and Rati Bartholomew to form the "Theatre Union" in 1979. Touring several colleges, community centers and commons, in and around Delhi, "Theatre Union" performed *Om Swaha* (1979) and *Dafa no. 180* (1981). *Om Swaha* protested against atrocities against women for dowry and *Dafa No. 180* addressed the lacunae in legislations regarding rape in India. Both the plays were urgent and appropriate to the moment, for the issues they dealt with, had already caught nation-wide attention. First produced by *Stree Sanharsh* (a Delhi based women's group), *Om Swaha* was patronized and re-produced with different casts by a number of women's groups. *Dafa No.180*, too, followed a similar course, for some proclaimed activists like Urvashi Butalia, Anuradha Kapur, Ragini Prakash, Vaid Sehgal, Ein Lall, etc. collaborated with Maya Rao and her team for its productions. Theatre and women's groups, therefore, in the 1980s proved complimentary to each other. The women's groups (following the strategy set by left/ right wing political activists) brought theatre out of the auditorium to the streets and *mohullas*; and affective/ interventionist as it is, theatre proliferated into different forms, such as the 'street theatre', 'engaged theatre','oppositional theatre', 'radical theatre', 'theatre of liberation', 'free theatre', 'applied theatre' etc. Hence the stimulus acquired by theatre from the women's movements in the late 1970s (and after) cannot be annulled.

Lights Out and *Getting Away with Murder* (none of which was composed to be performed as 'activist' plays), in their own rights, encapsulate what Helen Keyssar describes in *Feminist Theatre and Theory*. To Keyssar,

> 'productions of scripts characterized by the consciousness of women as women; dramaturgy in which art is inseparable from the condition of women as women; performance (written and acted) that deconstructs sexual difference and thus undermines patriarchal power, scripting and production that present transformation as a structural and ideological replacement for recognition; and the creation of women in the subject position (1).

The 1980s, provided playwrights like Padmanabhan and Mehta the necessary impetus for synthesizing politics and aesthetics in their plays but they also preserved their separation from being generalized as 'political' theatre activists.

Apart from engaging theatre and activism at the national level, the 1980s is notorious for the 'corporal turn' in academic feminisms worldwide, a nebulous reflection of which is also found in the plays chosen. Since violence on women is the epicenter of both *Getting Away with Murder* and *Lights Out,* the female body remains the site of major critical explorations. In this regard, the plays are in consonance with Indian feminist approaches to 'embodiment', which draw on the Western feminist notions of embodiment, but at the same time, are critical of them. While the 'First Wave' Anglo-American Feminism rarely focused on the body as a site of critical enquiry, engagement with body during the 'Second Wave' was structured by the inheritance of Cartesian dualism where the split between mind and body traditionally privilegedthe mind over body and associated women only with the latter. Unproblematised relegation of women to their body is also one of the reasons behind the separation between men and women in terms of their socio-cultural and political roles. For Simone de Beauvoir, the body is 'problematic' for women, because, it limits their 'freedom'. Arguing for a dematerialized view of gender, the liberal feminists accepted Beauvoir's position, but the radical feminists 'looked at the female body (nonetheless subordinated and controlled) as the source of empowerment and having the potential to produce social change in being the "source of actual lived and experienced pain, distress and pleasure"' (Howson, 49). Hence, a number of radical feminists like Koedt, Brownmiller, Greer, Millett and Firestone (to name only a few), writing in the 1970s, addressed the connotations that female body supplies to women's experience of subordination with respect to sexuality, rape, representation and reproduction (48). In accordance with Susan Bordo, Alexandra Howson argues that the radical feminist texts were 'grounded in a language of activism and quite explicitly engaged with a range of women's bodily experiences, 'from foot-binding, corseting to rape and battering to compulsory heterosexuality, forced sterilization, unwanted pregnancy, and explicit commodification"(48). In the 1980s, however, the female body came to be seen as 'specific, subordinated matter that could be important in transforming social relations and arrangements.' (49). Howson, therefore, lauds the 1980s' radical feminists such as Adrienne Rich for re-conceiving the ways in which the 'female subject' and the 'female embodiment' may be entwined inorder to comprehend the body as a "'resource' for women rather than as an inevitable psychological and biological destiny' (49).

Dina Mehta's *Getting Away with Murder*, explores the female body both as 'destiny' as well as 'resource' for a transformed social arrangement. The play revolves around three upper middle class women who are trapped within their 'private' psycho-social spaces of subordination and surrender, amidst the ambivalence of a re-formed social structure. It offers three different perspectives on the sexual/anatomical reductionism in gendered relations. Sonali, who has been a victim of child sexual abuse, is desperate to reassert her control over her body. Her friend, Mallika, though a successful entrepreneur, is apprehensive of defying the social norms in marrying Gopal (Sonali's brother and her fiancée) who is younger in age. Raziya is a medical doctorbut unquestioningly compromises with a cultural structure that compels her to carry on a failed conjugality with her husband who is set tomarry another woman. All three women in the play hail from the 'empowered' upper-middle-class section of the society and have enough scope for economic and individual liberty, but each one of them privately continue struggling with embodied social stratifications. Though the play is written in English and targeted to an educated urban audience, Mehta never projects a singular grand narrative on the living experiences of women in India. Gopal's display of photographs may be referred to as a dramatic technique for supplementing her contentions.

> Gopal: It's smeared with muck. That's Indumati. The mob at her heels is drumming her to the river, where they'll kill her and throw her in.

> ...

> Gopal: This one is a close-up (*switches off a light and projects picture on a wall*). See the tension in her neck? Her eyes looking straight at me, accusingly? I had snatched her moments of deepest dread and humiliation – and was about to walk away with them for public display, like a trophy. I ran all the way to the police station instead ... Indumati was saved in the nick of time.

> ...

Gopal: ... This is Dulkha Devi of Tharwar. The day after I snapped her in the bazaar, she was stripped naked within sight of the police station, her face blackened, head shaved, forced to run around the village while the men beat her with burning brands and sticks till she died (*switches off*).

...

The village priest denounced her as a witch. She had once repulsed him, it seems, so after her husband died of consumption the *pujari* took his revenge by accusing her of eating him up!

...

Gopal: And these are widows and deserted women who live in Chaibasa. (*Another projection*) Male relatives have accused them of being witches in order to usurp their land. Many such cases are pending in the courts.

...

Gopal: (*Offhand*): That? (*stammering suddenly*) She — she's from Barisola village. ...she's a widow — that's her 3-year old daughter with her — and their lives are in danger because her brother-in-law, who covets her land, has accused her of being a witch. (79 – 81)

The random presentation of slides, as a dramaturgic innovation, reflects Antonin Artaud's dramatic strategy of presenting forms of cruelty through minimum rhetoric and props. But most explicit is Mehta's strategy of projecting the difference in lived experiences of Indian women in different regions of the country. The Dulkha Devi of Tharwar is a victim of patriarchal violence, while Mallika and Raziya are trapped in the structures of socio-patriarchal expectations.

Sonali, on the other hand, is undergoing post-traumatic experiences of child sexual abuse, but also resistant against being subject to any further control. Hence, the images of women that emerge throughout the play, not only recognize the socio-patriarchal ideologies operating behind the reduction of women to their bodies, but also, suggest that women's reclaiming control over their body may transform the existing social arrangements.

With regard to the above proposition, the play is in sync with the Western materialist feminists of the 1970s and 1980s. They held that the female body's experience of discomfort or liberation is conditioned by its specific location in the socio-economic and political structures. The British sociologist, Ann Oakley situates women's bodily experiences within a social framework where capitalist structure is fused with the patriarchal. Exclusive women's experiences, such as the menstruation and the menopause, are never accommodated in the capitalist economic structure and even pregnancy sometime goes 'invisible' in a more oppressive frame. Though women's bodily experiences are strategically ignored, women's autonomy over their bodies did not go uncorrupt. The technological innovations in bio-medicine have situated woman's body (especially during the elaborate medical process of reproduction) not only under the patriarchal surveillance but reified the body in terms of parts and fragments. 'The surveillance of the female body', as Howson observes, is 'part of a more general shift towards visualizing the unseen' (52).Hence, questioning the socio-patriarchal 'normative' structures associated with the 'nature' of women's bodily experiences brought the materiality of women's experiences into more deliberate focus. But such attention conferred to the social shaping of experience, unwittingly associated experience with gender as a topic of sociological enquiry. Gender, therefore, is different from sex on the one hand and a blank category to be filled with socio-cultural assumptions and praxis, on the other. Consequently, the body came to be seen as a site where the social assumptions of gender are mapped on. The sex/ gender distinction thus sought, defines the hitherto capricious relation between the anatomy of a woman/ man and her/ his gender identity. For Christine Delphy, even sex is enmeshed within the 'practice of social and cultural determination that transforms 'a physical fact into a category of thought' (57). What follows then, is that, sex is not ahistorical but a culturally mediated social product constituted of historically acquired value. Thus, Indumati of Ranchi, Dhulka Devi of Tharwar, the widows of Chaibasa, Sonali, Mallika and Razia are similar in being looked upon and projected as 'sexed' bodies. Following Foucault's contention that 'body' is discursively constituted through forms of power which germinate not in the macrocosmic institutions of state but the 'micro-practices of everyday life' (73), and that power materializes through its operations on individual bodies, it may be argued that the female body continuously evolves as the produce of 'new knowledge and orthodoxies' (74), and involves itself in the social formation of femininity.

But considering the women characters in *Getting Away with Murder* as Foucaultian 'sexed' bodies, has its own problems. For, the notion of the 'sexed body', which was rooted in its specific genealogy of production and projected against the Cartesian privilege of the mind over body, has been criticized for failing to acknowledge the difference in gendered embodiment of male and female. This *difference*, however, has been addressed by Judith Butler in the context of self-other distinction using the post-Lacanian psychoanalytic framework which focuses on writing and textuality. For Butler, discourses are constitutive but not seminal to the body. The latter has 'something' in excess to what is constituted by the discourse. This 'something' is the 'imaginary space' that characterizes the 'excess of difference', which according to Hawson, 'can only be understood through knowledge of text rather than through substantive knowledge derived from observations and understandings of bodily experience rooted in material locations and practices' (85).But to look at the body as text, it is necessary to espouse the Derridian notion 'There is no outside-the-text'(Derrida, 841), which according to Derrida signifies that 'one never accedes to a text without some relation to its contextual opening that a context is not made up only of what is so trivially called text, that is, the words of a book or the more or less bio-degradable paper document in a library' (841). Hence, for Derrida, the 'context' of a text is very important. Moreover, for Derrida, *textuality* is characterized by *difference, deference* and *multiplicity* of meaning. Therefore the Derridian structure promotes an ambiguity within a system of shifting signifiers, which puts into rapture any constructed whole, and disturbs its fixity and encourages non-stability. Derived from the idea of textuality, and its 'undecidability', 'woman'for Derrida is 'undecidable'. For feminists, this 'undecidability' provides them, the greatest opportunity to break away from the 'fixed' binary categorization (Howson 86). Derrida's aim of 'destabilising the logocentricity, by rethinking the oppositional binary' (86) is championed by the feminists who advocated the rejection of male/ female binary. They used Derrida's deconstructive methods to 'demonstrate how women come to embody difference' (87). Likewise, some feminists have disrupted sex/ gender distinction arguing against the exclusivity of physiological or social category.

Padmanabhan's *Lights Out*, also, rejects the 'feminist' models that reduce woman to her anatomy. It discusses socio-political, cultural and ritualistic factors that collaborate in constituting the 'female' as a separate category. The protagonists of the play, an upper middle class couple (Leelaand Bhasker) are 'annoyed' by the 'spectacle' of gang rapes in their colony. They are gradually joined by a number of friends, viz. Mohan, Naina and Surinder (Naina's husband), but none of them come out of the apartment to help the victim(s). Instead, the scene becomes a cynosure of sex–battle among the male and female characters. Composed with a 'bystander effect', *Lights Out* recognizes the female body as subject to patriarchal control, repeated sexual abuse and a matter of continuous socio-cultural, political and religious debate. But at the same time, the play provides scope for reworking the sex/gender distinction as 'a stylized repetition of acts…understood as the mundane way in which bodily gestures, movements, and styles of various kinds constitute the illusion of an abiding gendered self'(Butler 140). Manjula Padmanabhan portrays Leela as the typical woman, and, Bhasker and Mohan as the typical men indoctrinated in gender roles. Leela is empathetic towards the women who are raped regularly in the colony but depends upon Bhaskar for acting against the atrocities. As an 'ideal' Indian wife, Leela remains passive, and subordinated to her husband throughout the play. But Padmanabhan introduces Naina as a foil to Leela. She not only challenges the vague masculine explanations of rapes, but also urges the men to act. Hence, both the women appear 'relational' to the 'material' condition they are situated in. As Judith Butler proposes, body acts as the medium through which each sex enacts itself both in acquiescence with and through the disruption of norms. For Butler, gender is not absolutely detached from sex, rather, it is mired in the complex structure of heterosexuality that not only creates but also attempts to establish 'an illusion of stability and fixity ... produced through repetition and enactments (typically interpreted as habitual practice) that make it seem as though gender (as identity) is fixed and attached to sex (as in the 'sexed body')' (111). The materiality of sex-gender dichotomy, therefore, is *not* a mere 'given'; it is a product of the process of materialization through repetitive practice which generates the 'effect of boundary, fixing and surface' (111). Body, as a result comes to be seen as 'matter (immutable) over time' (111). In *Bodies that Matter*, Butler develops her idea of 'materiality' and 'body'. While the former is constituted of 'power' that makes materiality seem 'given', the latter, for Butler, can only be comprehended through the process of linguistic signification because return to the body as matter, is possible only in return through signs. As a product of the system of signs, body emerges as 'relational'(30).

We can perhaps understand 'female body' in *Lights Out* as limiting and conscious of its boundaries which makes them physiologically separate from others. It is discursively produced in relation to a complex socio-political network of dependency/ interdependency/ non-dependency. Padmanabhan presents her characters through layered representations of gender performativity, which isat best an 'enactment' in relation to the 'compulsory' social norms that are made obligatory through the machinations of heterosexual hierarchical forms of power. Body, then emerges as the material site through which 'gender performatives' are enacted, ratified and questioned. The female body is especially intriguing here, because it has been historically compelled to undergo social, political, economic and 'religious' subjugation and denied human subjectivity and agency. But reading the body as text, argues Helene Keyssar, 'risks biological essentialism' (168). 'The body's role in theatrical representation poses some particularly complex issues for material feminists because, despite the extent to which 'gender' and 'character' may be social and/ or theatrical constructions, the facticity of the actor's biological sex always re-inscribes the performer with the cultural codes associated with his/ her gender' (168-9).This is in accordance with Jill Dolan's argument that body can never be free of connotative signs (Dolan 63). Hence, when a female body is presented on stage as a 'speaking subject', as it is also in the case of the plays by Indian women playwrights, the 'body' relatively acquires multiple significations. My main contention in this chapter, however, is to locate the thematic and dramaturgic uniqueness that Indian women playwrights arrive at, with respect to the female body when it is subject to violence. Though violence can take multifarious shapes (gendered violence, sexual violence, domestic violence, communal violence, religious violence, ethnic violence, 'medical' violence, taboos etc.) depending on the how, why and on whom it is enacted, my proposition is to look at violence as 'abuse'.

The Oxford Advanced Learner's Dictionary defines 'violence' as 'violent behavior that is intended to hurt or kill sb (somebody)' (bracketing mine) (1719). It defines 'abuse' as 'the use of sth (something) in a way that is wrong or harmful' (bracketing mine) (6) and 'unfair, cruel, or violent treatment of sb (somebody)' (bracketing mine) (6). The primary difference between violence and abuse, then, is that the former has more to do with the agent whose behaviour ('violent') is worked out on the victim, while the latter establishes the victim as a subject. My endeavor is to supplement the above difference with the representations of women experiences by Indian women theatre practitioners. However, to focus on the difference is not to see abuse as a non-porous compartment, rather, to build on the framework of violence while preserving the former's subtle separations from it.

With the publication of Susan Griffin's 1971 article, *Rape: The All–American Crime*, the 'Western' view on violence came to be recognized as gendered. Her essay refers to some cultures where violence is invariably equated with masculinity. The feminists in the late 1970s and early '80s have cited her essay in order to argue for the 'maleness' of violence (Price 11).R. Emereson Dobash and Russell Dobash define violence in conjugal terms. In *Violence Against Wives: A Case against Patriarchy* they argue that violence is 'the persistent direction of physical force against a marital partner or cohabitant' (11). Hence they argue for a heterosexual definition of violence, where woman is the obvious victim. Later, Anne Jones widens the scope of violence by identifying the use of physical force as only an aspect or form of violence, for the latter also includes 'Behaviour you might not think of as 'violence,' behaviour you might think of merely as getting things off your chest … if it coerces or frightens another person' (88). However, if causing fear is looked upon as the touchstone of violence/ violent behaviour, then it not only denies the misogynist dimension of male violence, but its sexual nature as well.

Sonali in *Getting Away with Murder* is a victim of 'sexual' abuse. Suffering from forced sexual subjugation, Sonali embodies the experience of discrimination between boy and girl. 'My mother used to exhaust herself over her household tasks – may be because she was grateful to Uncle for taking us in after Father died. She drove herself – and turned me into her satellite: I had to run her errands, mouth her opinions, feel her feelings … Of course, Gopal escaped all that because he was born with an extra set of accessories' (Mehta 59). Hence, the gendered nature of abuse can never be denied. Subject to sexual abuse, Sonali is reified both by her uncle and her mother, but with her 'body' under constant conflict of 'authorship', she emerges abnormally conscious of her anatomical existence. Hence, 'abuse' may have more complex results on the victim than mere 'violence'. But looked upon as violence, 'abuse' may be placed within the scope of the existing sociological discourse on the gendered nature of violence.

Lisa Price locates two schools of thinkers who understand violence and sex in two different ways – 'Violence is sex' and 'Violence *not* sex' (Price 18). She quotes Jill Radford, 'while men are murdered more frequently than women, men are rarely murdered simply because they are men' (16). For women, Radford says, it is the 'misogynous' attitude that causes their murder the most. Hence the obvious question that she raises is about the role of sexuality in violence. She builds up a feminist approach to 'rape' in order to vindicate the difference in positions of the aforementioned schools. That rape is a matter of violence which involves no sexuality, is a view espoused by Dorrie Klein, Judith Herman, Peggy R. Sanday and Carole J. Sheffield. For them, rape or for that matter even incest, though carried out on the body ('female'), are expressions of power and domination wrought with the patriarchal notion of control instead of being erotic. Price also includes Susan Brownmiller, who conceptualizes rape as a theft of property. In her book, *Against Our Will: Men, Women and Rape* (1975), she argues,

> Like assault rape is an act of physical damage to another person, and like robbery it is also an act of acquiring property: the intent is to 'have' the female body in the acquisitory meaning of the term. A woman is perceived by the rapist both as hatred person and desired property. Hostility *against her* and *possession* of her may be simultaneous motivations, and the hatred for her is expressed in the same act that is the attempt to 'take' her against her will. In one violent crime, rape is an act against person and property. (185)

Clark and Lewis agree with Brownmiller and consider rape to be simply an act of larceny of sexual property. They argue,

> A sexual attack is, in itself, neither better nor worse than any other kind of attack. ... to treat rape as a sexual offence simply because it involves a penis and a valuable vagina, only reinforces the connections between women as property and women's sexuality as the source of their property value. (179)

Hence, for Clark, Lewis, Brownmiller, and other proponents of "violence *not* sex', sexuality is always *absent* for both the victimizers and the victims. They leave altogether the very question of sexual identity. Among the notable advocates of 'violence is sex' proposition, are Carol Smart, Catharine MacKinnon and Susan Cole. For Smart, in its process of execution violence always incurs 'pleasure with power' (18). Speaking about the rapists, women murderers, the molesters and child abusers, Mackinnon's views are especially intriguing for she asserts that violence meted out to women by men are always already enmeshed insexual pleasure. Price cites her thus:

> [They] enjoy their acts sexually and as men, to be redundant. It is sex *for them*. What is sex except that which is felt as sexual? When acts of dominance and submission, up to and including acts of violence, are experienced as sexually arousing, as sex itself that is what they are. ... Violence is sex when it is practiced as sex. (19)

Therefore, for MacKinnon, sex and violence are not only complimentary but also emerge as synonymous when held in the context of masculine violence over women. Also worth mentioning is Susan Cole's reading of 'rape' through 'weapons' such as the 'broomsticks' instead of penis. She argues that even if weapons are used for rape, it does not erase the idea of sexuality involved in the act, for, in rape, weapons behave as substitutes to the penis. It is the involvement of certain sections of the woman's body, i.e. the erogenous zones, that makes explicit the ideas of sexual pleasure involved in rape. She says:

> That the penis is not a weapon in the assault does not mean that sex is not involved: saying rape is about power and not sex leaves out the crucial fact of where the attackers put their weapons. If rape is about power and not sex, why don't attackers just hit women, and exercise their power that way? Because *rape is sex to them.* (118)

When rape is sex, the theorists who equate violence to sex argue that the rape-victim remembers rape only as a forced traumatic sexual experience.

However, both the group of theorists who advocate 'violence *not* sex' and 'violence is sex', can be criticized on the ground that they take hard essentialist positions in arguing their cases. For the 'violence *not* sex' proponents, violence and sex are two extremely separate categories where the presence of one denies the other. But, for the 'violence is sex' theorists, violence and sex are so enmeshed in each other that they fail to appreciate the subtle differences between the two 'categories', owing to the socio-cultural contingencies of the bodies. Moreover, both the schools tend to theorise violence as a mere set of actions and sex as 'given'. The perpetrator of violence (considered male) – his intentions and instruments (penis or weapon) in fracturing/ dominating/ controlling/ causing fear/ sexually possessing the female body remains the privileged point of focus. My proposition here is to consider 'violence' both as a 'verb' and 'noun'; that one abuses the 'other' and the 'other' suffers the abuse; and then there is the third 'other': the witness who is party to the entire event, who may either reap pleasure or feel empathetic for the victim. Hence the affect must loom large. Leela and Naina in *Lights Out* are empathetic towards the women who are raped in the colony but Bhaskar and Mohan prefer only to discuss the non-credibility of the actions to be seen as an act of rape and rather seek to justify them as taboos or mere domestic brawls.

Lights Out recreates an eye-witness account of an incident that took place in Santa Cruz, Bombay, 1982. It may be mentioned here that in Bombay, in the period 1985 – 89, 504 cases of rape were registered, only 469 were charge sheeted, of which there were 15 convictions and 10 acquittals, and 441 were pending trial in 1990. Also a large number of convictions in the Sessions Courts were overturned on appeal, or the sentences reduced. At the end of the play there is 'no curtain call' (Padmanabhan 53). A dramatic innovation in the 1980s Indian theatre, some messages appear on the curtain in form of slides. The first slide reminds the audience of the 1982 Bombay incident of regular rapes. The next four slides build the familiarity with the incident and establish a bridge between the play and its context. Even though there is no formal end to the play, Padmanabhan's objective is reached. The play is not a general piece about crimes against women. With 'no curtain call' (53), the play travels with the audience wherever they go. It talks with the audience, making them *uncomfortable*. It arrests their attention and makes them relate the incidents on stage with their lived lives. Its production history reasserts the conviction that theatre, at best, is a collaborative art, where along with the actors, director(s) and members of the production, the audience participate in imagining/reimagining and exploring forms of realities. It reaffirms theatre as 'a cultural product of historical, geopolitical, and ideological conditions … capable of reconstructing those conditions by mediating sociopolitical formations' (Sengupta 3). And that theatre 'is as much a representation of offstage "realities" as a space where "realities" are equally formed and re-formed through human performance, exploring in the process a complex relationship between world, text, performance, viewing, and reception'(4). The 'objective reality', which nonetheless has its own structured and politically meditated presence, is an (in)authentic reference to actuality that is imitated by the actors on stage. Thereafter, the actors produce a reality, which in itself is a result of an interaction between the scoio-cultural and political condition of the actors, their training, dramaturgical techniques of (re)production and the source(s) of their reference(s). Lastly, and perhaps the most important form of reality amongst the triad is the *reality* that each member of the audience constitute for him/ herself, depending upon his/ her individual interaction with the performance on stage.

When *Lights Out* was adapted with some changes by "Lights Off" production for performance in the Alliance Francaise de Bangalore in 2012, it produced a similar impact on the audience as it did in its initial productions.

> The change that did get announced is that the play is no longer set in 1984 and is set in 2012, making this production of Lights Out, a contemporary version and an adaptation of the original and not an original in itself anymore. The audience was surely taken by surprise when the actors walked onto the stage from their seated position from amongst the very same audiences. This method of introduction or curtain call, if one may, definitely adds justice to the original play and its purpose to reach out to everyone in the audience. (Joseph)

The play was staged with a definite purpose of critiquing contemporary events in 2010. According to a report on 13th March, 2010 in The "Times of India", the play was performed on *Gyan Manch* by a Kolkata-based theatre group *Tree Hat*; the response of the audience was 'overwhelming': '*The full house attendance for ManjulaPadmanabhan's Lights Out was overwhelming to say the least.*' The director of the performance, Shubhayan Sengupta, is quoted, "Lights Out is our second production. We took a joint decision to stage Manjula's play that talks about social awareness. Though the actual events had taken place in the 80s, we don't see much of a change in the reaction of people to disturbing events happening right in front of them. Our play was intended as an eye-opener."(Dasgupta)

What emerges from these accounts of audience reception is that the play has evoked 'similar' tensions in the audience across regions and generations. Woman abuse therefore remains a common reference for experience in India, even though the country is making forays into international politics and establishing itself as one of the major players in world economics. The play suggests narratives of modern Indian response towards 'organised' sexual abuse. The characters in the play maintain their distance from the 'event' and indulge in discussions as to what if it's not rape? What if it is just a domestic brawl? Is it decent to interfere into other's familial matter (however violent it may be)? What if it's a religious taboo? Is it right to 'hurt' someone's religious sentiments (even if it abuses women) in 'secular' India? What if it's just a superstition or an act of 'exorcism'? What if the raped woman is a whore? Can a woman who is not 'decent' be raped at all? Is it being woman that makes one vulnerable to rape? If one has to act, how must he act? What weapons one must use? Knives? Bulbs? Acids? Petrol? Combinations of acid and petrol? Guns? Is it not better to click pictures before stopping the gang rape? Won't the live photos of gang rape earn money? Padmanabhan gradually points to the general urban reluctance in acting against someone else's misery. Such reluctance cohabits the common strategy of ignoring the desperate calls for help. Here one can definitely refer to a 'joke' cited by Slavoj Zizek in his book Violence:

> There is an old joke about a husband who returns home earlier than usual and finds his wife in bed with another man. The surprised wife exclaims: "Why have you come back early?" The husband furiously snaps back: "What are you doing in bed with another man?" the wife calmly replies: "I asked you a question first – don't try to squeeze out of it by changing the topic!" the same goes for violence: the task is precisely to change the topic, to move from the desperate humanitarian SOS call to stop violence to the analysis of that other SOS … (11)

Padmanabhan's intentions behind locating her characters at a 'remove' from the main incident, which, in turn removes the audience twice from the actual event, might have been to critique the 'ordinary' forms of theatre productions. In *Lights Out*, the audience is constantly informed about the rapes but never shown. They are teased throughout the play with gestures', 'actions' and even 'reactions' of the characters on stage. Hence the dramaturgy involves the Brechtian apparatus 'gest' to a good effect. In Leela, Padmanabhan portrays a woman who is in distress seeing/ hearing 'violence' unfold before her apartment. The audience may be drawn towards believing her but she is never authenticated throughout the play. She is constantly bullied by her husband and his friend, Mohan. Bhasker says, 'You're (Leela) making too much of it!'(Padmanabhan 5) (bracketing mine), '... Leela's hypersensitive these days' (35). However, the audience cannot believe Bhaskar either, for, through the entire course of the play he denies what isobvious in the colony. Hence the audience always finds itself in a position of 'uncertainty'. Praggnaparamita Biswas speaking on the play's dramaturgy says that,

'Padmanabhan's ... semiotic application by depicting three different sound effects: heart rending cry for help of the rape victim lady, Leela's hysterical outburst and Freida's constant reticence generates a series of antithetical verbal/ non–verbal gest which tries to configure the reality of barbarism. Crying is an oral gesture through which the raped lady wants to verbalize her inner turmoil and physical agony, while Leela's hysteria is a strong performative gest through which she likes to ventilate her suppressed emotional pangs of ignorance. Freida's silence indicates a kind of saturation and subsequent acceptance for survival. This three gradual diminishing of resonance modulations denote the fathom of violence against women. The bizarre sounds of screaming intermittently – screams emanating from a woman in the construction site – who is raped and brutalized every night in the midst of arch lights signaling to a gender oppressive society'. (371)

Such 'performative gest(s)' as mentioned above is also found in Dina Mehta's *Getting Away With Murder*, where the audience is provided subtle suggestions for weaving a complex narrative of psycho-social structure, projecting inter-sex battle in multiple levels. The play begins with Mallika, a successful businesswoman waiting in a restaurant for Sonali, an upper middle class housewife. As Sonali arrives and they talk her pregnancy, the waiter informs that the back wheel of Mallika's car has been punctured by someone. Mallika at once understands who has done it – 'I think I know who did it – that creepy bastard I brushed off!' (Mehta 65). Along with Mallika, the audience also knows that it was the *man* who tried to be 'cozy' (55) with Mallika before Sonali's arrival. The waiter's message suggests that a 'man' would never take a 'no' for a proposal from a woman and that if he anyhow fails, he may stoop so low as to harm the woman or at least something she possesses. But even more suggestive is Mallika's mature handling of the situation which bears enough suggestions of her 'habitus' in a so-called male dominated public world. Instead of being disturbed, Malu slights the matter saying 'Come on, Sonali, I'll drop you home in a taxi, then get to office and send Raju to take care of the Maruti. Get your things while I settle the bill' (65). The act of puncturing Mallika's 'red Maruti' shows the male tendency of asserting his superiority, while, Mallika's act of cool indifference is a 'performative gest' towards the ability of empowered women in managing the 'male world'.

Dramaturgic innovations and adjustments often allow the playwright-directors to comment on contemporary events. While Dina Mehta makes strong commentary on the nexus between caste tensions, upper class greed for land and the police administration, in referring to the reluctance of the police to stop women from being abused and stoned to death, Padmanabhan also makes subtle satirical references to the administrative machineries in *Lights Out*. In the play, Leela repeatedly pleads for calling the police. She believes that the state machinery will indubitably save her from experiencing the pain and fear she is forced to undergo in being exposed to the atrocities on women near her apartment. Even, Naina feels the same. But the men, who claim to know the 'real' 'public world', discourage them to expect the police to intervene in such 'petty' matters and if at all the police comes, the complex legal process will not take into consideration women's experiences. Bhasker advises Leela to go to the doctor instead of police. Mohan says that the police won't interfere in the matters of religion considering the spectacle of woman abuse to be ritualistic. What these accounts refer to is that the state in terms of its repressive apparatuses such as the police, works in collaboration only with the oppressor in order to bring about subordination/ domination/ control of the individual body/ bodies. Hence the body may be considered a site of control. The Dulkha Devi of Tharwar, subject of one of the snaps from Gopal's collections in *Getting Away with Murder*, is 'stripped naked within the sight of the police station, her face blackened, head shaved, forced to run round the village while the men beat her with burning brands and sticks till she died' (80). Gopal adds that she was killed only because she rejected the advances of a village priest. It would only be pertinent here to refer to the fact that the legal procedures concerning rape as public agenda of protest were put forward by the women's groups in the late 1970s only when Supreme Court acquitted 'the police rapists of a young tribal girl, Mathura' (Menon, 69)

Manjula Padmanabha, however, looks into rape in much wider light. While the women in *Lights Out* are extremely anguished for the regular rapes in the colony, Bhasker, who claims to have seen women being raped 'once or twice' (Padmanabhan 6), mentions the motif of enjoyment in the process (9). ButMohan presses on the act of looking at the 'rape' taking place. Both try to establish that the 'victims want us (them) to watch' (23) (bracketing mine). They graphically describe the actions—

Bhasker: Naked. They are usually naked. ... They start off clothed and then begin to loose them.

Mohan: All of them? The assailants too?

Bhasker: Well, the assailants tear the clothes off the victims and then, perhaps in the general excitement, remove their own clothes as well. (24)

The detailed discussions of the 'ceremony' of unclothing before the act of violence, points to the male sexual arousal at the description of sexual violence on women, defined as 'gorenography' by Jane Caputi:

This equation of sex and violence is the essence of gorenography, and I will see the term here to refer to those materials that, although not sexually explicitenough to qualify as pornography (that is, not enough close–up nudity or graphic sexual acts), nonetheless are pornography ... in that they present violence, domination, torture, and murder in a context that makes these acts sexual. (210)

While the act of sexual abuse on women can produce sexual arousal in men, the same, can create fear in women. Throughout the play, Leela complains that she is afraid and Bhaskar offers her different methods to keep the fear away. Leela exemplifies the 'timid body' and therefore is always sheltered, tamed and taught. She repeatedly asks Bhaskar to call the police but never calls herself. She refers to her children and the precautions she has adopted to protect them from the cynic effects of the spectacle of rape. Hence, in playing the ideal wife and mother, Leela ceases to be the 'speaking subject', which has the potential to cause turmoil in the 'toxic' socio–patriarchal normal. She remains a woman who is not only reified by the others, but also one who has reified herself.

Raziya in *Getting Away with Murder* is to a certain extent Leela's counterpart in *Lights Out*. Raziya, as we meet her in the play, is not the 'Razzle Dazzle'(Mehta 59) she formerly used to be. She has reduced herself to such an inner 'anxiety' that she will not claim or assert her sexuality any more. She confides to Mallika that her husband, Habib, is going to marry a young girl of 19, and she is happy that by the Islamic laws, she will continue to be the 'first wife' of her husband. In an apologetic tone, she divulges Malu that she can't give a child to her husband, 'the fault lies with me (her). The fatal flaw. I'm that joke of nature – a barren woman.'(Mehta 79) (bracketing mine). She is repentant about the fact that her body defies the 'fundamental' aspect of reproduction. It is not that Raziya is unaware of the discursive constructions of the body; that the present connotations of the body have been genealogically produced via the interaction of multiple discourses, but her helplessness is, as she herself puts it, 'an ancient tyranny at work within me (her) that makes me (her) believe that a man's desire for children must be satisfied' (78) (bracketing mine).

Though Raziya capitulated before the cultural expectations of a (barren) woman, Sonali who has been subject to repeated sexual abuse from the tender age of 8, is desperate to (re)claim autonomy over her body. She has experienced throughout, that her body is a site of other's control but she asserts her body as site of resistance too. We understand that Sonali's consciousness of the body is a result of the sexual abuse she has been subject to. She was made aware that the male penis is socially more desired and hence privileged over the female uterus and breasts. Her physical features aroused sexual desire in her uncle and reduced her to *his* 'possession'. The body, looked upon as a 'given', therefore, relegated as an object shaped by the social perspectives inscribed on it. Sonali remains traumatized. She feels being watched, controlled and constantly put under surveillance. She substitutes her mother-in-law with her uncle who wanted to see her naked every time she went to bath. Mehta draws Gopal in absolute contrast to Sonali. He was never taught to share, never expected to be responsible towards the house and therefore has grown up as a freelancer, committed to no serious relationship.

For Sonali, body remains the primary source of apprehension. Hence she has remained desperate to claim authority over it. She asks Mallika to request Raziya for a legally banned test, 'aminocentesis', which no doubt is an innovation in medical science, but at the same time, an instrument lending greater access to the woman body. But Sonali's own emphasis in doing the sex-determination test is shaped by her previous experiences. She wants to be sure if the foetus is a boy or a girl. If it's a girl, she would abort her pregnancy, for, 'To be born a girl is to be subject to violence and servitude' (Mehta 63). She wants to preserve her choice of a boy child, for, she remembers as a girl, the tickles and the touches of her uncle from her childhood; the discrimination between her and her brother; the social education that her mother left her with – if the husband physically abuses the wife, the latter must 'enjoy' it. Hence, the lack of penis looms large in Sonali's anatomical and social perception of the body. But, asMallika says, '... At least Sonali is tearing herself up – injecting chaos in her world – to disrupt an order she finds oppressive' (77).

Though Mallika finds Sonali impressive over Raziya, in her assertion of choice and desire for 'emancipation' (63), she is herself 'helpless' in her relationship with Gopal. She loves him but is apprehensive of marrying because she is six years older to him. Raziya condemns her for 'assessing yourself (her) through male eyes' (73) (bracketing mine). Mallika's reluctance in moving out of the relation with Gopal and repeated forgiveness of latter's 'mistakes' of getting into sexual liaison with different girls, may be read, as Mallika's reification of her own body as a result of her social and cultural indoctrinations. But at the same time, Gopal's inability to move away from Mallika, forces us to consider Mallika in a different light too. She may be argued to epitomize the major shift in woman's position from the desirable to the *desiring*. This may also be identified as Mehta's major breakthrough in understanding the changed location of the 'emancipated' working women.

However, Mehta is also aware of the hindrances that women face in industrialist capitalist structures. That women can be strategically reduced to their bodies even in corporate business is represented through Thelma, who was subject to the sexual advances of Mr. Pinglay, Mallika's business partner. When Thelma refused to succumb to the sexual desires, she was blackmailed for some trivial phone calls. Thelma's case may be explained by Adrienne Rich's use of Catherine A. Mackinnon's idea that '"sexualization of the woman" is part of the job. Central and intrinsic to the economic realities of women's lives is the requirement that women will market sexual attractiveness to men, who tend to hold the economic power and position to enforce their prediclictions'. (641) Also worth referring is Mr. Pinglay's chauvinistic attitude towards women in business. In one instance, Mallika complains to Sonali about Pinglay's high handedness thus:

> 'Yesterday Pinglay had the gall to tell me that women should stick to secretarial work – or, at best, PR work. Knowing full well that I'm out there on the front-line, getting all the business, running the entire office.' (Mehta 61).

While Mehta intelligently puts the 'feminist' concerns along with the masculine denial of women's capacity for cerebral works in the public sphere, Padmanabhan in presenting a debate over the visualization of rape in the colony subtly subverts the masculine rhetoric with a female one. When Leela finally comes out with a conviction that the brutality outside her apartment is nothing else than rape, Bhasker and Mohan deny it vehemently. They argue that the very act of repeating the abuses every night, must refer to a certain ritualistic exorcism which must be performed daily for the 'fits' come at 'regular times, every day' (Padmanabhan 38). Naina however rejects the explanation –

> Naina: Three men, holding down one woman, with
> her legs pulled apart, while the fourth thrusts his –
> organ – into her! What would you call that – a poetry
> reading? (39)

Bhasker immediately echoes the theorists who argue for 'violence' as not sex.

> Bhasker: But the beating, then? The brutality? If all
> that they wanted was a little *sex*, why would they go
> to the trouble of so much violence? (39)

Naina retorts, 'Most forms of rape, especially gang rape, are accompanied by extreme physical violence. (39) Hence, Naina apparently brings an end to the sex/violence debate, by positing violence as complimentary to sex in rape. To this, Bhasker and Mohan add a new dimension. They argue that women, who are 'raped' daily in the colony, may be whores and if they are whores, they cannot claim to be raped because only 'decent' women can be raped. Hence they shift focus from the *bodies* of the victims to the moral standards.

Naina questions why a whore can't be raped, for rape involves the questions of *choice* and a whore can exercise her choice, when she is choosing clients.

> Bhasker: Whatever rights a woman has, they are lost
> the moment she becomes a whore.(41)

Bhasker's words subtly suggest that choice is evocative of the desiring women, who must be looked upon as deviants. They can be hysterical but they cannot claim any rights. The extremely didactic stand that men take at this point also ventilates the general masculine anxiety of losing control over women's sexuality. A whore is sexually 'liberated' and not under the aegis of any particular male. Naina questions Bhaskar about the standards that separate a whore from the 'decent'. Bhaskar replies: 'It becomes difficult once their clothes are off and they're covered in blood and filth. (42). Hence, the entire debate between decent and non-decent comes down to the body as a plain slate which frustrates the processes of rationalization and cultural/ social/ political identification. The naked body emerges as an anatomy which is potentially devoid of any cultural signification. Naina, therefore, asks-

> Naina: By losing their vulnerability to rape, whores lose their right to be women? Is that what you mean?

> Mohan: Right. After all, finally, the difference between men and women is that women are vulnerable to rape.

> Bhasker: And men are not. (43)

Hence, Mohan and Bhasker consent to the fact that a woman's body is inscribed with sexual significance in terms of male desire. What follows, then, is that the 'male body', anatomically different as it is from the female, has no significance unless and until 'desired'.

Naina pulls the debate a little further, this time, with finer web of words, and Bhasker and Mohan fall in the strategic trap they themselves have framed until now.

> Naina (getting into the litany): And women believe they are vulnerable to rape –

> Mohan: And men do not.

> Naina: And women are decent enough to be raped ...

> Mohan: And men are not. ...

> Bhasher: After all ... what is a woman but someone decent enough to be raped?

Mohan: And what is a man but someone too indecent
to be raped?

Naina: But if men are too indecent to be raped does
it mean that men are whores? (43)

Hence, Naina, contriving a language of her own, at the end of
the debate subvert the man/ woman hierarchy in terms of decency,
body and abuse.

Manjula Padmanabhan and Dina Mehta, therefore, try to build
a vocabulary through which the gender/ sex dichotomy is not
only broached in terms of body and abuse/ violence but also re-
questioned, re-interpreted and finally subverted in a way that puts
them in separation from the feminist theatre practitioners of 'home'
and the 'world'.

CHAPTER

Women, Freedom, Desire: Fida and The Swing of Desire

Considering envy as the appropriate opposite of 'egotist self love', Slavoj Zizek argues that 'The problem with human desire is ... as Lacan puts it, ... "desire of the Other" in all senses of that term: desire for the Other, desire to be desired by the Other, and especially desire for what the Other desires.' (87). To him, the last form of desire i.e. the 'desire for what the Other desires' is what initiates envy but when all the three aspects of desire are understood with respect to women and theatre, they acquire nuanced social, political and aesthetic dimensions, because desire in these contexts can at once be 'liberating' and 'incarcerating', 'subverting' and 'complying', 'experimental' and 'traditional'. Hence, the present chapter takes up *these* issues in relation to Indian women playwrights and directors and examines how their engagement with desire (personal or acquired), espouses the idea of freedom in multiple dimensions.

The claim for freedom (in the political sense of the term) through theatre in India has a history of its own, which dates back to the first production of *Nil-Darpan* in 1872, but conceived in terms of socio-sexual liberty for women, the history of modern Indian theatre does not go beyond the plays composed in the late 1970s. Some of the earlier plays like Vijay Tendulkar's *Silence! The Court is in Session* (1963) or Girish Karnad's *Hayavadana* (1971) or *Nagamandala* (1988) took up themes of women's desire but only to expose the narratives of socio-sexual frustration for women. With women playwrights and directors increasingly harping on the issues of women's 'freedom' from the 1970s onwards, both the desire to be 'free' and the freedom to 'desire' gradually found their space in Indian theatre discourse. Mamta G. Sagar's *The Swing of Desire* and Neelam Mansingh Chowdhry's *Fida* (both appear in translations in Tutun Mukherjee's *Staging Resistance Plays by Women in Translation* (2005)), the two plays I take up for critical discussion in this chapter, are unique in presenting the contradictions inherent in the relation between desire and freedom when they are couched together against the backdrop of a patriarchal society. Directed by B. Jayashree in the 1990 National Theatre Festival, 'Expression', Sagar's *The Swing of Desire* is set in an urban household, where, two different forms of desires represented by Manasa and her sister-in-law, are caught in the cross fires of gender roles. On the other hand, Neelam Mansingh Chowdhry, who began as a theatre director by producing plays like Girish Karnad's *Nagamandala* in 1990 and her own, *Yerma* (1992), explored in *Fida*, facets of female desire where strong sexual passions are fraught with sense of guilt and fear of public criticism. In both the plays, the female sense of freedom, either in its socio-cultural or in its sexual form, is looked upon as the ultimate object of desire.

Mamta G. Sagar is a creative writer who has established herself as a poet, playwright, essayist and a translator (having translated contemporary African and Francophonic poems into Kannada). Though Sagar confessed that poetry has been her 'first choice for creative expressions' (Sagar Festival Internacional), the voice of the marginalized has always remained her forte: 'Through my poems

I explore language, formulated by men, to express and signify meanings in a highly marginalized world which has always alienated women' (Sagar Festival). *The Swing of Desire* is an English translation of the Kannada play *Mayye Bhara Manave Bhara*, one of the four plays she has written. The play involves four main characters and a chorus of men aligned with the ancient Greek tradition. Manasa (the word may be literally translated from Sanskrit as 'the desire of the mind'), the wife of Pratap (the word can be moderately translated from Hindi as 'power'), appears to be struggling for an independent identity of her own, at the outset of the play. Manasa displays extreme repugnance of the fact that she has been unjustly reduced to her husband's possession, and robbed of her own desire of becoming a professional dancer.

> I married him, believing his words of love and loved him wholeheartedly too… But, in no time his love showed itself as a possessive demonic lust that completely destroyed me. How could I guess that it would turn out like this, that a corrosive lust would ruin my life? Right from the beginning he loved me like a madman. Not my talent, not my success, just my body….(Sagar 232)

Manasa's anguish clearly reveals her resistance against being denominated as an object of male desire. In love with 'just my (Manasa's) body' (232) (bracketing mine), Pratap epitomizes the typical chauvinist who tends to impose restrictions on the female body. The masculine lust in Pratap has never been devoid of the desire to control and subjugate. Pratap and Manasa's relationship delineates almost all the characteristics that Kathleen Gough finds crucial in socio-sexual inequality in the domestic sphere. She lists them as: 'men's ability to deny women sexuality or to force it upon them; to command or exploit their labor to control their produce; to control or rob them of their children; to confine them physically and prevent their movement; to use them as objects in male transactions;

to cramp their creativeness; or to withhold from them large areas of the society's knowledge and cultural attainments.' (Gough 69–70) Pratap's endeavor to domesticate Manasa and stop her from pursuing a career in dancing, appears to be an attempt to control her 'sovereign will' which Polly Young-Eisendrath considers to be 'what a woman desires above all else' (25). The very act of controlling is associated with both recognition and subjugation of the other. The 'female' is feared to be the one which has the innate potential to defy the established norms of patriarchy, and hence the desperation to be 'in charge' of the feminine desire. Conventional gender roles tend to maneuver the female desires in ways which the patriarchal motives are achieved and sustained. Women are expected to generate desires which have possibilities only within the admissible domestic space. To Manasa, loss of a career of her choice is synonymous to the loss of her 'real self':

> I am Manasa ... How do I write these unwanted lines? The very thought irks me! *Chhi*! Disgusting memories ... The age between twenty and thirty is a precious time for a woman when she is not bothered by sneaking strands of grey. Nor is there any care for the world; no haunting thoughts of death. If one wished to do something in life, one should do it then – or never. ... Such a precious times, so many priceless moments ... but for me all gone ... all lost because of a selfish man! How do I write all this? What shall I write?-Was it a mistake to have married Pratap? Was I the only one there to quench his lust? Couldn't he find anyone else?' (232).

Though Manasa's passionate tirade is subject to the conditions of her own life, it is evocative for women of the age-group of twenties in general too. Leslie C. Bell, who interviews a number of women from the age group of twenty to thirty, in her book, *Hard to Get: 20-Somethings Women and the Paradox of Sexual Freedom*, however, argues that the sexual freedom acquired through constant socio-cultural struggles, is more often wasted than guided towards fruition.

> 'new in-between period of early adulthood for twenty-somethings ... offers women a mixed bag: opportunities, to be sure, but also retrograde messages about their identities as sexual beings, partners, and future mothers. And while they have plenty of training in how to be successful and in control of their careers, young women have little help or training, apart from the self-help aisle in their local bookstore, in how to manage these freedoms, mixed messages, and their own desires to get what they want from sex and love... The absence of such useful training combined with the new freedoms and mixed messages that characterize their twenties, contribute to a paradox of sexual freedom. Young women may appear to have more choices than ever before, but the opening up of cultural notions of what is acceptable for women generates great confusion, uncertainty, and anxiety'(ch.1).

Bell's point here is that freedom is never practiced as assumed by women and in the new age of 'liberating twenties'. This, she argues, is mainly due to feminisms' failure in providing appropriate 'definitions' and 'trainings' to enjoy the 'acquired' sexual freedom. Manasa, whose twenties, she feels, has been wasted in marrying and mothering is caught in the similar wilderness as the young, working and childless women whom Leslie interviewed.

Embodying the 'feminine' in a heterosexual social framework, Manasa has failed to assert her sexual/ political freedom. What ensues, therefore, is Manasa's rebellion against the patriarchal codes of sexual domination. She alleges, that Pratap has turned her into a 'child-bearing machine, an object of your (his) wanton desires' (Sagar233):

'How dare you use me and exploit my maternal
instincts to serve your selfish motives? Whenever
I think of it, I feel like strangling each one of my
children. Chhi! ... But why should I punish them for
your sins? You are the one who must be punished.'
(233)

Manasa is therefore subject to masculine desire and control by
the traditional emotional pronouncements of motherhood. One is
inevitably led to question the social institutions of care and sacrifices
built around the idea of motherhood. Pratap, however, uses them as
patriarchal strategies to not only invade and exploit Manasa's personal
spaces, but also questions her credibility as a woman and a mother:

What is your identity, your self-respect? Your pride as
a great dancer? Without caring a damn about others?
Is that what she makes you forget the love – starved
children of yours, deafening you with the applause?
How inhuman can you be? Tell me, what kind of a
woman are you, what kind of a mother? (233)

Limiting the physical movement of women within the framework
of motherhood has a history of its own. It has been instrumental in
controlling and imposing the presumptions of femininity on women.
Enforcing moral, social, physical and domestic hindrances on women
have historically cramped their 'creativeness' and suppress their
professional desires. While the frustration of desire for a successful
profession may amount to the suppression of sovereign will, 'desire',
in itself, is generative of multi-dimensional forms and complexities.

One of the traditional approaches to desire (male/ female) has
been that it is reproductive of suffering. In the Buddhist scheme of
things, it is 'desire' which is the primary source of all misery in the
world, and, is best destroyed, if one is seeking *nirvana* (liberation).
However, branding 'Desire' as a force that produces misery, requires
considering it as alien to the physical nature of existence which tends

to embody what it desires. In another approach, desire may be looked upon as fundamental to life and existence; viz. it is the desire of having children that bring forth the offspring, and it is the un-acknowledged desire of death that actively draws one towards his end. Hence it would be an anomaly to allege desire as the root cause of misery. Rather, it may be inferred that one of the primary cause of misery is *unfulfilled* desire. *Fulfilled* desire often results in unbridled joy. This also leads to the fact that one's desire can be relative and reflective of the social, cultural, political and sexual conditions s(he) is living in. Consequently, a man who is indoctrinated in the philosophy of killing desire, may be left with one great desire of destroying desire. Hence, desire emerges as one of the unavoidable rudiments of life. Mamta G. Sagar and Neelam Mansingh Chowdhry, therefore, take up the interplay of different forms of 'desire', placed in extremely different yet similarly complex contexts of the Indian socio-political milieu.

In *Kamasutra* (Aphorisms of Love), Vatsyayan attests to the view that *kama* (desire) along with *artha* (profit or resource) and *dharma* (virtuosity) are to be performed with respect to their relative importance in life. He explains: 'Any action which conduces to the practice of Dharma, Artha and Kama together, or of any two, or even one of them, should be performed, but an action which conduces to the practice of one of them at the expense of the remaining two should not be performed' (Vatasyayana 25). Hence, desire has definitely been part of the discourse in Indian aesthetics. *Kama* is regarded as one of the four healthy goals of *purusharthas*. *Kama* is generally defined as sexual desire but the concept broadly refers to any desire/ passion/ aesthetic enjoyment of life that may or may not involve sexual connotation. Indian theatre has explored both the sexual and asexual aspects of *kama* with respect to women. One can find immediate reference in Girish Karnad's *Hayavadana* and *Nagamandala*. Though different in their contexts, both the plays deal with women's desires (*kamana*). While *Hayavadana* harps on the complex game of intellectual desire on the one and sexual desire on the other, *Nagamandala* is thematically poised on a woman's passionate longing for carnal and emotional union with her husband. Padmini in *Hayavadana* is caught in the dilemma of her own desires of possessing the combination of her husband's intellectual prowess and Kapila's (husband's friend) physical features but Rani in *Nagamandala* displays such passion for a successful conjugality with her husband that an *ichhadhari naga* (self-willed snake) is drawn towards disguising himself as the husband. Though Karnad successfully projects subtle layers of women's desires, he chooses domestic frameworks for both the plays. Tripurari Sharma, however, brought woman's desire out of the domestic space and placed it in the context of national struggle in *Azizun Nisa: A Tale from the Year 1857.* In an interview given to me at the National School of Drama, Delhi, she confided that she has conceived Azizun Nisa's character as the one for whom more than the motive for her country it was the sense of freedom that she experienced in partaking a role outside the usual confines of her life as a courtesan. Hence, multiple aspects of women's desire have gradually found its place in the post-Independence Indian theatre.

But when it comes to incestuous sexual desire, Neelam Mansingh Chowdhry's *Fida* emerges as a unique reference. In her introduction to the play that appears in *Staging Resistance: Plays by Women in Translation,* Tutun Mukherjee observes that '*Fida,* inspired by Euripedes' *Hippolytus* and Racine's *Phaedre,* contains within it echoes of the Punjabi folktale of Luna. But Neelam's *Fida* is not a wanton woman like Luna or Euripedes' Phaedra; neither is she a victim of destiny like Racine's protagonist. Trapped by her own passion, she is rather like Abbie Putnam in O' Neill's *Desire under the Elms.*' (364). Though the play is a saga of irresistible passion, branding Fida as a woman 'trapped by her passion' (364) may appear a misnomer when understood at the backdrop of the absent presence of the socio-cultural and political framework. Chowdhry projects the character of Fida not in terms of an isolated woman who is caught in her personal cocoon of lust and desire but one who is constantly apprehensive of the turns her desires for Harsan, her step-son would take. While confiding her 'terrible lust for love' (Chowdhry, 409), Fida betrays the predicament she fears for her own desires:

> When I tell you about my fate, my sins, the shameful
> story of my life, believe me, my name will be more
> besmirched than before. (408)

With Bebo acting as a constant alter ego, Fida is always in a
hiatus between her desires as the mother of her son and the desire
to be desired by Harsan. The desires as the mother of her own son
has obvious social and cultural indoctrinations associated with it.
One of the predominant images of women in the male canon has
always been that of the mother (or comforter). It is the figure of the
mother which has been traditionally raised as the epitome of sacrifice
and the custodian of her child's rights (sometimes even at the cost
of her own). However, looked from the convex side, the mother
often emerges as the willing subject of sacrifice for her children. It
is through this sanctioned patriarchal matrix of domination, women
as mothers abandon their personal desires. In scene ii of the play, it
is reported that the king was missing after the battle and that in his
absence the throne can be claimed by three – Fida's son, Harsan (the
king's son from his first wife) and Asavari (the rightful heir who was
denied her ancestral property). Fida is caught between her passionate
desires for Harsan and prescribed motherly 'duties' towards her son.
Bebo desperately tries to dissuade Fida from her apparent sexual
frustration in not being able to express her desire for Harsan. It is
only motherly duty that deters her.

> Bebo: ... Your son needs you. If you live, he may
> be the king. As an orphan, who will care for him?
> He will be a servant to your rival's son. When he
> complains to the heavens, the gods will be angry
> with you and your ancestors will curse you. Don't
> you think you have reason now to live? ...
>
> Fida: Yes, you're right. If my motherhood stops me
> from death, I shall certainly live. (411).

While the motherhood 'trap' can prove 'evasive' for women, Manasa in *The Swing of Desire,* uses it as an effective instrument of constant torment for Pratap. She turns against him the 'ancient' masculine desires of having children and controlling woman's sexuality. While Pratap initially succeeds in *enforcing* motherhood on Manasa, she uses her children as pawns in her 'sex-battle' against him. She informs Pratap that one of her children is not from him and that he will never know who that child is. Manasa, therefore, simply subverts the 'game' she was subject to. Pratap later brands Manasa's pursuit of a career in dancing as 'prostitution' and blames her for staking his family name. Such branding, however, is reflective of the masculine frustration in failing to thwart women's movement outside the domestic pitch. But Manasa refuses to be subject to such patriarchal tirades and instead forces Pratap into an endless anxiety of losing his *control* over both her and her children. Pratap feels deceived and betrayed. The play however is unique in evincing that in the 'sacred' traditions of hetero-normative marriages, branding women as prostitutes, may appear extremely vilifying, but at times, it may seem annihilating for men too.

> PRATAP: (*Angrily*) You … what you've done is called prostitution. Do you know that?
>
> …
>
> PRATAP: I am not ready to forsake my honour and that of my family by making a public exhibition of my private life.
>
> MANASA: And I am not ready to strangle my dreams!
>
> …
>
> PRATAP: Will you stop your harangue! Are these words of a loving mother?

MANASA: Oh you can be sarcastic and flaunt the motherhood tag at me!

PRATAP: Who? Who is that man? Tell me, which one of my children is that bundle of sin?

(*He clutches her hand and swings her back.*) Will you tell me or not?

MANASA: (*With anger and pain*) I won't say … I won't. Whatever you do, I won't! Who is that child, who is its father, you'll never know. I will never tell you that.

PRATAP: (*Releasing her*) Oh God! What a farce! (*Sinks down.*)

MANASA: (*After a pause*) You know, I understood your plan to keep me tied down with child-bearing when I spoke to your sister. Then, I was in a more pathetic state than you are today. (Sagar 235)

While Manasa appears unpretentious in subjecting Pratap to a psychological 'turmoil' strong enough to pull down his male ego, she recognizes herself with the age old tradition of the 'hag bitch'. It is often expected of a woman that she must disguise her desires under the cloak of 'niceties and seductions' (Young-Eisendrath 15) but Manasa rejects the 'eggshell quality of female desire'(15) and clearly makes herself heard. That she is prepared to go the extreme for her career on the one hand and be famous on the other, harbors her earnest desire to be free. She betrays the secret desire to be 'wanted', but, this is not what is traditionally associated with the desire of becoming the beautiful muse. She lulls the desire to be the crowd's favourite, needless to mention, that the crowd is predominantly 'masculine'. In Scene IV of the play, a man from the audience comments,

She is a very good dancer! And, she is so beautiful!
Like sparkling gold, like a flawless pearl! Like, she was
born to be admired! How could she have given up all
this for a husband! Really, I can't imagine. I think I
have fulfilled my life's desire by watching her dance.
(Sagar 245)

Manasa is overjoyed: 'Aah! What sweet words! These are the
words that I have craved for, while I was with Pratap'.(245) Polly
Young-Eisendrath would call her 'responsible' to her own desires
because according to her, 'Being responsible means trying again and
again in different ways to say what you want, until it can be heard
and understood.'(30) The want to be wanted by the crowd rejects
the notion of being subject to only the husband's desire. Manasa
covertly emerges as the subject of her own desires. She is the desiring
subject that resists being transformed into Pratap's 'desirable'. But, if
looked upon as a 'hag', she is expected to display 'endless, voracious,
consuming' (25) desires, reinforcing the 'misogynist belief that a
demanding woman is to be dreaded and subdued' (14).

A threat to the male dominance, therefore, a 'hag' is better
tamed. Pratap warns Manasa of getting into 'great trouble' (Sagar
236) if she doesn't tell him about the child. His strategy of generating
fear and anxiety in Manasa is resultant of his 'masculine' frustration.
Displaying a tender scene between the child and Manasa where
she is willingly made to participate in her son's demand to be told
a bed-time story, Mamta Sagar suggests the actors of the story to
dress up in the Yakshagana or Chhau style. Blending the modern
proscenium with folk theatre forms, Sagar mentions the old legend
of 'Darling girl of Muttur' in order to suggest that women desire
sovereign will over material pleasure. The king in the story offers
the Muttur girl, 'jewels', 'silk' and 'palace' (237), but she rejects
everything. Displaying his 'majestic' chauvinism, he imprisons her:
'If that is so, then you should sing only for me. You should sing only
in my palace.'(237).The Muttur girl gave up singing and again sang
only when the Lord of the Wind played the flute. 'The girl showed

the world that her song was not for the king. But that made the king angry and he left his kingdom feeling humiliated'. (238).While Sagar uses the bed-time song to compliment the thematic movement of the play, Neelam Mansingh Chowdhry uses an introductory song at the beginning in order to provide the audience a peep inside the scheme of things, and a concluding song at the end of the play in order to leave them with an insight into the repentance of a guilt ridden mind. Neelam's first song is a dramaturgic installation which suggests the continuance of trouble in Fida because of a non–extinguished 'desire'. The last song on the contrary, is a commentary on the consequences of the *same*'desire'. Neelam is unpretentious in putting forward traces of sexual desire in the very first song. She uses subtle 'elemental' images at the very outset and later profusely carries them throughout the play. Chowdhry interplays 'river', 'thorns', 'yearning' and 'season' in the song to covertly suggests the maze of desire Fida is struggling with.

Desire and the flow of river are often closely associated in the indigenous *fakiri* traditions as well. The female body, symbolically harbours three 'rivers' of desire, viz., *Ira, Pinagala, Sushumna*, geographically (and cosmically) substituted as the Ganga, Yamuna and Saraswati. The *Ira* representing the tide and *Pingala*, the ebb of desire, blends with *Sushmana*, the bodily sap (*deha-rasa*). It is the *purusa* (the masculine energy) which has the potential and can be trained to drag the *Ira* down and push *Pingala* back along with *Sushumna* in order to use desire creatively. For Fida, however, desire remains parched forever. Both the masculine capacity and the feminine tide and ebb may change with the change of 'seasons'. But Fida is subject to ceaseless frustration in the absence of any 'masculine' desire for her in Harsan. Fida's 'cup of life' (408) has run 'dry' (406) in the lack of any passionate flow of desire, referred to as 'river' throughout the play. Even in the concluding song of the play, 'river' is alluded to in the phrase, the 'damp river bed' (426) but symbolizing the 'death' of all passions and emotions. Though thematically hinged with the events in the play, the songs may also stand on their own rights. However, if Neelam's use of songs be seen as a dramatic innovation, Mamta

Sagar's use of public comments on Manasa's dance performances and her relationship with Pratap, echoes the ancient Greek technique of using anonymous 'chorus' as commentary. In the *Swing of Desire*, her chorus does not participate directly in the main action of the play but both Pratap and Manasa are hugely affected by their comments. As the chorus of common men, named merely as A, B and C, converse amongst each other, both Pratap and Manasa are shown overhearing them. Sagar makes the chorus represent multiple perspectives that reflects the socio-patriarchal framework of thought. They begin by talking about Manasa's dance but soon identify her more as a woman than an artist. She is scrutinised as a woman 'who left her husband and had an affair with another man' (Sagar 244). With his own thought resonating among the chorus, Pratap is quick to respond, 'Yes, she is the same Manasa' (244). But indoctrinated in patriarchal morality, Pratap is also not ready to accept that he has been abandoned by his wife, 'A woman should always be good and honest to have a happy family life. She didn't leave her husband, her husband left her.' (244). When the chorus talks about professional 'success', they initially support Manasa's claims: 'Who wouldn't feel frustrated if such a talent had to be sacrificed for the sake of child-bearing?' (244).They make fun of Pratap but soon turn sympathetic towards him. The age old myth that a working woman can never take care of her family and children, resounds in them. It is Manasa who is now blamed for 'failing' to be the home-maker and the mother she is expected to be. Manasa protests vehemently:

C: How many children does she have?

B: Had she time for that? Her poor husband loved children, it seems. Heard that he has started an orphanage.

MANASA: No! No! This can't true! My children! My dear little babies. Not that I had fervently wished that they be born yet they are my children, after all. My lovely little darlings…

A: Family, wife and children, how nice! (245)

Sagar is therefore careful in presenting the debate between a woman's frustration and society's attempts to deride woman's desires. Manasa's passionate response to and rejection of the socially immanent patriarchal desire to 'arrest' a woman within her family, is also a proclamation of her love for freedom and self-will. She asserts that it is the fulfillment of desire, not sacrifice which leads a woman to her liberation.

> MANASA: He wasn't like you describe him. Yes, he has left me – forever, I suppose! But he deceived me. I feel the rage of that betrayal and the suffering. But he hasn't escaped the consequences either. He is still tortured for deceiving me. Even though he declares that he left me, that one arrow I shot hasn't let him rest in peace, and never will, I know that! No matter what a man does, society is ready to support and defend him. But for a woman, the smallest mistakes become monstrous. She is insulted and thrown out of the society. She belongs nowhere, has nowhere to go, no place to live.
>
> (Manasa moves to the chair and sits down as if preparing to write)
>
> Now I am back to what I love most – my dancing. I dance to forget the bitter moments of my life. I dance because I wish to. (246)

Though dancing, as she wishes to, is 'liberating' for Manasa, Sagar displays the 'swing' of desire through a completely contrasting image of woman in Manasa's sister-in-law. Throughout the play, Pratap's sister, who is also the wife of Bhava, remains anonymous and is just referred to as the Sister. Her anonymity probably suggests her voiceless existence. That patriarchy enforces itself on heterosexual marriage and is capable of generating multiple strategies in order to execute chauvinist domination on woman is what is substantiated by the Bhava-Sister relationship. If Pratap displays patriarchy's desire to enslave women's attempts towards socio-sexual liberation, Bhava demonstrates the patriarchal annoyance at women's successful mimicking of the 'prescribed' gender roles. While Manasa is blamed of failing as a homemaker, Sagar presents the Sister as a woman who has suppressed all her desires for her family and is desperate to enjoy her husband's love. In a dialogue between Bhava and the Sister, the former clears that he is annoyed with his conjugal relation because of the Sister's extreme ignorance in worldly affairs. The Sister's desperate attempts to hinge on to her relation with Bhava are not just rejected but also held responsible for the ensuing separation between the two. To the Sister, satisfying man's sexual appetite seemed enough for a happy marriage, but Bhava is inconspicuous in confiding that man's desires are not just associated with the body but also with the brains. Hence, it is patriarchy's insatiable desire to subjugate women in every possible term. But important is to recognize the tendency towards self-annihilation to uphold her socially recognized identity in a hetero-normative conjugal relation.

> SISTER: As if it's easy to break bonds ... look, I won't ask what you do outside. But, at home, with me, can't we be happy? Look here, we shouldn't part like this.

> BHAVA: Do you think I am computer? That I'd store all those feelings you want to feed into me? (After a pause) It's not enough, you see, that a woman satisfies one in bed. She should satisfy man's intellectual needs as well. So, there's no point. How will you ... you wouldn't understand at all.

SISTER: Why not? I understand everything. I may not rise up to your intellectual standards. But, I ... I love you so much!

(*She covers her face to stop herself from crying and sinks into a chair nearby.*)

BHAVA: (*Speaking to himself*) There's such a difference between innocence and ignorance. I appreciate your innocence, but your ignorance irritates me. You have suppressed yourself so much that I can't see you as my companion at all. (239)

What can be inferred from this argument is that patriarchy desires to subordinate women in every possible way. If restricting women's movements in the public, controlling their sexuality and objectifying are some of the patriarchal strategies of subordinating women to the masculine desires, those women who orient themselves according to the patriarchal institutions, are further pushed towards male 'ignorance'. The swing in *The Swing of Desire* therefore suggests the swing of patriarchal desire from 'controlling' to 'ignoring' and 'abasing' and not merely the swing of women's desire from being 'wanting to be wanted by one' to being 'wanting to be wanted by all'.

If the 'sister' in *The Swing of Desire* represents the desire to be desirable, Neelam Mansingh Chowdhry's Fida appears to be her mirror reflection. Exploring desirability, according to Polly Young-Eisendrath, is 'to encounter a hidden underworld of female sexual shame, embarrassment, confusion, frustration, and numbness'(57). Fida's desire to be desired by her step-son is drawn in a similar light. She is confused, ashamed, embarrassed and numbed:

FIDA: ... Where do my thoughts wander? God has numbed my senses. I'm ashamed of myself... wish I could hide in the darkness... why are my sinful thoughts being revealed to the world? I can't stop my

eyes from filling with tears of pain. What shall I do?
(Chowdhry 407)

One wonders what makes Fida apprehensive. The sexual desire
to possess a man is not what stalls her routine, but it is the sense of
amorality and guilt in her desire that unmakes her. Employing Bebo
as a social mirror who has access to the inner recesses of Fida's mind,
Neelam keeps the social and moral context constantly alive for Fida.

> BEBO: ... Look here, have you any right to forsake
> the life that is a gift of God? You're also betraying
> your children and him who married you. When your
> children lose their mother, they too will wander in
> the shadow of death. And what will happen to your
> son's dream of wearing the crown one day. The crown
> will surely go to the older queen's heir, the warrior
> queen's son Harsan. (407)

Bebo is quick to recognize that Fida's vulnerability goes against
the traditional 'grain' of women and therefore reminds her of her
role as a mother. She is 'expected' to control her sexual desires.
Polly Young-Eisendrath argues that 'The nineteenth and twentieth
century sexual ideology claimed that women were better equipped
than men to bring their sexual impulses and desires under control
because women are natural caregivers in being mothers'(62). But
Fida's desire has an element of uncontrollability in it which makes her
susceptible to the socio-patriarchal forces of containment. Young-
Eisendrath observes, 'By the middle and end of the nineteenth
century, doctors and scientists widely counseled that rampant sexual
desire in a woman could lead her to hysteria, criminal acts, and
violence' (62).Throughout the play, Fida exemplifies the observation.
Fida is a desiring woman, whose desire to be loved must be satiated.
In an extremely passionate conversation, she reveals that her first
encounter with Harsan reduced her to her 'elements'. In her attempts
to suppress her sexual desires for Harsan, she gets him banished. She

gains momentary freedom from her desires in her husband's love but is again 'enslaved' when Harsan returns and the King goes out for war. She realizes that there is no escape from this passion for it is strong enough to be tamed by the moral social commandments. But Fida's anguish lies less in her desires than in the sense of guilt her desires have produced. Quoting Fida at length gives access to the complex nuances of her mind expressed through Neelam Mansingh Chowdhry's use of typical organic symbols.

> Listen now to my only request: don't advise or scold –
> There's no point in correcting one close to death.
> Don't waste your breath to put out the fire that rages
> in my breast.
> There is no sense in guiding the wind and the water
> The fire will burn itself out –
> The trembling wind will fall –
> The rising water will calm –
> Let me take the course that I must. (410)

Chowdhry's use of 'water', 'fire' and 'wind' images suggest the irresistibility of Fida's passions but the saturating sense of guilt and incest advocates that she is not free from the moral educations that shape a woman's desire in society. A psychosexual appraisal of Fida's guilt and shame would reveal that she is caught in the tension between the impulses of her body and a socially indoctrinated mind. Her overwhelming desire to possess Harsan refuses being tamed by the principles of 'ideal' Indian wife but at the same time, the absence of Fida's husband does not free her from the socio-cultural aphorisms. She nonetheless fails to display the 'customary' behaviours of a wife whose husband is absent from the household as they are mentioned in Vatsyayan's *Kamasutra*. The 1st Chapter of the 4th *khand* (part) of *Kamasutra* is 'On the Manner of Living of a Virtuous Woman, And of Her Behaviour during the Absence of Her Husband'. The virtuous woman for Vatsyayana is the one 'who has affection for her husband, should act in conformity with his wishes as if were a divine being, and with his consent should take upon herself the whole care of his family'(128). An elaborate list of do's and don'ts for the virtuous woman follow that touch almost every aspect of domestic life. Speaking on behaviour of the virtuous during her husband's absence from the house, Vatsyayna sermonizes,

> She should wear only her auspicious ornaments, and observe the fasts in honour of the Gods. While anxious to hear the news of her husband, she should still look after her household affairs. ... She should look after and keep in repair the things that are liked by her husband, and continue the works that have been begun by him.... The fasts and feasts should be observed with the consent of the elders of the house. The resources should be increased by making purchases and sales according to the practice of the merchants and by means of honest servants, superintended by herself. The income should be increased and expenditure diminished as much possible. And when her husband returns from his journey, she should receive him at first in her ordinary clothes, so that he may know in what way she has lived during his absence, and should bring to him some presents, as also materials for the worship of the Deity. ... The wife, whether she be a woman of noble family, or a virgin widow remarried, or a concubine, should lead a chaste life, devoted to her husband, and doing everything for his welfare. Women acting thus acquire Dharma, Artha and Kama, obtain a high position, and generally keep their husbands devoted to them. (132 – 133).

Throughout the play, Fida shows overwhelming desire berating her from playing the ideal house wife. She fails to manage both her household as well as the kingdom. The public supports Harsan's claim to the throne and Harsan himself is ready to give major sections of the kingdom to Asavari and the son of Fida. Neelam constructs the drama as a triangle of desire, where both Fida and Asavari 'loves' and desires Harsan. Both feel that their desires remain un-satiated due to Harsan's ignorance. Both of them wish to emerge as the 'beautiful muse' for him. In wanting to be wanted, both wish to be the object of Harsan's desire. But the 'beautiful muse' has problems of her own. It always runs the risk of either being made subject to socio-patriarchal standards of morality or being frustrated by the masculine ignorance.

> Fida: I'm mad, yes, but didn't know what lay in fate
> Harsan, don't think that I call myself guiltless
> I'm aware of my sorrow and sinfulness –
> My shame, my guilt and my repentance.
> I'm like fire, burning all – myself almost of all.
> (Chowdhry 416)

Unrequited in her desire for Harsan, Fida is caught between 'shame', 'guilt', and 'repentance' because of her secret desire to be the ideal woman/ wife/ mother. She longs for freedom from the social indoctrinations but she is compelled by her role as a mother and a queen. Hence it is the double bind of desires that shoves her to 'hysteria, criminal acts, and violence' (Young-Eisendrath 62). In the presence of the king, she drives Harsan into banishment, subjects him to physical torture and throws him into prison. But in the absence of her husband, who represents the physical embodiment of socio-cultural manacles for Fida, her sexual desires for Harsan surfaces and she is driven into submitting them before her passions. Though rejected, Fida continues fanning her desires for Harsan and tries different methods to win his consent. When Bebo informs that Harsan is a misogynist, Fida assumes the general masculine hunger for wealth and power as his vulnerabilities. She asks Bebo to lure Harsan with the gifts of 'golden crown' and her own share of the kingdom in return of his love. However, when her husband returns, Fida is quick to blame Harsan, who is later killed on the charge of fostering incestuous desire for his step mother. Unlike Fida, Asavari is non-manipulative and unpretentious in her desire for Harsan. Harsan too reciprocates his love for Asavari. But pertinent is to see that, unlike Mamta G. Sagar who portrays extremely different contexts with respect to Manasa and her sister-in-law in *The Swing of Desire,* Neelam Mansingh Chowdhry draws Asavari's character with the same brush as that of Fida but achieves the expected difference in their own swings of desires. Asavari, like Fida, is willing to sacrifice any political or material benefits in order to be the subject of Harsan's desires. When Asavari learns from Asma that Harsan seemed enamoured by her beauty, she unpretentiously ventilates the joy of her 'requited' desire:

> ASAVARI: Oh tell me again, my friend, tell me all.
> That he'll come to me smiling, I cannot believe
> That he will year for me, I cannot hope
> No hope but my desire seeks that my hard – hearted
> lover
> shall meet. (412)

After being anointed heir to the king's throne, Harsan confides, he has been 'bewitched' by Asavari's beauty which makes the latter feel melodramatically liberated from the torment she has been subjected to. Harsan's gift of political rights to Asavari is accepted by her but at the same time she reveals that it is not the power over the land that she desires but his love.

> ASAVARI: … O Prince, I accept gratefully all your
> gifts. The Kingdom you want to give me may be
> great but it isn't the object I desire. It is something
> nearer to me that I seek…!(414)

In playing the 'beautiful muse' Asavari's desire to be wanted by Harsan is neither burdened with the psycho-social notions of incest nor is she propelled towards 'criminal acts', even though, the political hindrance in being from the 'enemy' camp still remains. Blending the 'naqqal' traditions of Punjab with the trained modern actors in her productions of the play, Neelam acquires a subtle distance between the actor and the character. The dramaturgic shift in the costume, gesture, speech and disposition from Fida to Asavari also shifts the audience's response towards the two otherwise similar characters. Both wish to be the 'beautiful muse', but, the 'excess' that features Fida both in her temperament and in her desires, forces the traditional belief that 'female power is unhealthy and overwhelming – a kind of soul sucking danger that needs to be warded off by women and men alike. So we can consciously support the male fantasy that the only legitimate power to be encouraged in girls and women, is, to be the Object of Desire.'(Young-Eisendrath 19). Hence, in desiring the excess (incestuous), Fida swings from the 'beautiful muse' to the 'hag bitch', while Asavari who is not 'too demanding, pushy, bossy... rush away from the hag-bitch... move towards the muse and her false power as the object of Desire. Although she appears to promise that female power is beauty, she denies a woman (herself) the right to her own sovereignty' (19) (bracketing mine).

Both *The Swing of Desire* and *Fida*, therefore, exemplify, that the desire to be 'worshipped' as 'beautiful muse' only produces a false notion of power and freedom. Playing the 'hag bitch' may suffer the same predicament as well. But being identified as 'desiring' in place of the 'desirable', increases the potential towards liberation from the masculine 'fantasy' of control and possession. Manasa's efforts in liberating herself from the emotional and economic dependence through her dance, not merely, frustrate the masculine 'fantasy' but also subvert the hetero-normative game of desire. Hence freedom as the sovereign will and women's exclusive desires are in constant interplay with socio-cultural contexts when the Indian women playwrights and directors are considered.

CONCLUSION

The last four decades in Indian theatre correspond with the period generally considered to be the most productive for women theatre practitioners. This is the period when women's voices finally came out of the 'closet' and explored different forms of theatre to find suitable expressions. Women playwrights and directors engaged with women's issues both thematically and dramaturgically. The early 1970s plays dealing exclusively with gender injustices were initially branded as feminist plays, but, from the late 1970s and the early 1980s, Indian theatre proliferated into multiple forms in order to accommodate the multitude of women's voices in theatre which was until then forced to remain content either with following the prevailing male-dominated theatre structures or imitating the 'Western' feminist theatre.

Having its inception in the socio-political activism in the 1970s and the contemporary experimentalist theatre, the 'feminist theatre' catered only to recognizing and exposing gender discrimination and subordination of women. But, it was never enough to mainstream the women's issues and destabilize the male gaze in exposing the social mechanisms that stereotype women and their roles both in the domestic and public spheres. Hence, the Indian women theatre practitioners sought to enhance the scope of theatre in India in order to produce a more inclusive dramaturgy that can accommodate not only the traditional approach to male-female relationship in the Indian context but also represent the ever-changing nature of the gender dynamics with respect to the change in socio-political, cultural, communal, religious and economic structures. Thematically, they widened the scope of writing plays in order to comprehend the issues of women living in the fringes as well as in the 'centre'; voice the regional concerns as well as the national; contextualize women's experiences instead of essentially valorizing the female. Hence, a host of plays were written on issues which ranged from domestic, public, ethnic, religious and political violence on women to challenging the stereotypical representations of women as either victims, comforters or seducers, from restructuring the position of women amidst the nationalist narratives, exposing the politics of class-caste matrix to engaging with women's economic, social and sexual freedom in a consumerist society, which though largely continues to be reserved for the masculine desires, is increasingly providing space for women's desires. But in producing such diverse plays the Indian women playwrights and directors have been often criticized for lacking any 'rudimentary ideology'.Kinnari Vohra argues in this regard:

> To start with, the plays … do not always provide a feminine aesthetic and sensibility. It is true that some of these plays … take up women's issues and their concerns in a relevant manner, but they are few and far between. But above all, what one detects is the absence of a rudimentary ideology. For women's theatre to proliferate, one will have to consciously contribute to a genre, which will have its own basic, underlying principles. (Vohra)

But, lack of any homogenous ideological position liberates Indian women theatre practitioners from any dogmatic approach. Free from committing to any rigid ideology, they could preserve their unique approaches with respect to the changing structures of society and politics. Though initially associated with either the Gandhian socialists or the Left, they remained largely at a distance from the mainstream political parties and sought to produce 'uncorrupt' criticism of the body of Indian socio-political culture. But in the early 1970s, any woman writer dealing with woman-centric themes would be easily categorized a feminist. In that case, either the mainstream national/ regional political parties tried to usurp the feminist voices or they were ignored as 'wishy-washy' feminists. B. Jayashree, Poile Sengupta, Gitanjali Shree, Irpinder Bhatia (Hindi), Neelam Mansingh Chaudhury (Punjabi), Binodini, Shanoli Mitra, Usha Ganguli, Sushma Deshpande, and Qudsia Zadie are some of the female playwrights who started their career as playwrights and directors during this period. Though most of the playwrights avoided 'radical' feminist approaches, a large number of plays were composed questioning the basic social structures. In their love of representing 'reality', they often espoused strong criticism of the conventional theatre structures and pilloried men in general. But such plays did not go unquestioned and hence attracted adverse reception too. Kinnari Vohra speaks of *Saavar Re*, a play by Mohan Agashe and Swati Chitnis, which was a revolt against the onslaught of some feminist plays in India. The play states quite clearly that the breach of trust between men and women in the Indian family structure is the product of unproblematic toeing of 'essential' feminist propositions such as Kate Millett's pronouncement against the continuance of the family system-'family must go' (Vohra 25). Vohra informs that *Saavar Re* exemplifies the anti-feminist stand in Indian theatre which considered the imitation of radical 'Western' feminist proposals as adversely harming the women in India instead of men.

The Indian Women playwrights and directors therefore gradually produced a theatre of their own which was free from following both the 'Western'feminist and the traditional Indian conventions of play-writing and theatre production. But simple rejection of the conventions did not imply the production of women's theatre, for 'even conventional forms can be used to depict the entrapment of women within social institutions'. (Mukherjee 17). The women playwrights and directors in India, instead, premised their plays on projecting women as 'conscious' and responsible subjects around whom the performances evolved. They explored variety of forms in order to accommodate the range of issues that the diverse social milieu threw up. As much as they represented the variety of Indian contexts, the forms of theatre production for women, the settings and the subjects, were decided by the 'agony, anger, and suspicion about *patriarchy*' (Kamble 33) (italics mine)identifying it and separating it from the 'male' as a set of ideologies that sought to promote gendered injustices.

For any playwright, according to Kamble, priority is that the plays should be comprehensible to the target audience and the performance should be participatory. Rather than offering entertainment for the audience and aesthetic appreciation for the readers and critics, they (playwrights) intend to educate, instruct, and inform' (33) (bracketing mine). While educating, instructing and informing through theatre have been traditionally realized through 'realistic' approaches to social events, they have also been criticized on the ground that too much of realism sometimes naturalizes 'the status quo of the patriarchal system and covertly positions the reader/ spectator within that ideology.' (Mukherjee 18) The purpose of women-centred theatre, instead of producing therapeutic effects on the audience, is to 'dislodge' their equipoise and make them recognize the contexts which either stereotype women or motivate them to revolt against the status-quo. But the history of post-independence Indian theatre reveals that it has always grappled with the questions of stage/ audience, text/ performance relationships. The stage was less looked upon as a separate platform held tightly with planks on either side but a place amidst an actively participating audience rather than an assembly of passive onlookers. Indian playwrights and directors like Ebrahim Alkazi (*Insaf ka ghera*, 1972), Rudraprasad Sengupta (*Kharirgondi,*1978), Habib Tanvir (*Sajapurki Shantibai,* 1982), and few others have drawn from Bertolt Brecht the techniques of engaging with the audience and presenting before them an alternative understanding of time and history through non-linear narratives and anti-realist staging in order to produce a rational rather than emotional effect. But the Indian women playwright-directors chose to espouse a dramaturgy that is interstitially located between 'realism and Brechtian non-realism'

(18). For example, C. S. Lakshmi's *Crossing the River* (2000), originally composed in Tamil is structured as a forum to equate a woman's voice from the stage with that of the voices of women in the audience. The play unfolds with only one character, Sita (from the epic Ramayana), and puts forward alternatives to the traditional representation of Sita as the epitome of silence. In this play, Sita embarks on a search for an authentic existence so that she can reframe her identity. Instead of building a conventional character, Lakshmi therefore chooses to 'trouble' the audience by making Sita assume multiple identities. She critiques the traditional one dimensional portraits of Sita as the victim of a patriarchal social structure. If considered as an exponent of Augusto Baul's 'forum theatre', the play must articulate the voice of the audience, but it refrains from following any set pattern of dramatic conventions. Lakshmi allows the content of her play to dictate the form. Neither realist nor absolutely non-realist, in its structure, the play foregrounds a multitude of questions which Sita answers with disgust, despair, wrath and conviction.

> Which Sita?
> Which Sita are you?
> Are you Kamban'sSita?
> Valmiki's Sita?
> Or
> Sita of Tulsidas?
> Are you the Maya Sita
> created
> to bear
> the pain and sorrow for the real Sita?
> Or
> are you the Sita of
> people's tales?
> A different Sita, are you?
> What difference does it make?
> Which Sita I am
> Which is the real Sita

and which
the false?
All are real and all false.
I am Sita
made up with words
bound in words
imprisoned in words.
I am Sita
made up with words
bound in words
imprisoned in words.
I am Sita
that authority creates.
I am Sita
that authority creates.
I am Sita brought up
with words,
Be this way
Stand this way
Sit this way
Lie this way
Think this way.
…
I am Sita of a kind,
Sita with many faces
living through
many times
many spaces.
I am
Another Sita
Another Sita.
…
I am a woman
I am a man
I am an object

I am the thing
ferreted out by rulers.
I am Ravan
if Rama so wishes:
...
I am you
all of you,
all of you asking questions.
I am the body of your questions.
There is strength
left still.
I shall cross the river
I shall cross the river
To see the new world
To assume a new form
to create a new Rajya.(Mukherjee 434 – 439)

Composed in verses, the play therefore aims at confronting the audience's state of mental equipoise. It also hints at a new project at the end. What Sita displays in the play is her disenchantment with the 'Ram Rajya'. She is led to explore not merely the *reality behind the illusion* of Ram Rajya but also to seek the *reality in illusion* in her search for a 'new world', 'new form' and a 'new Rajya' (439).

That the element of illusion or at least fantasy is always present in 'reality' in order to sustain its 'charms' and motivate the desired effect, has never been ignored by the Indian Women playwrights and directors in the last two decades. In *A Tale from the Year 1857: Azizun Nisa*, Tripurari Sharma recognizes the aspect of inherent fantasy in the idea of 'nationalism' which creates the ground for a distorted or at least a twisted texture of reality. Hence, it may be said to suggest a classic case of seeking *reality behind the illusion* as well as *illusion in the reality*. Azizun is indoctrinated in the idea of militant nationalism administered by the rebel soldier, Shamsuddin. Azizun is warned by her fellow courtesans not to involve herself in the rebellion and continue her pursuit of art. But she had already surrendered herself to the desire of participating in the rebellion which was touted as the nationalistic struggle. The desire to participate in the nationalistic struggle and prove herself as a rebel in the national cause leads her to a hysteric slaughtering of British women and children. This is how desire inscribes itself in the perception of reality – by distorting it (Zizek). The otherwise objective nationalism is transformed into an absolutely subjective phenomenon. Tripurari Sharma never justifies Azizun's choice of the bloody massacre of innocent British women and children. The indiscreet bloodshed is rather shown as the result of frustration in the unsuccessful armed rebellion of her fellow nationalists. Hence, the play displays Azizun's lack of objective perception into the ideals of nationalism and nationalistic struggles. She suspends the basic tenets of humanity and compassion before the 'desire' to be lost in the illusion intrinsic to the 'reality' of failure.

If desire distorts reality, Mamta G. Sagar in her *The Swing of Desire* identifies the recognition of reality to be inherently conditioned. Pratap's anonymous sister is caught in the patriarchal illusion that playing the docile submissive wife in conjugal relationship would assure her the status of 'muse' before the husband. The obvious intonation is towards the traditional masculine desire of control over women. But desire may have the element of insatiability in it and may produce complex ramifications soon after some initial fulfillments. Hence, the woman is expected to be conditioned according to the changing wishes of her husband. The play therefore suggests that the failure of marriage for the Sister is in misrecognising the nature of inscriptions of patriarchal desire on the institution of marriage. The Sister may have enjoyed libidinal pleasure while living in the illusion of marriage, but in failing to offer intellectual camaraderie to her husband, she is painfully driven to confront the reality of her husband's desire which now wishes for an intellectual partner in his wife than a woman who has reduced herself to his sexual desires. As an audience, looking at a play being unfolded on the stage may be subjected to similar forms of deceit but there always remains a certain amount of detachment. Unfortunately, the detachment has evaporated for the Sister, making her a slave to the illusion of 'happy' conjugality. The play, however, blames the Sister for the willing surrender of her ego before the husband's desire and instead of sympathizing with her, subjects her to further torture by making her the 'object' of ignorance for her husband. Courage to remain detached would have provided her the space to recognize the 'reality' inherent in the illusion of marriage, as it does to Manasa. The latter sees through the 'illusion' of her married life with Pratap and finally leaves him in order to build a career of her own. In fact, it is the realization of the 'reality' of self-abnegation in the marriage to Pratap that initiates Manasa's desire for the pursuit of her career.

One may consider Manasa's waking up to 'reality' as disenchantment with the traditional institution of marriage. But mere disenchantment is not enough. It must lead to a more appropriate cognitive reaction as well. Kusum Kumar has engaged with the representation of 'reality' in a more complex way in *Listen Shefali*. In the play, Shefali is portrayed as a woman who would never compromise with socio-cultural injustices. She had not only rejected all the 'benefits' endowed to her for being a woman from the lower caste, but also, moved out of her relationship with Bakul, the son of a politician in realizing that she was being used as a political tool for garnering minority votes. Throughout the course of the play Shefali emerges as a rebel against the political system which sustains caste discrimination through government sanctions and produces the illusion of social upliftment. Shefali, who is intelligent and educated enough to see through the 'political illusion', champions the cause of the lower caste women butdoes not represent them. Political trickery has the capacity of producing an overwhelming 'false consciousness' on the immediate everyday reality. To Shefali's mother, a marriage with Bakul would lend her family the opportunity to liberate themselves from poverty. Failing to convince Shefali, she marries her sister to Bakul. Shefali fails to 'demonstrate' the reality behind Bakul's marriage to her sister and reacts to her marriage with a stoic acceptance. Hence, Kusum Kumar recognizes and projects the subtle tension between the multiple forms of realities underlying the apparent dislodging of the 'illusion' of patriarchal and socio-political institutions. Shafali's failure to react in a cognitive way may seem incongruous with her nature, but Kumar intentionally ends the play at this moment, in order to sustain the tension between absolute frustration and stoic acceptance. This is typical to Indian women playwrights and directors for they are more concerned with sustaining the process of reaction than enforcing a therapeutic completeness.

In engaging with forms of reality, the Indian women playwrights have also provided serious space for subjective psychological articulations. Dina Mehta in *Getting Away with Murder* has portrayed Sonali as a troubled survivor of child sexual abuse, struggling to draw boundaries between actual perpetrators of violence and her caregivers. She has been subject to private surveillance of her uncle in her childhood and she continues to feel being 'looked at' by her mother-in-law, unknown to the fact that the latter has been employed by her husband only to prevent her from harming herself. For Sonali, her brother, Gopal escaped the child sexual abuses only because he was a boy and not a girl. She is desperate to regain control over her body and go through the pregnancy process only if a boy child is detected in her womb. Sonali's friend Razia is a doctor but caught in the expectations of an orthodox family, she has accepted the fact that the desire for child in a man must be satiated. Hence, the play articulates through Sonali and Razia the narratives of a male dominated society where women as victims of sexual abuse or patriarchal orthodoxy either continue living in psychosexual trauma or reduce themselves to passive recipients of social injustice. But in the course of the play, Dina Mehta seeks to redefine the traditional perceptions on patriarchy. While Sonali's uncle and Razia's husband are portrayed as male orthodox chauvinists, Sonali's husband on the other hand represents the man who is prepared not only to accept Sonali's decisions in child bearing but also to provide his wife the comfort and time to recover from the psychosexual trauma of her childhood. Gopal is presented as a man who champions the cause of the marginalized, especially the woman. Hence, instead of considering men as synonymous to patriarchy, Mehta argues that patriarchy is a set of ideas which is either endorsed or rejected, depending upon the process in which the individuals are indoctrinated.

Poile Sengupta drags Mehta's arguments further. Composed in 1994, her *Inner Laws* deals with the interpersonal relationships of women in a joint family system and instead of demonizing the male, critiques the social institutions of marriage and joint-family for women's experiences of domestic hostility. She identifies the traditional antagonism between the mother-in-law and the daughter-in-law as a forced relationship between two almost strangers expected to share the same home, kitchen etc. Sengupta opines, 'What makes the hostility even more serious is my belief that many women actually prepare themselves for the antagonism, much before the marriage is arranged. And this has to be seen in the larger context of marriage negotiations and the ubiquitous dowry system' (Sengupta 71). Using a woman-only cast of ten women representing ten different viewpoints, the play critically brings together contradictions not to destroy any but to put them in various contexts. Honest revisiting of the male-female relationship therefore has been a common feature in Indian women's theatre. This has provided the women playwrights and directors greater access to women's actual conditions of life and existence and helped them articulate the continuously changing dimensions of femininity and masculinity.

However, the need to put forward the female issue by reclaiming the spaces women have been traditionally denied, has remained the primary focus for the Indian women theatre practitioners. Plays were written and staged on the life, works and role of women who were notable yet denied historical importance. Plays on Binodini Dasi, one of the most talked about women theatre personalities in the early 20th century Bengal, Akka Madhavi, Meera Bai and Manimekalai (known for their contributions to the spiritual history of the country) and others who have participated in their own capacities to the fields of literature, science, politics, music etc., have contributed to the production of a new scape in the Indian Women's theatre canon. Amal Allana's *Nati Binodini*, Tripurari Sharma's *Azizun Nisa: A Tale form the Year 1857*and C.S. Mangai and V. Geetha's *Kaala Kanavu*, can be cited as examples here. Apart from digging deep into the Indian history for retrieving women's spaces and participating in consciousness raising drives, the Indian women's theatre has provided space for women working as sex-workers as well. Groups like Komal Gandhar, Sanlaap, Jabala, Veshya Anyay Mukti Parishad, etc. have been operating in different parts of the country and composing and producing plays on the daily lives, hopes, aspirations, frustrations and discriminations faced not only by the women sex-workers but also by their children. Plays like *My Mother, The Gharwali, Her Maalak, His Wife* (2006) and *I am that Woman* (2007) are notable for their accurate representations of the plight of women sex-workers.

Diverse in their range, the plays by Indian women playwrights therefore created enough scope for dramaturgic innovations. While theatre production has always been a collaborative affair, composing plays or rather developing the play script in collaboration has become commonplace for Indian women's theatre. Plays like *Umrao* (1993) and *Navlakha* (2001) have been developed, directed and presented on stage by Anuradha Kapur in collaboration with Vidya Rao, Geetanjali Shree and Nilima Sheikh. Often these plays have been criticized for not providing a clear 'convergence into' the climax (Subramanyam 212). But as Anuradha Kapur argues, narrative closure is a regular feature in the 'masculine way of telling the story, which has an ending.'(212). For the Indian women's theatre on the other hand, it is important to disengage with the masculine structures of narrative. Hence, a play like *Umrao* neither seeks to produce any well-built character nor does it aim at a convergent climax. It may rather look like a collage with uneven boundaries than a well-knit finished product. The last scene of *Umrao* may be specially mentioned here, for it provides an alternative mis-en-scene. Nilima Sheikh, a painter by profession, who has also designed several theatre productions has designed the framework of this scene:

> She painted eight scenes on wheels which had no particular locale, had nothing to do with a specific period, and in the end, these scenes

formed a configuration. Each one of them had a golden background, and depicted quotations from miniatures, a tree, kites, the edge of a cloud and other figuratives. These scenes would be moved on to the stage according to the lines of the play. At the end, the screens made a backdrop with Umrao lying down with her feet towards the audience, and the other characters standing around her like set pieces or memory images. Before Umrao lies down, the screens turn around and shed a golden light on her to provide an iconic element to the scene. As Umrao slowly turns around, one wanted to show her not only as growing old but also as moving beyond it, as one who has a beginning and an end, so that as one phase has finished another has started.(214)

Such elaborate stage designs which 'metaphorically' supplemented the actions of the play have become a regular feature in the Indian women's theatre. Neelam Mansingh Chowdhry may be specially mentioned here. Her productions are particularly marked with well thought out designs complemented by the use of delicate detailing in costumes, props, lights and 'make ups'. While in *Fida* (1996), there is a comprehensive use of daily rituals of worship, water and sand grains, in *Yerma* (1992),Yerma's joy, sexuality and passionate desire is embodied in the animated use of water which she splashes on herself. In *Kitchen Katha* she uses vegetables and food in order to access the human emotions. Chowdhry's productions are not merely unique for her use of props and designs but also female impersonators known as the Naqqals. The latter is a group of actors who performed the roles of women on stage. The constant shuffle between "doing' a woman on stage and being a 'man' in real life' (Mangai 124) have lend theatre with new problematics for the 'on and off stage selves do continually inform each other' (125). Veenapani Chawla too experimented with the traditional forms of theatre, dance and marshal art and combined them in her productions. She has presented

Vinay Kumar in the role of a woman, Brahhanala, for her production of *Brahhanala*, an episode from the Mahabharata. Kumar moves in and out of his characters of Brahhanala, the disguised dancer and Arjuna, the warrior and destabilizes the conventions of representing masculinity and femininity on stage (120).Anuradha Kapur's *Sundari: An Actor Prepares* further explores the nuances of performance both as man/ woman and woman/man. The slipping into the role of a woman on stage; the psychological and physical preparation for it and then reverting back to the gendered role of man in actual life, with a backdrop of a failed family life of the actor-director, Jaishankar Sundari, is a classic case for what Anarudha Kapur claims to be the concern of women directors in order to 'make visible this (the) process of showing ... how men and women are made' (bracketing mine) (Kapur 10).

While the use of female impersonators has enhanced the scope for complex representation in Indian women's theatre, engagement with folk forms and folk artists has further complimented it by going beyond mere synthesizing cultural legacy with new forms of theatre. Tripurari Sharma's collaboration with the Nautanki artists for her plays in Alarippu workshops and performances, not only provided Sharma deeper access to the lower rungs of the society but also addressed the gendered structures of the form itself. 'Nautanki women found the proscenium separation of actors and audience as granting them protection and dignity as artists and women which is a significant departure from viewing the art form as merely a colonial legacy' (Mangai 249). A. Mangai too have engaged with the traditional Therukkoothu form and drawn from them the techniques of impersonation, designs, costumes and make-ups for her play *Pani Thee*. Such use of indigenous forms of theatre and theatre workers may have been a regular feature for the Indian theatre practitioners but there has never been any attempt towards identifying them with the 'theatre of roots'. Indian women playwrights and directors have engaged with the folk forms and sought to evolve a dramaturgy that accommodates their own idiom.

While engaging with diverse forms of indigenous performance traditions has been a feature of Indian women's theatre, it has also increasingly problematised the importance of dramatic texts for theatre productions. I have discussed at length in the introduction of this book, about the evolution of play-texts from being written by an individual playwright to being adapted from novels or epics, from being assembled from multiple sources to being devised in collaboration with other playwrights, playwright-directors, novelists, lyricists, music composers etc., from piecing together interviews to being 'organically' grown in workshops. But the traditional method of translating play-texts into performances on stage is gradually receding and making way for autonomy of performances with little or no scripts. Instead of remaining true to the scripts, these performances seek to prioritize engagement with the audience. Propensity towards emancipating 'performance' from the dictatorship of dramatic texts, has initiated contemporary theatre practitioners like Maya Krishna Rao to perform on stage with minimal or no text to rely upon. Performing without the guidance of text and sometimes with minimum or no rehearsal, lends the actor the freedom to go beyond the conventions of theatre *making*, for, according to Rao, 'making' inherently involves the element of entering a 'precentered box'(Rao). Rejecting 'precentered box' for the sake of liberating performance from the authority of play-texts, has led towards the production of postdramatic theatre, a term introduced by Hans-Theis Lehmann in his book *Postdramatic Theatre* (1999).The *postdramatic* is associated with those *avant-garde* traits that seek to reject the conventions of dramatic theatre and evolve a performance aesthetic, unique in its own right. According to Deepa Punjani, 'postdramatic' in the context of Indian theatre may be seen as a term that provides 'historical insight into the multiplicity and diversity of Indian theatre traditions that defy mere conventional definitions of drama'. Punjani is also of the view that 'postdramatic' as an idea can be helpful in understanding 'the differentia as well as folk, classical, street, agitprop, immersive, site-specific, the praxis between art-installation and theatre, video art and theatre, theatre and contemporary dance, theatre of scenography and technologies – all of which are present in the Indian landscape' (Punjani). Maya Krishna Rao's *Loose Woman* and Neelam Mansingh Chowdhry's *Nachiketa* and *Naked Voices* may be considered as some of the examples. What is explicit in this evolution from script based productions to performance based productions is that there is a certain shift in the vocabulary. Chowdhry's opinion on her directorial style after a recent production of *Nachiketa* in London may be reiterated here: 'I don't do homework or follow any school. For me, the play emerges when actors' bodies move in spaces. I improvise and give meaning to the air in those spaces. Everything has to be instant' (Deepak). But such a shift in vocabulary of theatre production is not to vouch for the death of play-texts. Rather, it must be seen as one of the episodesin the evolution of theatre production, for, a quality play-text always retains the capacity to initiate and drive the action on stage. For an actor, words on the play-text, which almost always have a web of contexts associated with them, can still produce an impulse that conditions his performance on stage. But, at the same time, the trained actor has the ability and opportunity to not only improvise but also enhance the meaning of the words through his performance. The action, gestures, movements, pauses, modulation of breath, the *abhinay* only go on to add layers of meaning to the play-text. Hence, in the context of contemporary theatre production, play-text is no more the end but one among the many means of producing the theatre-viewing experience. The meaning of the play may change for the director and further change for the actor while performing. Hence, the play-text is reduced to a part of the collective that produces the 'theatre'for audience. Anuradha Kapur, while delivering her lecture on 'Is the playwright dead? The continued relevance of playwrights in today's multimedia world' in the Hindu Lit for Life 2014, rightly sums up the process of theatre making as follows:

> The writer, the word, the image is germane to theatre
> makingin the same way as the actor, the director, the
> mis-en-scene, the scenography is germane. Different

moments in history, different protocols of play-making stress different configurations. Sometimes, the story may drive the text and sometimes the mi-en-scene and sometimes the actor and hopefully altogether may drive what you experience. (Kapur et al.)

As the Indian women's theatre continues to evolve in its own right, inferences may be drawn referring to the seminars and the workshops that have been and are being often organized since the 1990s onwards. 'Expressions' organized by Madhushree Dutta and Flavia Agnes in 1991, provided a platform for women from various art forms across the country. The participants not only contributed to the concerns and commitments as women practitioners but also inspired the women's literary, theatre and art festivals. A. Mangai in *Acting Up* (2015) informs that along with Mina Swaminathan she formed *Voicing Silence* in 1993, whose performances ensured that at least half of their members were women. In order to encourage women's participation beyond the formal aspects of theatre, they started organizing *Kulavai* festivals and workshops. Mangai gives a detailed account of the *Kulavais* in *Acting Up*:

> In the first Kulavai held in 1996, we had a scroll on which the respective word for ululation in all the languages represented in the meet was recorded. It was like the quilt made by women and men acknowledging the abstract call of celebration made by women in many countries, including India. The 1996 Kulavai was a National Workshop-cum-Seminar on Women and Theatre; the 1997 Kulavai was a State-level workshop of Professional Women Artistes from various genres and districts of Tamil Nadu; the 1999 Kulavai was a Regional Workshop on Community Theatre at the South India level; in 2002, Kulavai was a National Seminar-cum-Festival of Women Directors titled 'Towards a Feminist Theatre'; the

last Kulavai in 2003 was a National Festival of solo shows by women' (Mangai 244).

The National School of Drama in Delhi organized the Asian Women's Theatre Festival in 2003 and South Asian Women's Theatre Festival in 2010 in order to initiate and enhance international dialogues on the participation of women in theatres across Asia. The international festivals were followed and complimented by the Government of India sponsored Women's Theatre Festivals throughout India (244). Jyoti Mhapsekar, Sushama Deshpande and Waman Kendre are credited with organizing the 8th International Women Playwrights' Conference in Mumbai, which was jointly hosted by the Academy of Theatre Arts, University of Mumbai and Stree Mukti Sanghatana, a Non-Governmental Organization working since 1975 for gender equality in diverse social and cultural fields. These are only a few among many seminars, workshops and festivals which are organized regularly with the specific purpose of increasing the dialogue amongst the Regional, National and International Women Playwrights and directors. Apart from these, some of the veteran Indian women playwrights, directors and playwright-directors like Usha Ganguli, Tripurari Sharma, A. Mangai, Neelam Mansingh Chowdhry, Maya Krishna Rao, have theatre groups and companies of their own which not only stage the plays written/ directed/ performed by themselves or in collaboration but also provide platforms for young Indian women playwright-directors. Hence, it may be said with conviction that in their attempts to exploit the traditional Indian theatre space, the Indian women playwrights, directors, 'auteurs' and performers have gradually produced a niche of their own, that can accommodate varied 'languages' of theatre production by women in India.

WORKS CITED

Introduction

Aston, Elaine. *Feminist Theatre*. n.p., n.d. Web. 2Apr 2015. <http://www.dramaonlinelibrary.com/genres/feminist-theatre-iid-2485>

Adalja, Varsha. "Mandodari". *Staging Resistance: Plays by Women in Translation*. ed. Tutun Mukherjee. India: Oxford University Press. 2005. Print

Ahuja, Chaman. "Diverse Activists". *Theatre India*. May 2001. Number 3.New Delhi: National School of Drama. 2001.Print.

Beteille, Andre. *Class, Caste and Power: Changing Patterns of Stratification in a Tanjore Village*. Berkeley, Los Angeles, London: University of California Press. 1971.Print.

Beauvoir, *de* Simone. *The Second Sex*. Trans. Constance Borde and Sheila Malovany-Chevallier. London: Vintage Books. 2011 Print.

Chawla, Veenapani. "The Hare and the Tortoise". Productions. Adishakti.n.d. Web.15 Feb 2018. <adishaktitheatrearts.com/productions/the-hare-and-the-tortoise/>

Chowdhry, Neelam M. *The Company.* Web. 24May 2015. <http://thecompanychandigarh.wordpress.com/fidaphaedra>

Deepak, Sukant. "Director Neelam Mansingh Chowdhry explores newer frontiers with the London debut of her opera Naciketa". *From The Magazine.* India Today. n.p.7 Dec 2013. Web.10 Dec 2013.<https://www.indiatoday.in/magazine/profile/story/20131209-director-neelam-mansingh-chowdhry-london-debut-of-opera-naciketa-768883-1999-11-30>

Editorial. *Negotiating new terrains: South Asian Feminisms.* Feminist Review. No. 91.n.p. Palgrave Macmillan Journals.2009. Web. 25May 2015. <http://www.jstor.org/stable/40663976>

Deshpande, Sushma. *SUSHMA DESHPANDE.* theatreforum.n.p.,n.d. Web.20 Mar.2015.<http://www.theatreforum.in/static/upload/docs/SUSHAMA_DESHPANDE.pdf>

Kapur, Anuradha. "A Wandering Word, An Unstable Subject". *WomenDirectors'Direction.* Theatre India. India: NSD.2001.Print.

Keyssar, Helen. *Feminist Theatre and Theory* U.K.: Palgrave Macmillan, 1996.Print.

Knowles, Ric. *Modern Drama: Defining the Field, Modern Drama, Vol. XLIII, No. 4.* Canada: University of Toronto Press, 2000.Print.

Lieder, F. K. *Not-Feminism: A Discourse on the Politics of a Term in Modern Indian Theatre.*n.p, n.d. Web.20Sept.2018.<https://muse.jhu.edu/article/592546/pdf>

Loomba, Ania, Lukose, Ritty A. "South Asian Feminisms:Contemporary Interventions". *South Asian Feminisms.* ed. Loomba, A. & R. Lukose. New Delhi: Zubaan, 2012.Print.

Mangai, A. *Acting Up: Gender and theatre in India, 1979 onwards*. New Delhi: Leftword, 2015.Print.

Mehta, Dina. "Getting Away with Murder". *Body Blows: Women, Violence and Survival.* Kolkata:Seagull Books,2000.55-92.Print.

Menon, Nivedita. *Seeing Like a Feminist.* New Delhi: Zubaan & Penguin Books.2012. Print.

Mohanty, C. T. *Feminism Without Borders: Decolonizing Theory, Practising Solidarity.* Durham & London: Duke University Press. 2003. Print.

Mohita, Negi. *Rise of Women's Theatre in India!* n.p., n.d. Web.20 Mar 2015.<http://www.yourarticlelibrary.com/essay/rise-of-womens-theatre-in-india/24346/>

Mukherjee, Ramkrishna. *Caste in Itself, Caste and Class, or Caste in Class.* Journal of World-Systems Research, VI, 2.2000. n.p. Web. 2 Apr 2015.

<http://www.jwsr.org/wp-content/uploads/2013/05/jwsr-v6n2-mukherjee.pdf>

Mukherjee, Tutun. *Staging Resistance: Plays by Women in Translation.* India: Oxford University Press, 2012. Print.

Nagar, Richa. *Mujhe Jawab Do! (Answer me!): women's grass-roots activism and social spaces in Chitrakoot (India).* Gender, Place and Culture, Vol. 7, No. 4, New York: Taylor and Francis, 2000. Web.<http://www.tandfonline.com/doi/abs/10.1080/713668879>

Padmanabhan, Manjula. "Lights Out". *Body Blows: Women, Violence and Survival Three Plays.* Kolkata:Seagull Books, 2000.1-54.Print.

"Performing Women/Performing Womanhood: Theatre, Politics and Dissent in North India". *Buy Performing Women/Performing Womanhood: Theatre, Politics and Dissent in North India Book Online at Low Prices in India. Performing Women/Performing Womanhood: Theatre, Politics and Dissent in North India Reviews & Ratings-Amazon. in.*Web.n.d.Amazon.

<www.amazon.in/Performing-Women-Womanhood-Theatre-Politics/dp/0198066937>

Sagar, Mamta G. "The Swing of Desire". Tutun Mukherjee. *Staging Resistance: Plays by Women in Translations.* India: Oxford University Press, 2005.Print.

Sengupta, Ashis. ed., *Mapping South Asia Through Contemporary Theatre,* palgrave macmillan, 2014.

Sharma, Tripurari. Personal Interview.18 Nov. 2015.

Singh, Anita. 'Performing Resistance, Re-dressing the Canon: The Emergence of Indian Feminist Theatre'.IISUniv.J.A. Vol.3(1), 1-11.2014. n.p. Web. <http://iisjoa.org/sites/default/files/iisjoa/2014/PDF/1%20Anita%20Singh.pdf>

Stephens, Julie. "Feminist Fictions: A Critique of the Category 'Non-Western Woman' in Feminist Writings on India". *Subaltern StudiesVI Writings on South Asian History and Society",* ed. Ranajit Guha. Oxford: Oxford University Press.1989.

Subramanyam, Lakshmi. *Muffled Voices: Women in Modern Indian Theatre.* India: Har-Anand Pub. 2002.Print.

Rao, Maya K., et al., *The Performative body as a Language of Resistance. 27th November 2015.*ILF Samanvay.13 Jan 2016. Web. 10 Dec 2017. <https://www.youtube.com/watch?v=QKURKB45IAO>

*Theatre: Classical meets Contemporary Veenapani Chawla.*India Foundation for the Arts.17 Feb 2014. Web. 10 Dec 2017.<https://youtube.com/watch?v=We_ZRpDGd6E>

Wandor, Michelene. *The Impact of Feminism on the Theatre.* Feminist Review. No.18. Cultural Politics. U.K.: Palgrave Macmillan Journals, 1984. Web. 11 April.2015.<http://www.jstor.org/stable/1394862>

Weber, Max., Gerth H. H., Mills C.W. et. all. *Max Weber: Essays in Sociology.* London: Oxford University Press. 1948.Print.

Woolf, Virginia. *Three Guineas.* U.K.: Blackwell Publishing. n.d. Web.20Mar 2015. <http://www.blackwellpublishing.com/content/BPL_Images/Content_store/Sample_chapter/9780631177241/woolf.pdf>

Chapter I

Barthes, Rolland. *Rhetoric of the Images.*8.n.p.,n.d.152-163.Web.18 Aug. 2014.<http://faculty.georgetown.edu/irvinem/theory/Barthes-Rhetoric-of-the-image-ex.pdf>

Bernett, R. James. "An interview with Girish Karnad" New Quest. No. 36, Nov.-Dec. 1982. 339-342.Print.

Deshpande, G.P. "Introduction". *Andhar Yatra.* Mumbai: Popular Prakashan,1995.Print.

Ferguson, Marry A. *Images of Women in Literature.* Boston: Houghton Mifflin.1973.Print.

Foss, Sonjonka K. "Theory of Visual Rhetoric." *Handbook of Visual Communication: Theory, Methods, and Media.*eds. Ken Smith, Sandra Moriarty, Gretchen Barbatsis, and Keith Kenney. Mahwa, New Jersey: Lawrence Erlbaum.2005.141-152. Print.

Juneja, R. *Women in Plays of Mohan Rakesh*. Journal of South Asian Literature, Vol. 19, No. 1, Miscellany (Winter, Spring 1984). Asian Studies Center. Michigan State University. 1984.Web.10 May.2016<http://www.jstor.org/stable/40872657>

Karnad, G. *The Fire and the Rain*. India: Oxford University Press,1998. Print.

Lal, Ananda. "A Historiography of Modern Indian Theatre". Bhatia Nandi (ed.). *Modern Indian Theatre A Reader*. India: Oxford University Press. 2011. Print.

Macgowan, Kenneth. & William Melnitz. *The Living Stage*. USA: Prentice Hall, 1955.Print.

Mee, Erin B. Mahesh Dattani: Invisible Issues. *Performing ArtsJournal. Vol.19, No.1*. India: Performing Arts Journal, Inc., 1997.Print.

Mee, Erin B. *Theatre of Roots: Redirecting the Modern Indian Stage*. India: Seagull Books, 2008.Print.

Muni, Bharata. *The Natyasastra*. Vol. I Chap. I – XXVII. trans. Manomohan Ghosh. Calcutta: The Royal Asiatic Society of Bengal.1950. Print.

Pandit, Maya. "Feminization of Politics: The Plays of G.P.Deshpande". Lakshmi Subramanyam(ed). *Muffled Voices Women in Modern Indian Theatre*. India: HarAnand Pub., 2013.

Singh, Lata. *Transgression of Boundaries: Women of IPTA*. Social Scientist. Vol.39. No. 11/12. Social Scientist, 2011.Web.11 May 2015.<http://www.jstor.org/stable/23076333>

Solomon, Rakesh H. "Towards a Genealogy of Indian Theatre Historiography". Modern Indian Theatre: A reader. New Delhi: Oxford University Press, 2009.Print.

Srampickal, Jacob. *Voice to the Voiceless*. The Power of People's Theatre in India. London & New York: Hurst & Company. St. Martin's Press,1994.Print.

Tendulkar, Vijay. "Kamala".trans. Priya Adarkar. *Five Plays*. Delhi: OUP, 2006.Print.

Tendulkar, Vijay. "Silence! The Court is in Session".trans. Priya Adarkar. *Five Plays*. Delhi: OUP, 2006.Print.

Tendulkar, Vijay. *Ghashiram Kotwal*. trans. Jayant Karve. Eleanor Zelliot. Calcutta: Seagull Books, 1999.Print.

Chapter II

Adalja, Varsha. "Mandodari". *Staging Resistance: Plays by Women in Translation*. ed. TutunMukherjee. India: Oxford University Press. 2005. Print.

Anderson, Benedict. *Imagined Communities*.48-59.n.p.,n.d. Web.11 Aug 2015.<https://www2.bc.edu/marian-simion/th406/readings/0420anderson.pdf>

Bellamy, Richard. *Citizenship*. A Very Short Introduction. Oxford: Oxford University Press. 2008.Print.

Boehmer, Elleke. *Stories of Women: Gender and Narrative in the Postcolonial Nation*. Manchester and New York:Manchester University Press.2005. Print.

Clausewitz, Carl von. Wikipedia. The Free Encyclopedia. Wkikpedia Foundation, Inc..,n.d. Web.10 Feb 2015. <https://en.wikipedia.org/wiki/Carl_von_Clausewitz>

Chatterjee, Partha. *The Nation and Its Fragments. Colonial and Postcolonial Histories.* New Jersey: Princeton University Press. 1993. Print.

Davis-Y N. and P.Werbner*Women, Citizenship and Difference.* India: Zubaan.2005.Print.

Dikshit, R.D. *Political Geography The Spatiality of Politics* (3rd Edition). New Delhi: Tata McGraw-Hill Publishing Company Limited, 2000. Print.

Foucault, Michel. *"Society Must be Defended"* Lectures at the College de France. Trans. David Macey, eds. Bertani, Mauro. & Alessandro Fontana. New York: Picador. 2003.Print.

Huntington Samuel P. *The Clash of Civilizations.* London: Penguin.1996.Print.

Mathur, J.C. *Hindi Drama.* Sangeet Natak. Sangeet Natak Academy. 2004.Print.

Mee, Erin B. Theatre of Roots: Redirecting the Modern Indian Stage. Kolkata. Seagull Books. 2008.Print.

Menon, Jisha. The Performance of Nationalism. Cambridge Studies in Modern Theatre. New York: Cambridge University Press. 2013. Print.

Menon, Jisha. *Rehearsing the Partition: Gendered Violence in Aur Kitne Tukde.* feminist review (84). *Postcolonial Theatres.* Palgrave Macmillan Journal.2006. Web.17 Feb 2016. 29-47. <http://www.jstor.org/stable/30232738>

Mitra, Shayoni. "Dispatches from the Margins: Theatre in India since the 1990s". ed. Sengupta Ashis. *Mapping South Asia Through Contemporary Theatre.* U.S. and U.K. Palgrave macmillan. 2014.Print.

Moraga, Cherrie. Queer Aztlan: The Reformatin of Chicano Tribe. *The Last Generation*. Boston, MA: South End Press. 1993.Print.

Mukherjee Tutun. *Staging Resistance: Plays by Women in Translation*, India: Oxford University Press, 2005.Print.

Pandey, Gyanendra. *Remembering Partition*. U.K.:Cambridge University Press. 2001.Print.

Poole, Ross. *Nation and Identity*. London and New York: Routledge.1999.Print.

Richmond Farely. *The Political Role of Theatre in India*. Educational Theatre Journal. Vol. 25, No. 3. The Johns Hopkins University Press.1973. http://www.jstor.org/stable/3205692

Samaddar, Ranabir. *The Nation Form*. Essays on Indian Nationalism. India: Sage. 2012.Print.

Sharma, Tripurari. "A Tale from the Year 1857: AzizunNisa".*Staging Resistance: Plays by Women in Translation*. ed. TutunMukherjee. India: Oxford University Press. 2005. Print.

Smith, Anthony. D. *Nationalism*. U.K.: Polity Press & U.S. A: Blackwell Publishing Inc. 2001.Print.

Sharma, Tripurari. Personal Interview.18 Nov. 2015. Delhi: NSD.

Woolf, Virginia. *Three Guineas*. U.K.: Blackwell Publishing. n.d. Web. 20Mar 2015. <http://www.blackwellpublishing.com/content/ BPL_Images/Content_store/Sample_chapter/9780631177241/ woolf.pdf>

Yuval-Davis, Nira. *Gender and Nation*. London: Sage.1997. Print.

Chapter III

Ambedkar, B. R. "Inter-caste marriage". *Thus spoke Dr. Ambedkar.*12 Jul.2007. Web. <https://ambedkarquotes.wordpress.com/category/inter-caste-marriage>

Agnihotri, Aditya N. Protest as Art: Contemporary Hindi Drama'. Sudhankar Pandey & Freya Taraporewala (eds.), *Contemporary Indian Drama.* New Delhi: Prestige Books,1990.Print.

Bhatia Nandi. *performing women/performing womanhood.* India: Oxford University Press,2010.Print.

Crompton, Rosemary. *Class and Stratification.* New Delhi: Rawat Publications, 2013.Print.

Dharwadker, Aparna Bhargava. 'Historical Fictions and Postcolonial Representations: Reading Girish Karnad's Tughlaq'. *Theatres of Independence: Drama, Theory and Urban Performance in India since1947.* Iowa: University of Iowa Press, 2005.Print.

Ganguli. Usha. "Rudali". trans. Katyal, Anjum. *Drama Contemporary India.* Baltimore and London: The John Hopkins University Press, 2001.Print.

Jalote, S. R. *Contemporary African American Theatre and Dalit Theatre: A Contemporary Study in Themes and Techniques.* Varanasi: Banaras Hindu University,2001.Print.

Katyal Anjum. ed. *Seagull Theatre Quarterly.* Issue 1. Kolkata: January. 1994.Kolkata:Seagull,1994.Print.

Katyal Anjum. *Metamorphosis of Rudali. Rudali From Fiction to Preformance.* Seagull Books, Calcutta. 1999.Print.

Kumar, Kusum. "Listen shefali".*Staging Resistance*. Tutun Mukherjee. Delhi:Oxford India Paperbacks, 2012. Print.

Marx, Karl. "The Future Results of British Rule in India"22 Jul. 1853. *Works of Karl Marx*. New York: New-York Daily Tribune, 8 Aug. 1853.Web. 15 Dec.2015. <https://marxists.catbull.com/archive/marx/1853/07/22.htm>

Mee, Erin B. (ed.) *Drama Contemporary: India*. Baltimore and London: The John Hopkins University Press, 2001.Print.

Mukherjee Tutun. *Staging Resistance*. Delhi: Oxford India Paperbacks, 2012. Print.

Roy Arundhati. 'The Doctor and the Saint'. Anand S. *Annihilation of Caste*. ed. B.R. Ambedkar Navayana, 2014.Print.

Subramanyam, Lakshmi. *Muffled Voices: Women in Modern Indian Theatre*. India:Har-Anand Pub. 2002.Print.

Taneja. Jaidev. 'Contradictions and Complexities: Women in Modern Hindi drama'. Lakshmi Subramanyam (ed.) *Muffled Voices. Women in Modern Indian theatre*. Delhi: Shakti Books,2002.Print.

Chapter IV

"abuse".Entry2.Oxford Advanced Learner's Dictionary.8th ed. India: Oxford University Press, 2010.Print.

Bennington, Geoffrey. 'Deconstruction is Not What You Think'. Martin, McQuillan.(ed.) *Deconstruction: A Reader*. London: Taylor and Francis,1989.Print.

Biswas, Praggnaparamita. Semiotic Encryption of Women, Violence and Hysteria in Indian Women Dramaturgy. Rupkatha Journal. Vol.

V. No.2. 2013.Web.11 Dec. 2016. <http://rupkatha.com/V5/n2/27 Indian Women Dramaturgy.pdf>

Butler, Judith. *Gender Trouble*. New York and London: Routledge, 2007.Print.

Butler, Judith. *Bodies thatMatter.On the Discursive Limits of "Sex"* .New York: Routledge,1993.Print.

Caputi, Jane. "Advertising Femicide: Lethal Violence Against Women in Pornography and Gorenography." Jill Radford and Diana E. Russell eds. *Femicide: The Politics of Woman Killing*. Burmingham: Open University Press. 1992.Print.

Clark, Lorenne M. G. and Debra J. Lewis. *Rape: The Price of Coercive Sexuality*. Toronto: Women's Press. 1977.Print.

Cole, Susan G. *Pornography and the Sex Crisis*. Toronto: Amanita Press. 1989.

Conroy, Colette. *Theatre& the body*. London: Palgrave Macmillan. 2010.Print.

Dasgupta, Priyanka. *This play was an eye opener*. Times of India. 13 Mar.2010. Web. <http://timesofindia.indiatimes.com/entertainment/events/kolkata/This-play-was-an-eye-opener/articleshow/5672404.cms>

Derrida, Jacques. *Biodegradables: Seven Diary Fragments*. Trans. Peggy Kamuf. Critical Inquiry 15(4). Print.

Dolan, Jill. *The Feminist Spectator as Critic*. Ann Arbor, Mich: University of Michigan Press.1988.Print.

Howson, Alexandra. *embodyinggender*. London: Sage Publications,2005. Print.

Jones, Anne. *Next Time She'll Be Dead: Battering and How to stop it.* Boston: Beacon Press, 1994.Print.

joseph, anish. *Lights Out by Lights Off production, a review on the play.*n.p.4 Jun. 2012.Web.<https://hi-in.facebook.com/notes/anish-joseph/lights-out-by-lights-off-production-a-review-on-the-play-by-anish-still-in-searc/10150937472968744/>

Mangai, A. *Acting Up* Gender and Theatre in India, 1979 Onwards. New Delhi: Leftword,2015.Print.

Mehta, Dina. "Getting Away with Murder". *BodyBlows:Women, Violence and Survival.* Kolkata:Seagull Books,2000.Print.

Nevitt, Lucy. *Theatre& violence.* London: Palgrave Macmillan, 2013. Print.

Padmanabhan, Manjula. *All Set for Harvest.*n.p. 29 Jul. 1998.Web. <http://www.rediff.com/news/1998/jul/29manju.htm>

Padmanabhan, Manjula. "Lights Out". *Body Blows:Women, Violence and Survival.* Kolkata:Seagull Books,2000.Print.

Price, Lisa S. *Feminist Frameworks* Building Theory Against Violence on Women. New Delhi: Aakar Books, 2009.Print.

Rich, Adrienne. "Compulsory Heterosexuality andLesbian Continuum". *Signs.* Vol.5 No.4.Women: Sex and Sexuality (Summer, 1980).Web.631-660.<http://www.jstor.org.iproxy.inflibnet.ac.in:2048/stable/pdf/3173834.pdf>

Sengupta, Ashis, ed. *Mapping South Asia Through Contemporary Theatre,* palgrave macmillan, 2014.Print.

"violence".Entry1.Oxford Advanced Learner's Dictionary.8th ed. India: Oxford University Press, 2010.Print.

Zizek, Slavoj. *Violence*. New York: Picador Paperback. 2008.Print.

Chapter V

Chowdhry, Neelam Mansingh. "Fida". *Staging ResistancePlays by Women in Translation*, ed. Tutun Mukherjee. India: Oxford University Press. 2005.Print.

Bell, Leslie C. "The Paradox of Sexual Freedom". *Hard to Get Twenty-Somethings Women and the Paradox of Sexual Freedom*. Berkley & Los Angeles. University of California Press.2013.Web.epub. <http://b_ ok.xyz/book/2370084/115ca5>

Gough, Kathleen. "The Origin of the Family". *Toward an Anthropology of Women*, ed. Reiter, Rayna R. New York: Monthly Review Press. 1975.Print.

Kamasutra. Wikipedia. The Free Encyclopedia. Wikimedia Foundation, Inc.n.d. Web.10 Dec.2017. <https://en.wikipedia.org/ wiki/Kama_Sutra>

Sagar Mamta G. "The Swing of Desire". *Staging ResistancePlays by Women in Translation*, ed. Tutun Mukherjee. India: Oxford University Press. 2005.Print.

Sagar, Mamta. Internacional de Poesia de Medellin, Prometeo, Latinoamerican Poetry Magazine No 81 – 82 July 2008.n.p., n.d. Web.10 Dec. 2017.https://www.festivaldepoesiademedellin.org/en/ Revista/ultimas_ediciones/81_82/sagar.html

Vatasyayana. *Kamasutra*. http://www.pitbook.com/English/texts/ pdf/kamasutra.pdf n.p., n.d. Web.10 Dec.

Young-Eisendrath, Polly. *Women &Desire Beyond Wanting to be Wanted*. UK: Piatkus.2000.Print.

Zizek, Slavoj. *Violence*. New York: Picador Paperback. 2008.Print.

Conclusion

Deepak, Sukant. "Director Neelam Mansingh Chowdhry explores newer frontiers with the London debut of her opera Naciketa". *From The Magazine*. India Today. n.p.7 Dec 2013. Web.10 Dec 2013.<https://www.indiatoday.in/magazine/profile/story/20131209-director-neelam-mansingh-chowdhry-london-debut-of-opera-naciketa-768883-1999-11-30>

Kamble, Rahul. Teaching Plays by Indian Women in a Postgraduate Class: Conventions and Post-conventions. The EFL Journal Vol. 6 No.02. 2015.Hyderabad: The English and Foreign Language University. Web. 10 Jan.2019. <http://www.openhumanitiesalliance.org/journals/eflj/article/view/84/76>

Kapur, Anuradha. "A Wandering Word, An Unstable Subject..." *Theatre India. National School of Drama's Theatre Journal*. Number Three. May 2001.pp10. New Delhi: NSD,2001.Print.

Kapur, Anuradha et al. "The Continued Relevance of Playwrights in Today's Multimedia World." You Tube, The Hindu Lit For Life 2014, 5 Feb. 2014. <www.youtube.com/watch?v=b1gcaB0Y5lE>

Mangai, A. *Acting Up: Gender and theatre in India, 1979 onwards*. New Delhi: Leftword, 2015.Print.

Mukherjee, Tutun. *Staging Resistance: Plays by Women in Translation*. India:Oxford University Press, 2012. Print.

Punjani, Deepa. "Initial Thoughts on the Curious Case of Postdramatic Theatre in the Indian Context." *Critical Stages/Scènes Critiques*, Dec. 2018, www.critical-stages.org/18/initial-thoughts-on-the-curious-case-of-postdramatic-theatre-in-the-indian-context.

Vohra, Kinnari. "Women that Men Created". *Theatre India.* May 2001.Number 3.New Delhi: National School of Drama. 2001.Print.

Vohra, Kinnari. *Theatre: From a Woman's Point of View.* India: Mumbai Theatre Guide.n.d. Web.21 Oct.2018. <https://www.mumbaitheatreguide.com/dramas/features/05/mar/kinnari_vohra.asp#>

Sengupta, Poile. "Inner Laws". *Women Centre Stage. The Dramatist and the Play.* Delhi: Routledge,2010.Print.

www.ingramcontent.com/pod-product-compliance
Lightning Source LLC
Chambersburg PA
CBHW030429290526
45786CB00001B/198